Key Concepts for Understanding Curriculum

The Falmer Press Teachers' Library

Fundamentals of Educational Research
Gary Anderson, *McGill University, Canada*

Search and Re-Search:
What the Inquiring Teacher Needs to Know
Edited by Rita S. Brause, *Fordham University, USA* and John S. Mayher,
New York University, USA

Doing Qualitative Research:
Circles Within Circles
Margot Ely, *New York University, USA* with Margaret Anzul,
Teri Friedman, Diane Garner and Ann McCormack Steinmetz

Teachers as Researchers:
Qualitative Inquiry as a Path to Empowerment
Joe L. Kincheloe, *Clemson University, USA*

Key Concepts for Understanding Curriculum
Colin Marsh, *Secondary Education Authority, Western Australia*

Key Concepts for Understanding Curriculum

Colin J. Marsh

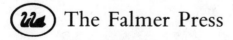 The Falmer Press

(A Member of the Taylor & Francis Group)
London • New York • Philadelphia

UK   The Falmer Press, 4 John St, London WC1N 2ET
USA   The Falmer Press, Taylor & Francis Inc., 1900 Frost Road, Suite 101,
        Bristol, PA 19007

© Colin Marsh 1992

L B

1570

.M3668

1991

First published 1992

1S8009

**A catalogue record for this book is available from the British
Library**

Feb.1993

**Library of Congress Cataloging-in-Publication Data are
available on request**

ISBN 0-75070-008-4
ISBN 0-75070-009-2 (pbk)

Jacket design by Caroline Archer
Typeset in 10/11.5 Bembo by
Graphicraft Typesetters Ltd, Hong Kong

*Printed in Great Britain by Burgess Science Press, Basingstoke on paper
which has a specified pH value on final paper manufacture of not less than 7.5
and is therefore 'acid free'.*

Table of Contents

List of Tables   x
List of Figures   xii
Series Editor's Preface   xv
Preface   xvii

Introducing This Book   1

Part 1: **Student Perspectives**   13
  1 Learning Environments   15
    — Student Needs and Person–Environment Fit   15
    — Physical Environment Factors   16
    — Reflections and Issues   18
    — References   18
  2 Hidden Curriculum   20
    — Functionalist Perspective   20
    — Critical Perspective   20
    — Reflections and Issues   22
    — References   24
  3 Curriculum and Gender   25
    — Major Issues   25
    — Practical Classroom Ideas   27
    — Reflections and Issues   28
    — References   30
  4 Students' Role in Curriculum Decision-Making   32
    — Points For and Against Participation   32
    — Levels of Participation   33
    — Reflections and Issues   36
    — References   36
  5 Examinations   38
    — Points For and Against Public Examinations   39
    — General Certificate of Secondary Education (GCSE)   39
    — Reflections and Issues   40
    — References   41

Part 2: **Teacher Perspectives**   43

6   Teacher Empowerment   45
    — Empowered versus Disempowered   45
    — Some Approaches to Empowering Teachers   46
    — Reflections and Issues   48
    — References   49
7   Textbooks   51
    — Some Definitions   51
    — Different Expectations About Textbooks   53
    — Features of Textbooks   53
    — Checklists to Evaluate Textbooks   55
    — Reflections and Issues   57
    — References   57
8   Leadership and the School Principal   58
    — Leadership Qualities   58
    — Principal Styles   59
    — Reflections and Issues   62
    — References   63
9   Teacher Appraisal   64
    — Why, What and Who   64
    — Criteria and Methods   66
    — Reflections and Issues   68
    — References   69

Part 3: **Curriculum Planning and Development**   71

10 Curriculum Frameworks   73
    — Characteristics   73
    — Advantages and Disadvantages   74
    — Examples from the UK, Australia and Canada   75
    — Reflections and Issues   76
    — References   78
11 Situational Analysis/Needs Assessment   79
    — Situational Analysis Factors   79
    — Needs Assessment Procedures   81
    — Reflections and Issues   82
    — References   83
12 Aims, Goals and Objectives   85
    — Characteristics and Examples   85
    — Criteria for Use   86
    — Reflections and Issues   90
    — References   91
13 Selection of Method   93
    — Methods of Imparting Content   93
    — Methods of Organizing Content   96
    — Reflections and Issues   99
    — References   100

14 Assessment, Grading and Testing   102
    — Characteristics and Issues   102
    — Commonly Used Techniques   103
    — Reflections and Issues   105
    — References   106
15 Tyler's Model of Planning   107
    — Planning Steps   107
    — Advantages and Disadvantages   109
    — Reflections and Issues   110
    — References   111
16 Walker's Deliberative Approach to Planning   112
    — Naturalistic Model   112
    — Advantages and Disadvantages   114
    — Reflections and Issues   115
    — References   115
17 Teachers as Researchers/Action Research   116
    — Action Research Processes   116
    — Examples of Action Research   117
    — Reflections and Issues   120
    — References   121
18 Centrally-Based Curriculum Development   123
    — Characteristics   123
    — Advantages and Disadvantages   125
    — Reflections and Issues   126
    — References   127
19 School-Based Curriculum Development   128
    — Types and Characteristics   128
    — Problems that Participants can Experience with SBCD   131
    — Reflections and Issues   131
    — References   133

Part 4: **Curriculum Management**   135

20 Innovation and Planned Change   137
    — Phases of Planned Change   137
    — Characteristics and Contexts of Innovation   140
    — Change Agents and Strategies   142
    — Reflections and Issues   146
    — References   147
21 Managing the Curriculum: The Collaborative School
    Management Model   149
    — Phases of the CSM Model   149
    — Advantages and Disadvantages   155
    — Reflections and Issues   156
    — References   157
22 Effective Schools and School Improvement   158
    — Effective Schools — Factors and Examples   158

— School Improvement Targets and Factors 160
— Reflections and Issues 162
— References 163
23 School Councils and Governing Bodies 165
— Characteristics and Major Factors 165
— Advantages and Disadvantages 167
— Reflections and Issues 169
— References 170
24 School Evaluations/Reviews 171
— Reasons for Undertaking Evaluations 171
— Techniques for Collecting Evaluative Data 172
— Examples 173
— Reflections and Issues 178
— References 179
25 Curriculum Implementation 180
— Factors Affecting Implementation 181
— Problems of Describing/Measuring Implementation 182
— Two Perspectives of Implementation 184
— Curriculum Alignment 186
— Reflections and Issues 186
— References 187

Part 5: **Curriculum Ideology** 189

26 Curriculum History 191
— Uses of Curriculum History 191
— Examples 192
— Reflections and Issues 194
— References 195
27 School Subjects 196
— School Subjects as Social Systems 196
— Examples 197
— Reflections and Issues 199
— References 200
28 Curriculum Theorizing and the Reconceptualists 201
— Theorizing Principles of the Reconceptualists 201
— Achievements and Problems 202
— Reflections and Issues 203
— References 205
29 Sociology of Knowledge Approach to Curriculum 206
— Proponents and Their Principles 206
— Achievements and Problems 208
— Reflections and Issues 209
— References 209
30 Curriculum Reform 211
— Ideology Stances 211
— Types of Reforms 212

— Reflections and Issues   214
— References   215

Concluding Issues   217

Index   218

List of Tables

Table 1.1	Analysis of six synoptic curriculum texts	3
Table 5.1	Advantages of a public examination	39
Table 5.2	Disadvantages of a public examination	39
Table 7.1	Inventory of evaluative criteria stated as adjectives	56
Table 8.1	Domains in which the principal is expected to demonstrate leadership	59
Table 8.2	Three different styles of principal	61
Table 8.3	A training programme based on the principal profile	61
Table 9.1	An example of a self-appraisal check list	67
Table 11.1	Situational analysis factors	80
Table 11.2	Situational analysis techniques	81
Table 11.3	Steps involved in needs assessment	82
Table 11.4	Advantages of using needs assessment	83
Table 11.5	Disadvantages of using needs assessment	83
Table 12.1	Some reasons for using instructional objectives	89
Table 12.2	Some problems in using instructional objectives	90
Table 13.1	Some major methods of imparting content	94
Table 13.2	Groupings of teaching methods	96
Table 14.1	Commonly used assessment techniques	104
Table 14.2	Rating scales for skills development	104
Table 14.3	Semantic differential example	105
Table 21.1	Guidelines for establishing the Collaborative School Management (CSM) cycle	150
Table 21.2	Preparing policies on non-contentious and contentious issues	153
Table 22.1	Dimensions of effective schools and schooling	159
Table 22.2	Key factors of effectiveness in elementary schools in the Inner London Education Authority	160
Table 23.1	Some unanswered questions about school councils	166
Table 25.1	Factors affecting implementation	182
Table 25.2	Some important factors in promoting successful implementation practices	183
Table 30.1	Types of curriculum reforms and examples	213

Table 30.2 Taxonomy of reform proposals in the USA during the
1980s 214

Table 30.3 Reform proposals and their implementation in the UK
during the 1980s 214

List of Figures

Figure 1.1   Concepts included in 'Student Perspectives'   4
Figure 1.2   Concepts included in 'Teacher Perspectives'   5
Figure 1.3   Concepts included in 'Curriculum Planning and
              Development'   6
Figure 1.4   Concepts included in 'Curriculum Management'   8
Figure 1.5   Concepts included in 'Curriculum Ideology'   8
Figure 1.6   Concepts included in a 'Cooperative, democratic,
              decision-making' theme   10
Figure 1.7   Concepts included in a 'Performance driven, student
              outcomes, academic excellence' theme   10
Figure 4.1   Student participation continuum at two levels: (a)
              individual classroom, and (b) school-wide   33
Figure 12.1   Relationships between educational aims, goals,
              objectives and instruction   87
Figure 12.2   Comparison between perceived and preferred goal
              emphasis (social, academic, personal and vocational) for
              students, teachers and parents   89
Figure 15.1   Ralph Tyler's principles   108
Figure 15.2   Tyler rationale for curriculum   108
Figure 16.1   Walker's naturalistic model   113
Figure 17.1   The action research spiral   119
Figure 18.1   An authority model for a state education system   124
Figure 19.1   A matrix of SBCD variations   130
Figure 20.1   Educational change process   139
Figure 20.2   Tactics and their potential effects   144
Figure 21.1   Phases in the Collaborative School Management (CSM)
              cycle   151
Figure 24.1   Stages in the traditional evaluation model   174
Figure 24.2   The five stages of the institutional review and
              development process   176
Figure 24.3   Teacher-oriented model of evaluation, using the
              analogy of a space rocket   177

To Glenys

Series Editor's Preface

The starting point for this series comes from the memorial plaque to Lawrence Stenhouse: 'It is teachers who in the end will change the world of school by understanding it.'[1] This is of course to subscribe to a pedagogy of hope. But there is nowhere else to go. (Were we without hope we would say history teaches us that politicians, bureaucrats and their academic collaborators will connive to deprive teachers of understanding).

Colin Marsh's value position is an eloquent testimony to the pedagogy of hope for he places 'considerable emphasis upon student, parent and teacher inputs into curriculum'. He provides a 'menu' of thirty concepts through which to investigate curriculum and further our understandings. Each conceptual study guide is free-standing and is provided with its own follow-up section on 'reflections and issues'. In the spirit of the Falmer Press Teachers' Library he therefore provides a learning tool for teachers and others to develop their own further understandings of the school curriculum.

I have long admired Colin's commitment to policy and practice — a commitment perhaps best epitomized by his recent move from a university position back into the Secondary Education Authority in Perth. In his work in this book (and I hope in this series generally) we see a commitment to develop a counter-culture which will derive from and inform school practice. In doing so it is our hope to begin a reversal of the dominant modalities of educational research as conducted in so many academic settings. Rob Walker and I recently judged that as academics:

> 'we have over-valued the accolades of the invisible college, and undervalued the worlds of policy and practice. We have invented and sustained self-indulgent and arrogant realms of discourse.'[2]

This series in general, and this book in particular, seeks a reversal of these tendencies by placing the teacher's understandings at the centre of our endeavours.

Ivor Goodson
University of Western Ontario
Canada
July 1991

Notes and References

1. Ruddolk, J. and Hopkins, D., 'Research as a Basis for Teaching'. Readings from the work of Lawrence Stenhouse. Heinemman London, 1985.
2. Goodson, I. and Walker, R., *Biography, Identity and Schooling. Episodes in Educational Research*, (Falmer, London, New York and Philadephia 1991), p. 202.

Preface

The diversity and pace of change in curriculum policy and implementation continues unabated in many countries in the Western world. In addition, the players who are taking leading roles in policy formulation are changing, with increasing pressures coming from politicians and employer groups, as well as from community interest groups, parents, teachers and students.

A number of these individuals and groups have very limited understanding of curriculum theories, principles and processes, even though they are prepared to commit enormous amounts of energy to advance their preferred solutions to specific curriculum problems.

The book is intended especially for those who will be commencing full-time careers in schools, namely students who are taking teacher education degrees (BAs in education, BEds, Diplomas of Education, Diplomas of Teaching and PGCEs). Another major group who is likely to be very interested in the book include those practising teachers who are embarking upon professional development programmes. Parents and community members involved as school governors and members of school councils, boards and districts, will obtain considerable assistance from the succinctly stated commentaries about major curriculum concepts.

The book provides details about thirty major concepts in curriculum. Various ideas about how the volume might be used are given in 'Introducing this Book'. Readers are advised to use the book selectively and flexibly rather than reading it straight through from cover to cover. My value orientation has been to place considerable emphasis upon student, parent, and teacher inputs into curriculum and this will be evident from the arrangement of the modules in specific sections. Yet there are various other ways of rearranging the modules in keeping with technocratic or community or discipline-oriented stances, as detailed in the next chapter.

The thirty concepts cover a wide range of important topics in curriculum. In such a small space each concept module cannot provide an exhaustive treatment of each concept, but every attempt has been made to highlight major features, controversies, strengths and weaknesses. In particular, the follow-up questions challenge the reader to reflect further upon specific issues relating to each concept and the listing of recent references at the end of each module (including an enormous range of Falmer Press publications), facilitates this task.

I acknowledge various colleagues in curriculum, both within Australia and in the United Kingdom, United States of America and Canada, who have helped me hone my ideas over the decades about curriculum. They include Michael Fullan, Gene Hall, Paul Klohr, Michael Huberman, Bill Reid, Helen Simons, Kerry Kennedy, Eric Hoyle, Ray Bolam, Michael Connelly, Christine Deer, David Smith, Noel Gough, Chris Day, Ivor Goodson, Brian Caldwell, Paul Morris and Malcolm Skilbeck. This volume is very different to synoptic texts that I have published in the 1980s, and to this extent, it has been a most exciting and rewarding challenge for me.

For permission to reproduce figures and tables I am most grateful to Brian Caldwell, Chris Day, Meredith Gall and Barry Fraser. A special word of thanks is due to Lynne Schickert for her expert secretarial assistance in the preparation of the manuscript.

Colin Marsh
Secondary Education Authority
Osborne Park
Western Australia

Introducing This Book

Preliminary Comments

We make sense of our world and go about our daily lives by engaging in *concept building*. We acquire and develop concepts so that we can gain meaning about persons and events and in turn communicate these meanings to others. Some concepts are clearly of more importance than others. The *key concepts* provide us with the power to explore a variety of situations and events and to make significant connections. Other concepts may be meaningful in more limited situations but play a part in connecting unrelated facts.

Every discipline and field of study contains a number of key concepts and lesser concepts which relate to substantive and methodological issues unique to that discipline/field of study. Not unexpectedly, scholars differ over their respective lists of key concepts, but there is nevertheless, considerable agreement. With regard to the curriculum field there is a moderate degree of agreement over key concepts.

Key Concepts in Curriculum

To be able to provide any commentary on key concepts in curriculum assumes of course that we have access to sources of information that enable us to make definitive statements. A wide range of personnel are involved in *making curriculum* including school personnel, researchers, academics, administrators, politicians, and various interest groups. They go about their tasks in various ways such as planning meetings, informal discussions, writing reports, papers, handbooks, textbooks, giving talks, lectures and workshops.

To ensure that a list of key concepts is comprehensive and representative of all these sources would be an extremely daunting task. A proxy often used by researchers is to examine textbooks, especially *synoptic textbooks* (those books which provide comprehensive accounts and summaries of a wide range of concepts, topics and issues in curriculum).

Schubert (1980) undertook a detailed analysis of textbooks over the period 1900–1980 and this volume provides a valuable overview of curriculum thought over major historical periods. Marsh and Stafford (1988) have provided a similar historical analysis of major curriculum books written by Australian authors over the period 1910–1988.

More recently, Rogan and Luckowski (1990), have produced a useful analysis of nine major synoptic curriculum texts produced by American authors. Their purpose in undertaking this analysis was to portray major concepts within the curriculum field. They noted that all texts included an analysis of four major themes, namely paradigms, conceptions of curriculum, history, and politics, but that there was little consensus on preferred positions within each of these topics. This diversity of stance within topics may reflect the nature of the curriculum field compared with the apparent singularity of purpose and methodological procedures followed in some science disciplines.

A Sample Analysis

To illustrate the organization of concepts included in this volume I undertook a review of six major synoptic curriculum books that are widely used at the college/university level. As indicated in table 1.1, they include: two from the USA (McNeil, 1985, third edition; Schubert, 1986); two from the UK (Kelly, 1977; Lawton, 1986); one from Canada (Robinson, *et al.*, 1985); and one from Australia (Brady, 1987, second edition).

It is very evident that the two American texts are far more comprehensive in their coverage of topics than the others. In size alone, these volumes have double the number of pages of the UK and Australian texts. The two authors (McNeil and Schubert) cover very similar topics if we use the broad categories of:

Conceptions of curriculum/models/approaches
Curriculum history
Curriculum policy and policy-makers
Curriculum development procedures/planning steps
Curriculum change/improvement
Politics of curriculum
Issues and trends/problems/future directions

By contrast, the two UK authors (Lawton and Kelly) are far more limiting in that their major focus is upon only two categories, namely 'conceptions of curriculum' and 'curriculum development procedures'. Lawton (1986) has additional chapters on 'politics' and the 'democratic curriculum' and Kelly (1977) has an additional chapter on 'social contexts'. It is interesting to note that both authors consider the 'common curriculum' in some detail and that this topic is not covered in any of the other texts included in the sample.

The Canadian text (Robinson, *et al.*, 1985) has 'curriculum development procedures' as its major focus and the majority of the chapters focus upon

Table 1.1: Analysis of six synoptic curriculum texts

USA McNeil (1985) 398 pp.	USA Schubert (1986) 478 pp.	United Kingdom Kelly (1977) 201 pp.	United Kingdom Lawton (1986) 161 pp.	Canada Robinson et al. (1985) 353 pp.	Australia Brady (1987) 262 pp.
Conceptions of Curriculum — humanistic, social, reconstructionist, technology, academic subjects	Curriculum domains Philosophies and theories Curriculum models Tyler, Schwab, critical theorists, reconceptualists	Planning approaches Common curriculum	Curriculum definitions Cultural analysis Common curriculum	Psychology models Learning models	Contributing disciplines Models School-based curriculum development
Historical perspective	Curriculum history				
Curriculum policy Policy makers	Curriculum policies Policy makers Educational contexts and interest groups	Social contexts			
Selecting content Selecting learning opportunities Evaluation Designing curricula	Purposes/objectives Selecting content Planning phases Learning experiences Organization Evaluation	Objectives Selecting content Curriculum integration Evaluation	Objectives Planning Evaluation Accountability	Goals Objectives Organizing sets Growth schemes Instructional strategies Assessment Problem-solving Curriculum materials	Situational Analysis Objectives Selecting content Selecting method Evaluation Evaluation models Evaluating curriculum Programming
Curriculum change	Curriculum improvement Teacher in-service		Planning for plural society Democratic curriculum		
Politics of curriculum Issues and trends Directions of theory and research	Curriculum problems Future directions		Politics		

various aspects of this topic. With the exception of several chapters on learning models, no chapters address the other six categories included in the American examples. The Australian text (Brady, 1987), is also very limited and only includes chapters in the two categories presented by Robinson, *et al.* (1985).

Categories of Concepts Included in This Volume

After examining a wide range of synoptic curriculum texts, including the six described above, I made a decision to include material relating to the following categories:

Student Perspectives
Teacher Perspectives
Curriculum Planning and Development
Curriculum Management
Curriculum Ideology

Figure 1.1: Concepts included in 'Student Perspectives'

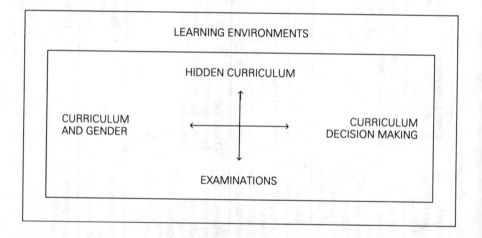

For each category a number of brief chapters, termed *modules* were developed. Each module focuses upon a *key concept* in terms of its major characteristics, strengths and weaknesses. Follow-up questions and references are also included in each module.

Student Perspectives is the first category and contains five modules. The titles of these concepts are listed in figure 1.1. The five modules are closely inter-related in that they portray various aspects of the classroom life of the student, such as client, colleague, resistor, and passive recipient of instruction.

Figure 1.2: *Concepts included in 'Teacher Perspectives'*

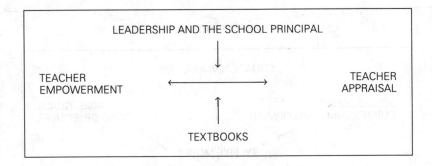

Gender issues (module 3) can be a major source of conflict in schools and can often lead to sex role stereotyping and lack of self-esteem for girls. The *hidden curriculum* (module 2) of the classroom, in terms of its rituals and rules, can exacerbate the problems for females and can discriminate markedly against minority groups.

In some schools there may be opportunities for students to participate in *curriculum decision-making* (module 4) and where this occurs, more cooperative and satisfying learning can result for both students and teachers. However, *examinations* (module 5) often loom large and this can limit the opportunities for creative planning and cooperation between students and teachers. Examinations can also have the effect of encouraging didactic forms of teaching.

The *learning environment* (module 1) in terms of the physical arrangement of furniture and resources and appropriate levels of noise and temperature, can facilitate or hinder learning. Some open planned classrooms can provide a liberating atmosphere for students whereas some traditional architectural forms can be sterile and forbidding.

The concepts included in these five modules emphasize student interests and problems of unequal power relationships between students and teachers. Questions are raised about functions of schools, about schools as a source of conflict for students and about the legal and moral rights of students as clients and consumers.

Teacher Perspectives is the second category and this contains four modules, consisting of 'empowerment', 'textbooks', 'leadership' and 'appraisal' (see figure 1.2). It can be argued that 'empowerment' and 'appraisal' are two of the most contentious issues facing teachers today. Some writers maintain that teachers are taken too much for granted, that they are only permitted to undertake technical tasks and that over recent years they have become de-skilled and disempowered. Others argue that there are opportunities for teachers to become *empowered* (module 6), and one such opportunity is via *teacher appraisal* (module 9) schemes which can provide valuable feedback and professional development experiences for teachers. Teacher appraisal provides opportunities for teacher self-monitoring and for staff members as a

Figure 1.3: *Concepts included in 'Curriculum Planning and Development'*

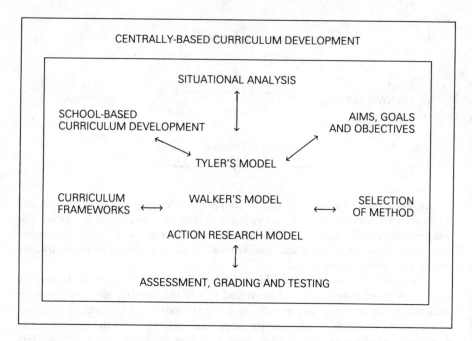

collectivity, to systematically develop and build upon their strengths and interests.

Leadership skills (module 8) emanating especially from the school principal, are of considerable importance in encouraging teachers and giving them opportunities to achieve greater intrinsic rewards. Excessive use of *textbooks* (module 7) by teachers is symptomatic of teacher disempowerment and domination by multinational publishers. Yet, an informed understanding of the purposes and limitations of textbooks can lead to them becoming a valuable resource for students and teachers.

The concepts dealing with the teacher perspective endeavour to examine some of the human aspects of teaching — the crutches that some teachers use (for example, textbooks), the pressures which can bear down upon teacher creativity and initiatives, and yet the opportunities which exist for professional growth.

Curriculum Planning and Development is the third category and contains ten modules. These are listed in figure 1.3. A useful starting point is to examine the three planning models (module 15, 'Tyler's Model of Planning'; module 16, 'Walker's Deliberative Approach to Planning'; and module 17, 'Teachers as Researchers/Action Research').

These modules represent three very different approaches to curriculum planning. The Tyler model provides an explicit set of procedures for planning which is based upon a scientific-rational orientation. Walker's model is far less precise and emphasizes the amount of dialogue and interaction (deliberation) which needs to occur between members of a planning team. The Action Research model highlights the need for classroom teachers at a school to take responsibility for their curriculum development. The emphasis in this model is upon using classroom problems as the basis for collaboration, for searching out solutions, and for implementing changes.

The different value stances implicit in these three modules are also reflected in the remaining seven modules. For example, 'Curriculum Frameworks' (module 10) can be construed as being a useful platform to demonstrate commonalities between subjects and is consistent with ideas contained in Walker's model. Then again, some writers argue that curriculum frameworks are an important control mechanism — an instrument of compliance. These writers link frameworks with the Tyler model and conclude that they are overly restrictive.

'Assessment, Grading and Testing' (module 14) has links with the three models, with the intensity of the connection being affected by the value orientations described above.

The modules 'Aims, Goals and Objectives' (module 12) and 'Selection of Method' (module 13) have special relevance for the Tyler and Walker models and to a lesser extent, to the Action Research model. By contrast, 'Situational Analysis/ Needs Assessment' (module 11) and 'School-Based Curriculum Development' (module 19) are directly related to the Action Research model and less so to the other two models.

The module 'Centrally-Based Curriculum Development' (module 18) is depicted in figure 1.3 as being separate from the other nine concepts. The reason for this is that centralized modes of curriculum development operate at a different level. For example, centrally-based curriculum development is often controlled by senior administrators and increasingly, politicians. They are the ones who have access to the knowledge and information and they make decisions as a superordinate group. Eventually these decisions are transmitted to the subordinate group, the teachers.

In total, it can be seen that the ten concepts included in this category are closely interrelated. All are involved in one or more of the processes of curriculum planning and development.

Curriculum Management is the fourth category and contains six modules. These are listed in figure 1.4. 'Innovation and Planned Change' (module 20) is of major importance because it refers to a variety of change processes. For example, 'Curriculum Implementation' (module 25) is one of the specialized change processes. 'School Evaluations/ Reviews' (module 24) are often undertaken by management groups to pinpoint changes needed in schools.

'Effective Schools and School Improvement' (module 22) considers some of the changes which tend to be prescribed for schools via state legislation and mandates, as well as other initiatives. Some of these efforts over recent years have been successful but many have faltered, which points to insufficient attention being given to important implementation factors.

'School Councils and Governing Bodies' (module 23) have been chang-

Figure 1.4:   Concepts included in 'Curriculum Management'

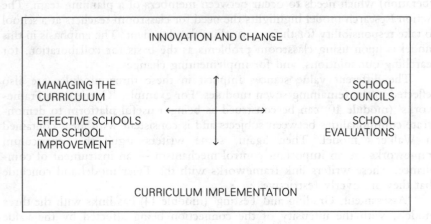

Figure 1.5:   Concepts included in 'Curriculum Ideology'

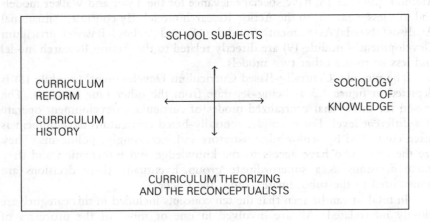

ing quite markedly, especially in the United Kingdom and Australia. These developments raise important questions about decision-making, and about appropriate representation of community interests.

'Managing the Curriculum: The Collaborative School Management Model' (module 21) is included as a model of change which has been very successful in a number of schools in Australia, the United Kingdom and New Zealand. Management of the decision-making is undertaken by a policy group (which can include parents) and by various project teams of teachers.

Curriculum Ideology is the fifth category and contains five modules, as listed in figure 1.5. An overview of competing ideologies is included in 'Curriculum Theorizing and the Reconceptualists' (module 28). Theorizing involves reflecting about curriculum matters and seeking meaning and direction to curriculum experiences.

A specialized example of theorizing is included in the module 'Sociology of Knowledge Approach to Curriculum' (module 29) which argues that schools reproduce the values and attitudes needed to maintain dominant social groups.

'School Subjects' (module 27) examines the coalitions of interests which occur between sub-groups in a discipline. This seems to lead inexorably toward academic or pedagogic or utilitarian emphases for individual subjects.

'Curriculum History' (module 26) also examines ideological emphases. In this module the focus is upon ideological changes over the decades. The dominance of the technological emphasis is given special attention. It is argued that studies of curriculum history have value because they provide valuable insights about the complex relationships between the past, present and future.

'Curriculum Reform' (module 30) examines some of the ideological bases for reforms initiated recently, especially the current emphasis in several countries upon excellence, and economic productivity. Some of the reforms currently being proposed are pluralist and even contradictory, while others are closely integrated and presented as a total package of reform by the groups concerned.

The five categories described above provide a framework for discussing the thirty concepts. Each category does have specific characteristics and there is some logic in the modules allocated to each. Yet it must be stressed that each module is treated separately and independently. The reader is not expected to read the modules in any set order and there are no prior readings required of earlier modules to master later ones. After reflection and discussion, the reader may discover that there are different combinations of concepts that are more meaningful to him/her. Some of these alternatives are discussed in the following section.

Some Alternative Groupings of Concepts

A theme which is very evident in the curriculum literature relates to '*cooperative, democratic decision-making at the school-level*'. It assumes shared decision-making between teachers, parents and students. The emphasis is also upon the development of appropriate physical and human resources to bring about maximum learning for students. The listing of modules in figure 1.6 links together ten concepts that are related to this theme.

The 'Collaborative School Management Model' (module 21) is a very good example of cooperative decision-making. Other modules such as 'School Councils and Governing Bodies' (module 23) and 'Situational Analysis/Needs Assessment' (module 11) all contribute to our understanding of school-based decision making.

Figure 1.6: Concepts included in a 'Cooperative, democratic, decision-making' theme

Learning Environments	(module 1)
Students' Role in Curriculum Decision-Making	(module 4)
Teacher Empowerment	(module 6)
Situational Analysis/Needs Assessment	(module 11)
Teachers as Researchers/Action Research	(module 17)
School-Based Curriculum Development	(module 19)
Managing the Curriculum: The Collaborative School Management Model	(module 21)
School Councils and Governing Bodies	(module 23)
School Evaluations/Reviews	(module 24)
Curriculum Theorizing and the Reconceptualists	(module 28)

Figure 1.7: Concepts included in a 'Performance driven, student outcomes, academic excellence' theme

Examinations	(module 5)
Textbooks	(module 7)
Assessment, Grading and Testing	(module 14)
Tyler's Model of Planning	(module 15)
Centrally-Based Curriculum Development	(module 18)
Effective Schools and School Improvement	(module 22)
School Evaluations/Reviews	(module 24)
Curriculum Implementation	(module 25)
Curriculum Reform	(module 30)

Another theme which is also frequently cited in the literature can be depicted by the terms '*performance driven, student outcomes, and academic excellence*'. This theme is concerned with economic indicators, rational planning and observable student performances. The listing of modules in figure 1.7 links together nine concepts that support this theme.

The use of textbooks (module 7) and the influence of examinations (module 5) are clearly related to a performance-driven theme. So too are such concepts as 'Tyler's Model of Planning' (module 15) and 'School Evaluations/ Reviews' (module 24).

Many other themes might be also described but these two examples are sufficient to illustrate the combinations that can be formed.

There are benefits for the readers in reflecting upon each concept and considering examples from their teaching experiences which tend to support or do not support the statements included in a module. The questions at the end of each module should also stimulate the reader to ask probing questions and to explore matters further, perhaps by making use of the references included at the end of each module.

There are no simple answers or recipes for major issues in curriculum. However, the time spent in reflecting extensively over curriculum matters can be most rewarding. It is to be hoped that the key concepts presented in this volume provide an accessible entry-point for readers embarking upon this journey.

References

BRADY, L. (1987) *Curriculum Development*, 2nd edn, Sydney, Prentice Hall.

KELLY, A.V. (1977) *The Curriculum: Theory and Practice*, London, Harper and Row.

LAWTON, D. (1986) *Curriculum Studies and Educational Planning*, London, Hodder and Stoughton.

MARSH, C.J. and STAFFORD, K. (1988) *Curriculum: Practices and Issues*, 2nd edn, Sydney, McGraw Hill.

McNEIL, J.D. (1985) *Curriculum: A Comprehensive Introduction*. 3rd edn, Boston, Little, Brown and Company.

ROBINSON, F.G., ROSS J.A. and WHITE, F. (1985) *Curriculum Development for Effective Instruction*, Toronto, OISE Press.

ROGAN, J.M. (1991) 'Curriculum Texts: The portrayal of the field', Part II, *Journal of Curriculum Studies*, **23**, 1.

ROGAN, J.M. and LUCKOWSKI, J.A. (1990) 'Curriculum Texts: The portrayal of the field', Part 1, *Journal of Curriculum Studies*, **22**, 1.

SCHUBERT, W.H. (1980) *Curriculum Books: The First Eighty Years*, New York, University Press of America.

SCHUBERT, W.H. (1986) *Curriculum: Perspective, Paradigm, and Possibility*, New York, Macmillan.

Part 1

Student Perspectives

Chapter 1

Learning Environments

Classroom environments are an integral part of the learning process and no teacher or student can be unaffected by their presence. In any school, the class teachers and students have to adjust to the building architecture — the overall space, the position and number of doors and windows, the height of ceiling and the insulation qualities of the walls. Teachers and students have the opportunity to 'express their "personalities" through the arrangement and decor of the environment and the arrangement of space' (Ross, 1982, pp. 1–2). However, creative arrangements need to be undertaken in the knowledge that specific physical conditions and space allocations can have important consequences on the attitudes, behaviours and even the achievements of students.

Student Needs and Person-Environment Fit

Students have a number of needs with regard to classroom patterns of use and these include:

(a)   A need for them to be seated at points in the classroom where they can comfortably undertake the learning activities. This might include being close to the teacher to see and hear him/her clearly without straining; to be able to read the blackboard/whiteboard/ overhead projector in comfort; to be close enough to the teacher and centrally located to ensure that they will be fully engaged in the interactions (questioning, discussions) with the teacher.

(b)   A need for them to be located with peers with whom they have a close and mutually positive relationship (Woods, 1990).

(c)   A need for them to have learning goals and value orientations consonant with those adopted by the classroom teacher (and which would be reflected in the teacher's use of classroom space and activity segments).

A teacher may desire to organize his/her class on the basis of *territory* or by *function*; the former focuses on a teacher-dominated purpose while the latter emphasizes a resource specialization, student-initiated focus.

In classrooms organized by territory, the major decision is how to allocate and arrange student desks and chairs. It is assumed that each student has his/her own domain/work space and that this is the basis for considering how certain learning activities will occur. The teacher may produce some rather different configurations of desks in his/her efforts to encourage particular kinds of interactions between students, but the focus of each activity segment and the location of the desks will be such that the teacher remains the central figure.

Classrooms organized on the basis of function are commonly found in junior grades in primary schools and in specialist subject areas (for example, Media, Science or Woodwork) in many secondary schools. In this case, the allocation of space is based upon what specialist materials/activities can be accommodated in a given area, and the matter of the location of desks is only of minor consideration. If several different functional areas are to be included in the one room, then additional considerations need to be made about how each area should be arranged in relation to the others.

It is desirable to try to obtain the optimal *person-environment fit* for students and teachers. Inventories have been developed which provide background data about teachers' styles of teaching (including learning goals and value orientations) and students' preferences. These can assist greatly in obtaining a desirable person–environment fit.

For example, the *Classroom Environment Scale Manual* (Moos and Trickett, 1978) has been widely used in the USA. This instrument measures nine different dimensions of the classroom environment including students' interpersonal relationships, personal growth, and teacher control.

'*My Class Inventory*' is an instrument developed by Fisher and Fraser (1981) and is used to gain information about students' perceptions of classroom goals and value orientations. The items require students to make ratings on actual classroom environments as well as preferred environments. This information can be of great interest to class teachers who are concerned about providing instructional environments which are more in accord with those preferred by students.

Physical Environment Factors

Colour

The media are very aware of the use of colour and it is little wonder that colour television, colour inserts in daily newspapers, glossy colour magazines and colour computer games are so popular. So it is in classrooms. The list of items which can add colour to a classroom are endless. Newspaper clippings, pamphlets and photographs are an integral part of many classrooms and they can add to the visual impact. So too can three dimensional models (for example, of landscapes, buildings and animals) and dioramas. Even the latest nooks and cubicles for microcomputers found in many classrooms add to the diversity of colours in the typical classroom.

Noise

Sounds are all around us but when certain sounds are unwanted it is generally termed 'noise'. Bell, Fisher and Loomis (1976) make this point when emphasizing that noise involves a physical component (by the ear and higher brain structures) but also a psychological component when it is evaluated as unwanted.

As far as the classroom is concerned, it is important that the physical environment provides acoustics which enable participants to hold discussions in a normal conversational voice. The level of desirable noise will vary in different settings such as a manual arts workshop with noisy lathes and electric drills to an extremely quiet library. Each instructional setting has its own noise level requirements to the extent that each person can hear clearly what is needed to be heard and not be distracted by other noises (Eriksen and Wintermute, 1983).

Every classroom has a background noise level due to the operation of various ventilation and audiovisual appliances (for example, oscillating fans, recorders, computer keyboards, calculators, etc.). Background noise level (BNL) is typically measured in decibels. According to the Department of Education and Science (1975) in the United Kingdom, a teacher can communicate clearly in a quiet voice when BNL rises to 35 dB. A normal voice will carry quite well over a BNL of 40 dB, but once a BNL of 45 dB or 50 dB is reached a teacher (or student) has to speak in a very loud voice. Inevitably the exchange of conversation in a loud voice can lead to irritation, stress and fatigue. Of course the irritation is generated by disagreements over what is being said as well as the level of noise which is being created by the sender. A particular noise, of itself, may or may not be wanted. More often it is the unpredictability or lack of control over the source of noise which is the major cause of the frustration.

Temperature

Common sense would indicate that there is a fairly limited temperature range in which school students might be expected to work at their best. High temperatures will tend to make some students irritable and uncomfortable. In extreme cases students can become lethargic and even nauseated. Then again, cold temperatures seem to bring out aggression and negative behaviour in some students.

Judgments about temperature control in schools are typically made at head office in that decisions about the architectural design of schools and the use of specific building materials are made at this level. The use of particular designs, the siting of buildings and the use of insulating material will clearly affect maximum and minimum temperatures.

Within each school, a principal may be able to seek additional equipment to maintain the temperature at moderate levels. For example, oscillating ceiling fans are commonly used now in many schools and the traditional hearth and wood fires have given way to oil and gas-fired heaters.

Reflections and Issues

1   Judging from what is said and from what is available as a measuring stick, schools are architecturally and environmentally sterile ... Their structure is insipid, cavernous and regimented. They are only now and then really creature-comfortable. Their designs maximize economy, surveillance, safety and — maybe — efficiency (George and McKinley, 1974, p. 141).

[Open planned classroom environments] are a liberatory measure capable of emancipating children from the authority of teachers (Cooper, 1982, p. 268).

Compare and contrast these two statements about schools.

2   The classroom environment is such a potent determinant of student outcomes that it should not be ignored by those wishing to improve the effectiveness of schools (Fraser, 1986, p. 1).

In what ways does the classroom environment determine student outcomes? What can a class teacher do to maximize the positive elements of a classroom environment?

3 According to Evans (1990), a school is both the temple and the exhibition hall of the modern world. Brightly coloured curtains and carpets are part of the intentions to display desired features to the public. But important aspects of teaching and administration remain hidden. In fact, care is often taken to indicate the 'official' way into the school.

Do you agree with this statement? To what extent do the physical forms of schools give out messages to the public?

References

BELL, P.A., FISHER, J.D. and LOOMIS, R.J. (1976) *Environmental Psychology*, Philadelphia, W.B. Saunders.

COOPER, I. (1982) 'The maintenance of order and use of space in primary school buildings', *British Journal of Sociology of Education*, **3**, 3.

DEPARTMENT OF EDUCATION AND SCIENCE (1975) *Acoustics in Educational Buildings*, London, HMSO.

ERIKSEN, A. and WINTERMUTE, M. (1983) 'Students, Structure, Spaces: Activities in the Built Environment', ERIC Research in Education, ED233796, Washington DC.

EVANS, K. (1990) 'Messages Conveyed by Physical Forms', in LOFTHOUSE, B., *The Study of Primary Education: A Source Book, Volume 2, The Curriculum*, London, Falmer Press.

FISHER, D.L. and FRASER, B.J. (1981) 'Validity and use of the "My Class Inventory"', *Science Education*, **65**.

FRASER, B.J. (1986) *Classroom Environment*, London, Croom Helm.

GEORGE, C.J. and MCKINLEY, D. (1974) *Urban Ecology*, New York, McGraw-Hill.

MOOS, R.H. and TRICKETT, E. (1978) *Classroom Environment Scale Manual*, Palo Alto, Consulting Psychologist Press.

ROSS, R.P. (1982) 'The Design of Educational Environment: An expression of individual differences or evidence of the "press toward synomorphy"?', Paper presented at the Annual Meeting of the American Educational Research Association, New York.

WOODS, P. (1990) *The Happiest Days?*, London, Falmer Press.

Chapter 2

Hidden Curriculum

Phillip Jackson (1968) first coined the term 'hidden curriculum' in his book *Life in Classrooms*. He used the term to indicate that the social requirements of learning at school are often hidden but are extremely important. He emphasized three elements of the hidden curriculum as being:

(a) the crowded nature of the classroom — pupils have to cope with delays, denial of their desires and social distractions;
(b) contradictory allegiances required of both teachers and peers;
(c) unequal power relations given to teachers over pupils.

The key aspect of the term 'hidden curriculum' is its hiddenness but can there be degrees of hiddenness (Seddon, 1983)? Can the effects of the hidden curriculum be beneficial as well as detrimental? According to Seddon (1983), the hidden curriculum involves the learning of attitudes, norms, beliefs, values and assumptions often expressed as rules, rituals and regulations. They are rarely questioned and are just taken for granted. The judgment about whether a hidden curriculum is positive or negative depends upon the value stance of the person concerned.

Functionalist Perspective

Jackson's analysis of hidden curriculum is labelled as a *functionalist* perspective because it is assumed that schools promote the goals and functions of the wider society. That is, Jackson was intent on explaining how structures within schools operate or function.

Critical Perspective

There have been many critical perspectives about 'hidden curriculum'. For example, Bowles and Gintis (1976) argue that schools function to maintain the capitalist system because of particular social relations which occur in schools, namely:

(a) the hierarchical division of labour between teachers and pupils;
(b) the alienated character of pupils' school work;
(c) the fragmentation in work (and the destructive competition among students).

They argue that a student's social class/race/gender all have significance in determining the social experiences they have at school — that is, there is not a unitary hidden curriculum but *many*.

Michael Apple, in several major books (1979, 1982, 1986), argues from a slightly different critical stance. Apple (1979) argues in *Ideology and Curriculum* that there is high-status and low-status curriculum knowledge. The poor and minorities are excluded from the high-status (technical) knowledge and this is used as a device to filter for economic stratification and future career prospects. In *Education and Power*, Apple (1982) argues that schools are producers of culture and its reproduction in schools is presented in forms which are either accepted (by career-oriented bourgeoisie) or contested and resisted (by lower classes). In *Teachers and Texts*, Apple (1986) describes how reproduction occurs through the control of teachers and textbooks in schools. He argues that the variety of textbooks and curriculum packages on the market causes teachers (and especially females as they are in the majority in the teaching profession) to be deskilled.

A very powerful impression of the hidden curriculum at work is contained in Paul Willis (1977) *Learning to Labour*. He portrays how twelve 'lads', observed at a northern county secondary school, resisted the authority of the school system and developed their own counter culture. The boys were able to penetrate the arbitrariness of the power relationship between teachers and students and in fact developed their own powers within the school environment (Lynch, 1989, p. 17). But in practising their resistance at school they reproduced their male working-class position, which is likely to lead to a subordinate social position in adult life. Willis argues that it is not school structures which are important in understanding the hidden curriculum but pupil resistances.

Lynch (1989) argues that inequality is perpetuated via the hidden curriculum because of *universalistic* and *particularistic* aspects of schools. Many of the universalistic qualities of schools are highly visible and include such elements of provision as syllabuses, prescribed content, length of school periods and examination procedures. They apply to all students regardless of social class and background. Particularistic aspects of schools apply more to consumption elements such as streaming and grading, timetabling practices and reward systems. These elements are more familiar to some social groups and are used by them to further their own ends. It is the particularistic elements that increase inequalities but they are not widely known or understood and are 'hidden' from many groups.

In her study of ninety schools in Ireland she discovered that schools which were predominantly middle and upper class maximized the consumption of educational resources among all students (frequent assessments, strong academic climate) whereas in schools with large numbers of working class students, consumption was maximized only for a minority of the higher achieving students. Whitty (1990) suggests that policies included in the Education Reform Act for England and Wales (1988) will also produce this differentiation with LEA schools becoming yet again the paupers compared with the public schools.

Examinations seem to carry a hidden curriculum of their own (see also module 5). Although the major purpose of examinations is to assess students' performance they can also have a considerable effect upon:

(a) methods of teaching,
(b) students' levels of motivation,
(c) assignment of senior teachers to particular classes,
(d) interactions between a teacher and students.

Turner (1983) suggests that for some students the hidden curriculum effects of examinations are to stimulate conformity to teachers' demands. However some students may seek deviant behaviour because it is more attractive to them than passing examinations. Some of the very able students may be very selective and only conform in activities that they perceive are directly related to the passing of examinations.

Reflections and Issues

1 Is the hidden curriculum a process *or* an outcome of learning *or* both? Use examples to illustrate your answer.

2 To make sense of the hidden curriculum means that schools have to be analyzed as agents of legitimation, organized to produce and reproduce the dominant categories, values, and social relationships necessary for the maintenance of the larger society (Giroux, 1981, p. 72).

Provide arguments to support or refute this stance.

3 The reason why the term 'hidden curriculum' has become so accepted is that by definition its mechanisms are so difficult to uncover; cause and effect remain largely at the speculative level and it is a convenient concept to explain the large part of school life rarely open to quantitative research, but full of conjecture (Davies, 1984, p. 188).

Discuss.

4 Whose interests are served by a hidden curriculum? Is it possible to

reveal and incorporate a hidden curriculum into a 'taught' curriculum?

5   Consider the matter of school uniform:

What rule violations are ignored by teachers?
Are the rules more prescriptive for boys or girls?
Does the school uniform try to play down sex differences?
What are some symbolic meanings of schools uniform (for example, hair length)?
What aspects of ingenuity by students are tolerated so that students can compete with current fashions?

Reflect upon these matters and provide answers based upon your teaching experiences and point of view.

6   Schools uphold certain limited kinds of academic skills — particularly logical mathematical and linguistic intelligences — and demean and marginalize the rest (Lynch, 1989).

Discuss.

7   The differences in social, racial, ethnic and class backgrounds that students bring to schools are *maintained* or *magnified* as a result of their interaction with its organizational structures (Bullivant, 1987, p. 15).

Discuss.

8   Individual competition is only fair if one competes in a world with equally privileged peers. In a materially and culturally hierarchical society, competition between equals is impossible without either handicapping the privileged or compensating the relatively disadvantaged (Lynch, 1989, pp. 147–8).

Discuss.

9   Cornbleth (1990) describes the following as examples of hidden curriculum:

(a)   arrangement of time, facilities, materials and examinations.
(b)   compartmentalization of school programme into separate subjects.
(c)   texts treated as the most authoritative sources of knowledge.
(d)   grading systems.
(e)   district policies, school rituals.

Comment upon the extent to which you consider these examples are significant in the light of your teaching experiences.

10   Walker (1991) distinguishes between the teacher in the formal situa-

tion where he/she is constantly the centre of attraction and the informal situation when the teacher can be less conspicious and more personal. Do hidden curriculum elements assume greater importance in formal or informal learning situations? If so, what are the implications for teachers?

References

APPLE, M.W. (1979) *Ideology and Curriculum*, London, Routledge and Kegan Paul.
APPLE, M.W. (1982) *Education and Power*, London, Routledge and Kegan Paul.
APPLE, M.W. (1986) *Teachers and Texts: A Political Economy of Class and Gender Relations in Education*, London, Routledge and Kegan Paul.
BOWLES, S. and GINTIS, H. (1976) *Schooling in Capitalist America*, New York, Basic Books.
BULLIVANT, B.M. (1987) *The Ethnic Encounter in the Secondary School*, London, Falmer Press.
CORNBLETH, C. (1990) *Curriculum in Context*, London, Falmer Press.
DAVIES, L. (1984) *Pupil Power: Deviance and Gender in School*, London, Falmer Press.
DE CASTELL, S., LUKE A. and LUKE, C. (Eds) (1988) *Language, Authority and Criticism*, London, Falmer Press.
GIROUX, H.A. (1981) *Ideology, Culture and the Process of Schooling*, London, Falmer Press.
HAMMERSLEY, M. and HARGREAVES, A. (1983) *Curriculum Practice: Some Sociological Case Studies*, London, Falmer Press.
JACKSON, P.W. (1968) *Life in Classrooms*, New York, Holt, Rinehart and Winston.
LYNCH, K. (1989) *The Hidden Curriculum*, London, Falmer Press.
SEDDON, T. (1983) 'The Hidden Curriculum: An Overview', *Curriculum Perspectives*, **3**, 1.
TURNER, G. (1983) 'The Hidden Curriculum of Examinations', in HAMMERSLEY, M. and HARGREAVES, A., *Curriculum Practice: Some Sociological Case Studies*, London, Falmer Press.
WALKER, R. (1991) 'Classroom Identities', in GOODSON, I.F. and WALKER, R., *Biography, Identity and Schooling: Episodes in Educational Research*, London, Falmer Press.
WHITTY, G. (1990) 'The New Right and the National Curriculum: State Control or Market Forces?', in FLUDE, M. and HAMMER, M. (Eds) *The Education Reform Act, 1988: Its Origins and Implications*, London, Falmer Press.
WILLIS, P. (1977) *Learning to Labour*, London, Saxon House.

Chapter 3

Curriculum and Gender

'Gender' must be considered along with 'class' as a major source of power. The problem is that our understandings of the world are based on a male experience. There is a need to either *integrate* aspects of women's studies into the curriculum and into all the disciplines or to establish *autonomous* women's studies as a subject in its own right.

Major Issues

Women's experiences of life have largely disappeared from our knowledge of the past. Most people are ignorant of past women's achievements and of their everyday lives (Porter, 1986). Porter (1986) suggests that:

(a) we have a distorted history but one which is not seen to be distorted.
(b) the male experience is seen as central to life and female experience is seen in *relation* to male experience and hence is peripheral.

The differentiation of schooling experiences according to sex has been critically examined over the last two or three decades in most Western countries and found to be unacceptable. In these countries equal opportunity legislation and appropriate agencies have been established in an attempt to eradicate discriminatory practices.

However, many vestiges of differentiation still remain such as the traditional pattern of recruitment to subjects according to sex ('girls' subjects and 'boys' subjects); sexual divisions in the home and labour market; teachers' attitudes, expectations and their inadvertent discriminatory behaviour.

Schools tend to demand gender-related behaviour and this is conveyed via the official curriculum and the hidden curriculum (see module 2). Administratively, gender distinctions are made because they are useful to the school goals or ease of operation. Examples include:

(a) separate assemblies on occasions for boys and girls;
(b) health and safety reasons given for limited access of girls to certain courses;
(c) separate sporting teams and fixtures with major rewards being linked to male teams;
(d) forms of discipline for boys and girls;
(e) rules about school uniform (especially restrictions for females; Davies, 1984; Clarricoates, 1990; Lesko, 1988).

Gender problems are not confined to schools. There are massive sexual inequalities in the home and in the workplace. Some major issues, according to Anderson (1989) and Acker (1989) include:

(a) the double load of many females of following a career and taking most responsibility for rearing children and the guilt that often occurs in not being able to provide enough time to do both;
(b) families tend to reinforce negative aspects about female status and achievements and these attitudes persist through their children when they enter school;
(c) in the workplace there are still major inequalities for females in terms of salaries, promotional opportunities.

Sex-role stereotyping is very evident in our society. For example, papers and magazines include many sexist cartoons depicting masculinity and femininity. Career opportunities for girls are more restricted than for boys. Advertising in the media exploits females and males. It is a major responsibility for all teachers to provide class activities to students to reduce sex-role stereotyping habits.

Recent Research Studies

Wyn's (1990) study of working-class girls in schools in Melbourne concluded that they

(a) had as career goals, traditional work such as 'working with kids', hairdressing;
(b) they were interested in male dominated occupations but were usually pressurized by family or peers to go for traditional female occupations;
(c) they wanted predominantly to be able to establish themselves as adults and to develop stable friendships;
(d) they saw school as boring, irrelevant and at times a source of conflict and developed their own strategies for coping with this by 'mucking about'.

Lustig-Selzer (1991) argues that male historians have largely determined the structure and content of the Australian History curriculum at Year 12 level in Victoria during the period from the 1940s to the late 1970s. She cites as evidence that:

(a) membership of the history committee up until the 1980s has been predominantly male;
(b) the content of the syllabuses between 1940s to the 1970s has been the public world of men, their politics, diplomacy, economy and culture;
(c) an analysis of eight major textbooks for the period shows that they highlighted males as the active agents making and shaping our history.

Some Practical Classroom Ideas

Sex bias against females occurs across all subjects taught in primary and secondary schools. For example, Hillman and Parker (1987) remind us that there is a lot of stereotyping and frequent omission of women in social studies textbooks. It might be useful for you to do your own survey of a social studies text. Start by analyzing the following:

the number of men listed in the index,
the number of women listed in the index,
the number of illustrations depicting men,
the number of illustrations depicting women,
the number of illustrations depicting both,
the names of women found in each index (Yanonne, 1983, p. 10).

Hillman and Parker (1987) argue that if teachers work toward achieving sex equity they need to be constantly asking themselves the following questions:

Do I consciously look for sex bias in my situation, that is, in written or oral statements, organization and policy?
If I find sex bias, do I attempt to correct the situation, look for support or ignore and accept it?
Do I consider that some activities, tasks, etc. are more appropriate for males than females?
Do I allocate tasks on a basis of sex, race and ethnic origin?
Do I consciously arrange groups of mixed sexes?
Do I have specific expectations for a particular sex?
Do I actively encourage resistance to stereotypes?
Do I consciously attempt to avoid using sexist language?
(Curriculum Development Centre, 1976, pp. 18–19)

There are many useful activities to heighten awareness among students about sex and gender issues. Consider the following questions:

What does it mean to say someone is:

> male?
> masculine?
> female?
> feminine?

What are the differences between men and women?
How many of these are inborn and have a biological basis?
How many are the result of upbringing, of conditioning?
(Tasmanian SEMP Team, 1979, p. 9).

Not all recent policy developments in curriculum build upon advances in reducing female discrimination in schools. For example, Miles and Middleton (1990) argue that the Education Reform Act (1988) in the United Kingdom is not greatly concerned with equal opportunities for male and female students, rather the emphasis is upon raising educational standards to meet the needs of the economy and of industry. These authors consider that:

(a) the privileged position of mathematics, science and technology in the new national curriculum tends to reflect and reinforce masculine modes of thought and understanding.

(b) the greater emphasis on assessment will affect girls' performance because external tests tend to disadvantage them compared with boys.

(c) the chronic shortage of teachers and imminent use of untrained graduates will have a detrimental effect on girls' education.

(d) in-service training will concentrate on traditional content and assessment and not on gender and multicultural issues.

Reflections and Issues

1 What kinds of arguments would you provide against the following propositions:

(a) equity for women diverts resources from other groups in need.

(b) sex equity has now been achieved and there is no problem any more (Sadker et al., 1989).

2 How do teachers express their own sexuality, consciously or unconsciously?
Can teachers ever be sexually neutral in the classroom?
Does a teacher's sex-role ideology affect his/her interactions in the classroom?

3 The term 'inclusive curriculum' is sometimes used to promote the need for social justice for all students. What are the implications of this term for curriculum planners?

4 The differences between girls and boys in the choice of options subjects at school are closely related to sexual divisions in the home and the labour market (Hammersley and Hargreaves, 1983).

Discuss.

5 The evidence is far from clear that girls have low self-esteem or that schools have a detrimental influence on girls' self-esteem — the differences between girls' and boys' self-esteem are related more to sex role stereotyping (Renshaw, 1990).

From your teaching experiences do you agree or disagree with this statement?

6 Learning theory has tended to assume a gender-neutral pupil but it does seem that gender needs to be put into the study of the curriculum (Measor, 1983, p. 189).

Give examples of how learning theory is not gender-neutral. What strategies can teachers use to overcome this discrimination against females?

7 Teachers' life-styles are an important factor affecting gender-based differentiation in schools. They bring to the classroom various attitudes, expectations and behaviours and these can vary over teachers' life cycles (Goodson and Walker, 1991).

Give examples of how teachers affect classroom interactions between males and females. How might teachers' behaviours vary over their teaching life cycles due to such issues as teacher stress and burn-out; amount of recognition given for innovatory actions; opportunities for management and evaluation.

8 As teachers we can gain considerable insights about gender differentiation in schools by reflecting upon our own behaviour. We need to consider, write about and interpret our teaching experiences (Grumet, 1989).

How would you go about this process? What data would you try to collect about your own teaching?

9 For young women in high schools, school status and opportunities are not the result of just what they know or do in subjects but that their position in a school organization and among peers is strongly influenced by how they control or fail to control their bodies. For girls, the curriculum of the

body appears to be an implicit, accepted and powerful basis for differentiation and stratification (Lesko, 1988, p. 139).

Do you accept this argument? Give illustrations to support your point of view.

References

ACKER, S. (Ed.) (1989) *Teachers, Gender and Careers*, London, Falmer Press.

ANDERSON, B. (1989) 'The Gender Dimensions of Home-School Relations', in MAC-LEOD, F. (Ed.) *Parents and Schools: The Contemporary Challenge*, London, Falmer Press.

CLARRICOATES, K. (1990) 'Gender Stereotyping: Another Aspect of the "Hidden Curriculum"', in LOFTHOUSE, B., *The Study of Primary Education: A Source Book, Volume 2, The Curriculum*, London, Falmer Press.

CURRICULUM DEVELOPMENT CENTRE (1976) 'Non-Sexist Curriculum', background paper No. 5, International Women's Year Conference 1, Melbourne, August.

DAVIES, L. (1984) *Pupil Power: Deviance and Gender in School*, London, Falmer Press.

GOODSON, I.F. and WALKER, R. (1991) *Biography, Identity and Schooling: Episodes and Educational Research*, London, Falmer Press.

GRUMET, M. (1989) 'Feminism and the Phenomenology of the Familiar', in MILBURN, G., GOODSON, I.F. and CLARK, R.J. (Eds) *Re-Interpreting Curriculum Research: Images and Arguments*, London, Falmer Press.

HAMMERSLEY, M. and HARGREAVES, A. (1983) *Curriculum Practice: Some Sociological Case Studies*, London, Falmer Press.

HILLMAN, W. and PARKER, L. (1987) 'Women's Studies', in MARSH, C.J. (Ed.) *Teaching Social Studies*, Sydney, Prentice Hall.

KENWAY, J. and WILLIS, S. (Eds) (1990) *Hearts and Minds: Self-Esteem and the Schooling of Girls*, London, Falmer Press.

LESKO, N. (1988) 'The Curriculum of the Body: Lessons from a Catholic High School', in ROMAN, L.G., CHRISTIAN-SMITH, L.K. and ELLSWORTH, E. (Eds) *Becoming Feminine: the Politics of Popular Culture*, London, Falmer Press.

LUSTIG-SELZER, A. (1991) 'Androcentricism in Australian History at Year 12 Level, Victoria', *Curriculum Perspectives*, **11**, 2.

MEASOR, L. (1983) 'Gender and the Sciences: Pupils' Gender-Based Conceptions of School Subjects', in HAMMERSLEY, M. and HARGREAVES, A., *Curriculum Practice: Some Sociological Case Studies*, London, Falmer Press.

MILES, S. and MIDDLETON, C. (1990) 'Girls' Education in the Balance: the ERA and Inequality', in FLUDE, M. and HAMMER, M. (Eds) *The Education Reform Act, 1988*, London, Falmer Press.

PORTER, P. (1985) 'The Sexism You Have When You Aren't Having Sexism: Issues of Women's Role and Influence in Education', keynote address to the Women in Education Conference, April, Perth.

PORTER, P. (1986) *Sociology of the School: Gender and Education*, Geelong, Deakin University Press.

RENSHAW, P. (1990) 'Self-Esteem Research and Equity Programmes for Girls: A Reassessment', in KENWAY, J. and WILLIS, S. (Eds) *Hearts and Minds: Self-Esteem and the Schooling of Girls*, London, Falmer Press.

SADKER, M., SADKER, D. and STEINDAM, S. (1989) 'Gender Equity and Educational Reform', *Educational Leadership*, **46**, 6.

TASMANIAN SEMP TEAM (1979) *Women and Men: Teaching the Concepts*, Canberra, CDC.
WYN, J. (1990) 'Working-Class Girls and Educational Outcomes: Is Self-Esteem an Issue?', in KENWAY, J. and WILLIS, S. (Eds) *Hearts and Minds: Self-Esteem and the Schooling of Girls*, London, Falmer Press.
YANONNE, D.S. (1983) 'No Sexist History in this Class! Social Studies Awakens to the Study of Her Story', *Media and Methods*, 2.

Chapter 4

Students' Role in Curriculum Decision-Making

Points For and Against Participation

Some Reasons For Enlisting Student Participation

(a) Students do more than just 'receive' a curriculum — they become engaged with it, and they can become active initiators and reactors to it (Measor, 1984). It might be anticipated, therefore, that a more broadly based group of persons discussing curriculum matters should lead to more informed decisions being made.

(b) Students should be perceived as clients in the educational situation. In business dealings clients have certain rights and expectations and a relatively high standing. After all, they are the recipients — the ultimate audience for certain learning activities.

(c) Students, especially at the secondary school level, are already participating in leadership positions in other spheres such as sporting clubs, leisure groups, religious organizations and clubs. These students have already developed effective leadership and communication skills and therefore have the potential to be effective participants in curriculum-planning activities.

(d) Students have legal rights which cover various aspects of schooling including curriculum decision-making. Some of these legal rights have in fact been tested in the courts, especially in the USA since the 1960s. A number of court decisions have upheld student rights regarding outcomes of schooling (for example, basic literacy) and the rights to enrol in particular programmes.

(e) Collegial relationships between teachers and students can be advanced considerably if students are permitted to become active participants in curriculum decision-making.

Figure 4.1: *Student participation continuum at two levels: (a) individual classroom, and (b) school-wide*

(a) Individual classroom level continuum		
Students consulted	Students take an active role in planning	Students share in decision-making for most classroom activities
(e.g. needs analysis)	(e.g. research projects)	(e.g. all subjects require negotiated conditions)

(b) School-wide level continuum		
Students consulted	Students take an active role	Students share in the decision-making
(e.g. school evaluation)	(e.g. Student Representative Council)	(e.g. School Council)

Some Reasons Against Enlisting Student Participation

(a) Decision-making should be left to the professionals. Teachers are given intensive training in such areas as child development and learning styles, philosophical studies, educational measurement, subject methods.

(b) A classroom teacher spends inordinate amounts of time creating a particular classroom climate, producing order and stability out of a sea of faces, a cacophony of requests and comments, and a bewildering array of behaviours. It is an extremely difficult task. The creation and maintenance of a productive working environment requires respect for and harmonious interactions between teacher and students. Providing students with opportunities to participate in decision-making can break down all the established norms and codes of behaviour essential for class discipline and a positive class tone. A teacher must maintain his or her respect from students as the professional decision-maker.

(c) External constraints, such as public examinations, give little scope for teachers to deviate from established and relatively narrow academic syllabuses. There is little point therefore in encouraging student participation in curriculum planning if, in fact, there is no viable alternative to an academic syllabus which is textbook- and examination-oriented.

Levels of Participation

Student participation can be conceptualized at two different levels, at the *individual classroom* and the *total school* levels. At each level it is useful to consider a continuum ranging from minimal to high degrees of student participation (see figure 4.1).

Student Participation at the Individual Classroom Level

Within an individual classroom teachers have the opportunity to encourage student participation in the planning and implementation of particular curricula; or they can restrict it, and perhaps stifle participation opportunities quite deliberately.

Students consulted
At the minimal participation end of the continuum (figure 4.1), students are not given opportunities to participate directly in the planning of their curricula, but teachers may, in various ways, seek out student needs and interests.

The type of input from students is largely that of *receiver* to questions asked by a teacher. It could be almost entirely a *passive role*, in that the teacher might make certain planning decisions based upon his or her observations of the class of students in different learning situations (Davies, 1984).

Students take an active role in planning certain activities
A middle position on the 'individual classroom' continuum is where students take an active role in planning *selected classroom activities*. Although it might be possible to provide some choice to students in lower primary grades it would appear to be more relevant to older students such as upper primary and secondary school students.

It is very much a compromise position, with teachers relinquishing a certain degree of control in areas and activities where it is considered that students could become highly self-motivated and innovative in their approaches.

Students share in the decision-making
This type of decision-making (see figure 4.1) refers to students becoming active participants in all subjects at the classroom level.

Publications, such as Griffiths (1986) provide numerous suggestions about how students might become active participants in classroom-decision-making. Suggestions include:

(a) Students negotiate with the teacher about the types of assessment that might be used (including self-assessment procedures).
(b) Students negotiate with the teacher about the teaching methods/ organizational procedures that might be used to accommodate a variety of student backgrounds.
(c) Students negotiate with the teacher about how classroom activities will be monitored and evaluated, to inform future decision-making.
(d) Students negotiate with the teacher about contracts (individual or group) for doing certain tasks/activities within subjects. As an example, contracts involving computer-assisted tasks are becoming increasingly popular and it is an area where students have developed considerable expertise (Griffiths, 1986).

Student Participation at the School-Wide Level

When we turn to school-wide activities there are several ways in which student input can and should be obtained, as illustrated on the continuum in figure 4.1.

Students consulted
Schools are becoming increasingly involved in periodic *school reviews* and *evaluations*. In these various school review efforts, the studies typically examine a number of formal and informal school activities, including of course the teaching and learning activities of teachers and students. Many of the evaluation studies seek data from students because it is realized that this is a valid and reliable source of information. A number of recent research studies (for example, Marsh and Overall, 1979; Aleamoni, 1981; Farley, 1981) indicate that:

(a) students can make consistent judgments.
(b) students can make reliable descriptions of classroom activities.
(c) students can make accurate judgments about specific teachers whom they see every day.

And that:

(d) students do not typically provide inflated or distorted judgments.
(e) students are usually very candid in their comments, and they can be brutally honest.

Students take an active role (for example, Student Representative Council)
The middle and right-hand position on the 'school-wide' continuum indicates quite active student participation. Rather than students merely being consulted on matters such as school reviews, this position involves more elaborate efforts to have students participating in school-wide activities.

In many schools in Victoria, Australia, activities have led to the formation of student representative councils (SRCs). These SRCs are very different from the traditional student councils, usually nominated by staff and typically having token responsibilities such as organizing the annual school ball. The SRCs as they are developing are intended to provide truly representative decision-making for students. As a result, students get involved in many activities (for example, student newspapers, lunchtime meetings, weekend seminars). In so doing, they often require permission to be absent from certain classes, and there are sensitive matters to resolve such as whether they should have access to confidential school documents or not.

Reflections and Issues

1 Students are the only group who can portray the lived-in quality of schooling (Vallance, 1981).

Do we seek information and understandings from students? What might be some gains for curriculum planning?

2 Examine the following list of legal rights of students:

- the right to an effective education, as measured by outcomes of schooling;
- the right to have access to schools that are geared to respond effectively to different needs and cultures;
- the right to be provided with an educational environment that is comfortable and conducive to learning;
- the right to equality of educational opportunity;
- the right of access to and instruction in all things that affect their social development (Fitzgerald and Pettit, 1978, p. 34; Blakers, 1980, p. 1).

To what extent are these legal rights provided at your school? Have any of these ever been contested in local courts? What were the outcomes?

3 Do you agree that there tends to be little opportunity for high levels of student participation in curriculum decision-making in government secondary schools and independent (public) schools? Give reasons to support your stand.

4 It is important that teachers find out the ways which their students receive school subjects, and their reactions to different areas of the curriculum (Measor, 1984). Do students receive school subjects differently? If so, can this cause problems for the typical classroom teacher?

5 To what extent do you consider that discipline problems in schools and truancy might be alleviated if students had greater opportunities to be involved in planning school activities? Are there additional deep-seated reasons for student opposition to schools?

References

ALEAMONI, L.M. (1981) 'The Students' Ratings of Teachers', in MILLMAN, J. (Ed.) *Handbook of Teacher Evaluation*, Beverly Hills, California, Sage Publications.

BLAKERS, C. (1980) 'Principals Seven', ACSSO Discussion Paper, Canberra.

DAVIES, L. (1984) *Pupil Power: Deviance and Gender in School*, London, Falmer Press.

FARLEY, J.M. (1981) 'Student Interviews as an Evaluation Tool', *Educational Leadership*, **39**, 3.

FITZGERALD, R.T. and PETTIT, D.W. (1978) *Schools in the Community: A Growing Relationship*, Canberra, Schools Commission.

GRIFFITHS, B. (1986) *Negotiating the Curriculum*, Melbourne, Ministry of Education.

MARSH, H.W. and OVERALL, A.U. (1979) 'Long-Term Stability of Students' Evaluations', *Research in Higher Education*, **10**.

MEASOR, L. (1984) 'Pupil Perceptions of Subject Status', in GOODSON, I.F. and BALL, S.J. (Eds) *Defining the Curriculum: Histories and Ethnographies*, London, Falmer Press.

VALLANCE, E. (1981) 'Focus on Students in Curriculum Knowledge: A Critique of Curriculum Criticism', paper presented at the Annual Conference of the American Educational Research Association, Los Angeles.

Chapter 5

Examinations

Examinations have always figured prominently in education systems in most countries. In China they have been in use as early as the Han dynasty (202BC–190AD). At that time formal examinations were introduced to select persons for key posts in the Imperial household. Examinations are still used extensively in the twentieth century although there has been a shift in some countries to remove examinations from the primary school level and to retain them at senior secondary school levels.

Examinations tend to be administered by independent or quasi-independent agencies consisting of assessment specialists, university personnel and teachers. In some countries, such as the People's Republic of China, examinations are administered by the central government.

The term 'public' examination is commonly used to describe examinations open to persons of any age and background. Public examinations are used predominantly to select students for entry to tertiary institutions, and in some countries, for selection into senior secondary school.

Public examinations are of major importance as regulators of selection into tertiary studies. To date no credible alternatives have been accepted and they are still viewed as legitimate gatekeepers for entry into universities (Broadfoot, 1986).

Public examinations enable persons to be selected for occupational roles using criteria other than birth and social class. This growth of a meritocracy has endured ever since it developed in Western countries during the nineteenth century. Some specific assumptions underpinning this use of public examinations include:

(a) schools rather than another social agency select persons of merit via the examinations.
(b) failure in an examination is the fault of an individual and not the fault of a school.
(c) examination procedures can provide rational, equitable and acceptable forms of selection.

In some cases examinations are 'external' in that each paper is set and marked by external individuals or groups but an increasing number are combinations of school assessments and external examinations.

There appears to be a trend toward greater control by the teaching profession over public examinations via initiatives taken to incorporate school assessments as a significant portion of the total examination scores.

Points For and Against Public Examinations

Some of the commonly listed advantages and disadvantages of public examinations are contained in tables 5.1 and 5.2:

Table 5.1: Advantages of a public examination

(a) It can provide an objective assessment of a student's performance.

(b) It can define common standards of performance required for adequate completion of a syllabus.

(c) It has status in the wider community.

Table 5.2: Disadvantages of a public examination

(a) It can only cover a limited part of the course syllabus.
(b) It can capture only a small sample of a student's performance, even on the topics tested, within the period of time allotted.
(c) It can be biased against students who do not perform well under examination pressures.
(d) It may encourage a concentration in teaching on those aspects of a course which are most readily assessed by an external examination.
(e) It may encourage didactic teaching and rote learning.
(f) It can often be biased in favour of particular social and cultural groups.
(g) It can often involve inaccuracies of marking and subsequent variations in the marks awarded for the same piece of work.
(h) It is expensive in terms of development costs and operating and administrative costs.

General Certificate of Secondary Education (GCSE)

The General Certificate of Secondary Education (GCSE) is a new public examination introduced in the United Kingdom in 1988 for fifth-formers and is a useful case study example. The *purposes* of the GCSE are:

(a) to improve the quality of education and to raise standards of attainment;
(b) to produce a system which is fair to candidates;
(c) to motivate teachers and pupils by setting clear targets;
(d) to enhance the esteem in which the examinations are held;
(e) to promote improvements in the secondary school curriculum (Kingdon and Stobart, 1988; Grant, 1989).

Major Features

(a) Positive achievement — all candidates should be able to demonstrate what they know, understand and can do.
(b) Differentiated examinations (examinations set at different levels of difficulty within the subject) are available to meet the needs of candidates with different levels of ability.
(c) All syllabuses for the GCSE contain some teacher-assessed components.

Implications

(a) The school-based elements will require more time to be spent by teachers on preparing and grading tests and more time by students in preparing major papers and preparing for tests.
(b) It is far more demanding for chief examiners to have to set differentiated examination papers.
(c) It has caused teachers in schools to work cooperatively with each other on assessment tasks and has provided an impetus for teachers upon wider assessment issues.

Reflections and Issues

1   It is important not to overestimate the influence examinations have on teachers ... Teachers are not passive subjects of controlling forces. They may even be able to play some sources of power off against others (Horton, 1987).

Give examples of how teachers may be able to use these sources of power to their own advantage.

2   Over recent years examination structures have changed whereby there is now a greater measure of internal freedom in both syllabus and assessment, while preserving the authority of an external examining agency (Kay, 1978).

Has this been the case in your experience? Give reasons.

3   It is certainly the case that success in competitive examinations is, for most people, an essential prelude to the legitimate exercise of power, responsibility and status throughout modern societies (Eggleston, 1984).

Do you agree with this statement in the 1990s? Give reasons for your acceptance or rejection of the statement.

4   Examinations, perhaps more than any other single factor in the schooling process, are widely regarded as having an

educationally undesirable effect on schools and as represent-
ing a significant constraint on curriculum innovation (Hammersley and Hargreaves, 1983, p. 11).

Can these claims be justified? Is there any empirical evidence? Alternatively, do examinations form a normal and natural part of
teaching?

5 Some commonly attributed negative effects of examinations include:

- they are an unreliable measure of learning achievement
  (Nuttall, 1986).
- they are strongly correlated with social class and occupational attainment (Scarth, 1983).
- they play a key role in selective assessment for cultural
  reproduction (Broadfoot, 1984).

Critically analyze these statements in the light of your teaching
experiences.

6 Arrangements for assessing the national curriculum in the
United Kingdom include the use of teacher assessments and
a variation of public examinations termed standard assessment tasks (criterion-referenced tasks to be undertaken by all
students at particular age levels). This assumes a whole-
school approach to assessing, recording and reporting
achievement (Flude and Hammer, 1990).

Is this a feasible assumption to make? What do you envisage as some
possible difficulties in UK schools?

References

BROADFOOT, P.M. (Ed.) (1984) *Selection, Certification and Control: Social Issues in Edu-
cational Assessment*, London, Falmer Press.
BROADFOOT, P.M. (1986) 'Alternatives to Public Examinations', in NUTTALL, D.L.
(Ed.) *Assessing Educational Achievement*, London, Falmer Press.
EGGLESTON, J. (1984) 'School Examinations: Some Sociological Issues', in BROADFOOT,
P.M. (Ed.) *Selection, Certification and Control*, London, Falmer Press.
FLUDE, M. and HAMMER, M. (Eds) (1990) *The Education Reform Act: 1988*, London,
Falmer Press.
GRANT, M. (1989) *GCSE in Practice*, London, NFER-Nelson.
HAMMERSLEY, M. and HARGREAVES, A. (1983) *Curriculum Practice: Some Sociological
Case Studies*, London, Falmer Press.
HORTON, T. (1987) *GCSE: Examining the New System*, London, Harper and Row.
KAY, B.W. (1978) 'Monitoring Pupils' Performance', in HOPKINSON, D. (Ed.) *Stand-
ards and the School Curriculum*, London, Ward Lock Educational.
KINGDON, M. and STOBART, G. (1988) *GCSE Examined*, London, Falmer Press.
NUTTALL, D.L. (Ed.) (1986) *Assessing Educational Achievement*, London, Falmer Press.
SCARTH, J. (1983) 'Teachers' School-Based Experiences of Examining', in HAMMERS-
LEY, M. and HARGREAVES, A., *Curriculum Practice: Some Sociological Case Studies*,
London, Falmer Press.

Part 2

Teacher Perspectives

Chapter 6

Teacher Empowerment

The term *teacher empowerment* has various meanings associated with it in the education literature. Examples include as a slogan for class struggle; as a term to connote collegial learning with students; and to connote increased expertise due to technological advances.

Empowered versus Disempowered

'Power' can be defined as control but in terms of educational settings it is more useful to consider power as 'doing or acting'. Opportunities for teachers to try out new approaches, to problem-solve and to inquire, assist them in becoming *empowered*. Empowerment of teachers (and students) occurs when they have opportunities to create meaning in their respective schools. By contrast, *disempowered* teachers are those who teach defensively and control knowledge in order to control students (McNeil, 1988). In these situations schooling becomes an empty ritual, unrelated to personal or cultural knowledge.

Teacher empowerment is seen by writers such as Giroux (1982) as a significant concept in understanding the complex relations between schools and the dominant society. He argues that teachers and students need empowerment to resist and to struggle against the domination in society produced by capitalism.

Some writers argue that teachers are becoming steadily *disempowered* (Apple, 1986; Ozga and Lawn, 1981). For example, Apple (1986) argues that teachers face the prospect of being deskilled because of the encroachment of technical control procedures into the curriculum in schools. He cites as examples behaviourally-based curricula, prespecified competencies for teachers and students and testing activities.

Empowerment can also be considered as teacher and student empowerment, *jointly developed* (see module 4). Boomer (1982) and Green (1988) argue that students must be given opportunities to contribute to and modify the curriculum, so that they will have a real investment both in the learning processes and the outcomes. The negotiation process between a teacher and his/her students empowers both groups as they share commitments and make decisions about class activities. Green (1988) refers to the affective and cognitive tensions in the classrooms as a teacher and his/her students permit and commission various *power* sanctions. Different learning situations will permit or require certain actions. Actions of power occur with great subtlety and include legal power, informational power, charismatic power, physical power and many other forms exercised by both teachers and students.

Some Approaches to Empowering Teachers

Teachers can become *empowered* through increased resources, such as technology. Recently, educators have been proposing that broad-based use of computer technology (for example, word processors, spreadsheets and data bases) can enhance teaching and teachers can match the technology to their own creativity (Valdez, 1986).

With computers, teachers and students can learn together — they can share experiences as they try out new programmes — both groups can become empowered as they master additional uses and ends of computer technology. Individuals use computers in different ways and allow the machine to be integrated into their sense of identity — that is the big payoff.

Some writers consider that teachers are not interested in empowerment because of limiting factors in the culture of teaching. For example, Hargreaves (1989) argues that teachers are present-oriented, conservative and individualistic. They tend to avoid long-term planning and collaboration with their colleagues.

McCutcheon (1988) takes a more positive stance. She admits that there are teaching situations in a number of countries where the curriculum to be taught by teachers is specified, so that it can be controlled by administrators or national reformers. Examples which are occurring currently are teacher competency tests and student achievement tests. Yet, each classroom teacher can still make important decisions about what he/she will teach. The teacher is the filter through which the mandated curriculum passes (McCutcheon, 1988). Teachers filter the objectives and conceive of ways of enacting them, they make sense of the teaching context and make the necessary adjustments.

Teachers can and do identify problems and progress to defining them and seeking resolutions. Teachers are dedicated, responsible and morally-committed professionals. They are empowered to inquire into matters critically, in order to improve their own practice. The inquiries and reflections can occur in *preactive* mental planning of lessons, *interactively* during lessons and in *post-lesson* reflections. They can also occur individually or collaboratively among a group of teachers.

School administrators have the resources and the opportunities to empower teachers. They can provide leadership opportunities for outstanding staff members. They can increase opportunities during the school day for teachers to interact on teaching problems (Nias, 1990).

Effective *reward* systems can be used to increase:

(a) teacher motivation
(b) acceptance of personal accountability
(c) continuous professional development
(d) acceptance of an enlarged definition of teacher work responsibilities.

Reward systems need to be a mixture of intrinsic satisfactions (for example, exciting work, positive working conditions, interesting co-workers) and extrinsic benefits (for example, promotions, public recognition; Mitchell and Peters, 1988).

Ideally teachers can become increasingly empowered by:

(a) working together on joint projects.
(b) talking to one another at a level of detail that is rich and meaningful.
(c) shared planning or evaluation of topics.
(d) observing their colleagues in peer observation arrangements.
(e) training together and training one another (for example, teaching others about new ideas and classroom practices).
(f) having access to appropriate levels of material and human support/resources (Little, 1990).

A problem for teacher groups becoming empowered is that teachers are trained to survive in the system as *individuals*. Teachers have few ways of sharing their experience. As noted by Walker and Kushner (1991, p. 194), 'precious time available for staff meetings tends to be gobbled up by scheduling arrangements and by the need to consider closely each individual child's progress.' There is little opportunity for schools to reflect on their practices. This can be a major deficiency because major problems for teachers are problems of organizations.

Clark and Meloy (1990) suggest that problems of schools as organizations can be greatly reduced by developing *democratic* structures, incorporating the following principles:

(a) designated leaders (for example, the principal) should be chosen by the teachers.
(b) the school must be built on shared authority and responsibility, not delegation of authority and responsibility.
(c) all staff should have terms of work as administrators as well as classroom teachers.
(d) formal rewards to the staff (for example, forms of promotion) should be under the control of the staff.
(e) the goals of the school must be formulated by and agreed to through group consensus.

47

Reflections and Issues

1   We must preserve and protect those teachers (and materials) who without fear examine the problems of our society realistically (Littleford, 1983).

Are teachers discouraged from openly discussing societal issues in your experience? Give reasons.

2   Teachers are thinkers who make many decisions that create the curriculum in classrooms. They have an important function in shaping what students have an opportunity to learn (McCutcheon, 1988).

Are teachers sufficiently empowered to undertake this function?

3   At the root of many ill-conceived panaceas of the past is that teachers have been taken for granted and have been treated as classroom furniture rather than as thinking human beings (Shanker, 1986).

Discuss.

4   The three major factors that facilitate empowerment include *acquisition of support* (for example, endorsement by the principal), *information* (for example, technical data) and *resources* (for example, human services). Do you agree that these are important factors? Give examples to support your answer.

5   Teachers seeking empowerment have to resolve the common tensions between management and curriculum. Decisions are often made in favour of management which emphasizes the need to survive above the urge to learn and to develop (Walker and Kushner, 1991).

Is this the typical pattern in your experience?
How can both groups' ends be served more appropriately?

6   We are certain of one thing. We will never move within the bureaucratic structure to new schools, to free schools. That structure was invented to assure domination and control. It will never produce freedom and self-actualization. The bureaucratic structure is failing in a manner so critical that adaptations will not forestall its collapse. It is impractical. It does not fit the psychological and personal needs of the workforce (Clark and Meloy, 1990, p. 21).

To what extent do you support this stance?
If the bureaucratic structure is failing why has it survived so long?
Are there potential pitfalls with a democratic alternative?

7   As well as influences such as commitment and interests bearing on teachers from within themselves, as it were, there are

forces from without, over which the teacher may have little control (Woods, 1990, p. 15).

What are some of these external constraints? How does a teacher typically cope with them? Can this lead to conflicts between personal goals and external constraints?

8   Teachers are generally isolated from one another and receive little recognition from either colleagues or administrators ... Everybody does their own thing and nobody helps anybody else. As a consequence, the school becomes atomized and the educational enterprise is hopelessly segmented (Webb, 1985, p. 84).

Explain how teacher isolation deprives teachers of power and leads to powerlessness about school-wide decisions.

9   Bureaucratic rationality dictates that effective and efficient means be found that match predetermined ends. In pursuit of effectiveness and efficiency, the administrators need to influence the motives of their subordinates, and control and direct them in such ways as to produce maximum benefits to the organization (Rizvi, 1989, p. 71).

Is this an accurate portrayal of what typically occurs in schools with which you are familiar? What strategies can teachers use, if any, to empower themselves within this structure?

References

APPLE, M.W. (1986) *Teachers and Texts*, New York, Routledge and Kegan Paul.

BOOMER, G. (Ed.) (1982) *Negotiating the Curriculum*, Sydney, Ashton Scholastic.

CLARK, D.L. and MELOY, J.M. (1990) 'Recanting Bureaucracy: A Democratic Structure for Leadership in Schools', in LIEBERMAN, A. (Ed.) *Schools as Collaborative Cultures: Creating the Future Now*, London, Falmer Press.

GIROUX, H.A. (1982) 'Power and Resistance in the New Sociology of Education: Beyond Theories of Social and Cultural Reproduction', *Curriculum Perspectives*, **2**, 3.

GREEN, B. (Ed.) (1988) *Metaphors and Meanings*, Perth, Australian Association for the Teaching of English.

HARGREAVES, A. (1989) *Curriculum and Assessment Reform*, Milton Keynes, Open University Press.

LITTLE, J.W. (1990) 'Teachers as Colleagues' in LIEBERMAN, A. (Ed.) *Schools as Collaborative Cultures: Creating the Future Now*, London, Falmer Press.

LITTLEFORD, M.S. (1983) 'Censorship, Academic Freedom and the Public School Teacher', *Journal of Curriculum Theorizing*, **5**, 3.

McCUTCHEON, G. (1988) 'Curriculum and the Work of Teachers', in BEYER, L.E. and APPLE, M.W. *The Curriculum*, New York, State University of New York Press.

McNEIL, L. (1988) 'Contradictions of Control, Part 2, Teachers, Students, and Curriculum', *Phi Delta Kappan*, **69**.

MITCHELL, D.E. and PETERS, M.J. (1988) 'A Strong Profession through Appropriate Teacher Incentives', *Educational Leadership*, **46**, 3.

NIAS, D.J. (1990) 'A Deputy Head Observed: Findings from an Ethnographic Study', in SOUTHWORTH, G. and LOFTHOUSE, B. *The Study of Primary Education, A Source Book, Volume 3, School Organization and Management*, London, Falmer Press.

OZGA, J. and LAWN, M. (1981) *Teachers, Professionalism and Class*, London, Falmer Press.

RIZVI, F. (1989) 'Bureaucratic Rationality and the Promise of Democratic Schooling', in CARR, W. (Ed.) *Quality and Teaching*, London, Falmer Press.

SHANKER, A. (1986) 'Teachers Must Take Charge', *Educational Leadership*, **44**, 1.

VALDEZ, G. (1986) 'Realizing the Potential of Educational Technology,' *Educational Leadership*, **43**, 6.

WALKER, R. and KUSHNER, S. (1991) 'Theorizing a Curriculum', in GOODSON, I.F. and WALKER, R., *Biography, Identity and Schooling: Episodes in Educational Research*, London, Falmer Press.

WEBB, R.B. (1985) 'Teacher Status Panic: Moving Up the Down Escalator', in BALL, S.J. and GOODSON, I.F. (Eds) *Teachers' Lives and Careers*, London, Falmer Press.

WOODS, P. (1990) *Teacher Skills and Strategies*, London, Falmer Press.

Chapter 7

Textbooks

Textbooks play a major role in the structure and day-to-day teaching activities in the classroom. Textbooks are the tools used by a teacher to motivate students and to give them maximum understanding about a topic or problem. The well-organized teacher will use textbooks in different ways to suit different levels of students.

If teachers are not aware of it, textbooks can greatly influence and determine what they teach and how they teach it (content and values).

Some Definitions

A Student Textbook

(a) is written at a level suitable for particular groups of children;
(b) is carefully sequenced and illustrated;
(c) includes exercises and questions.

A Teachers' Guide

(a) offers advice to teachers about teaching a specific subject;
(b) is written in practical terms but can include easy and difficult sections;
(c) includes content and methodology suggestions;
(d) includes resource details;
(e) can sometimes include student textbook sections.

A Syllabus

(a) contains explicit details about objectives, content and assessment procedures for a unit or course;

(b) can include recommendations about teaching methods and resources;

(c) is usually very brief and concise.

Curriculum Materials

Curriculum materials are any physical objects, representational in nature,
which are used to assist the learning process. They can be:

(a) printed matter;
(b) physical models;
(c) audiovisual items;
(d) combinations of all of these.

Each item or object represents something else and has no instructional
significance in itself. That is, a textbook has no significance until a teacher
and students interact with it. A floppy disk has no significance until it is
inserted into a computer.

A number of studies reveal how much teachers rely upon textbooks and
related curriculum materials.

Examples

A USA study

● of the total teaching time in Grade 5 classrooms, 78 per cent of it
involved students using textbooks.

A USA study

● the dependence on textbooks varies with different subjects: Social
Studies (72 per cent), Science (49 per cent), Mathematics (45 per
cent), Language Arts (44 per cent).

A UK study

● textbooks are by far the most commonly used curriculum materials.
Other important ones include worksheets, maps and pictures, globes
and models.

Different Expectations About Textbooks

What Principals Expect

(a) up-to-date content,
(b) material that is easy to understand,
(c) relatively cheap to purchase.

What Teachers Expect

(a) some new content or rearranged content,
(b) new ideas about organizing their teaching,
(c) up-dated resource lists,
(d) an up-to-date summary on a particular topic.

What Students Expect

(a) information that is easy to understand,
(b) information that is an up-to-date summary on a particular topic,
(c) material that is directly related to the syllabus and the examinations that they have to pass.

What Authors Expect

(a) that they can present up-to-date information in an interesting way,
(b) that their textbook is unique and special,
(c) that teachers and students will recognize its usefulness and use it in class.

Is it possible for textbooks to satisfy all four groups? What about expectations of parents? What are some conflicts that can occur between these groups?

Features of Textbooks

Instructional Load

(a) This is the subject matter to be communicated to the reader.
(b) It is usually the stated purpose for which the book was written.
(c) There is also unintended material included (biases, stereotypes).
(d) The instructional load represents the knowledge which is considered most worthy to be transmitted.

Mode of Presentation

(a) This is the mode in which the instructional load is presented. It might be a hard-cover or soft-cover book.
(b) It might be aimed at students or teachers or both.
(c) It might include audio-visuals and computer software.
(d) The mode of presentation apparatus will depend on the subject, level of teaching, financial constraints, space and equipment constraints.

Illustration Features

(a) This usually consists of photographs, art work (cartoons, drawings) and tables and graphs.
(b) The combination and sequence can vary enormously.
(c) They can have an enormous impact on the use of a textbook.

Access Features

(a) These include the table of contents, headings and sub-headings, indexes, glossary, etc.
(b) They are the key to a textbook's information system.

Display Features

They include such things as the cover, chapter openings and other devices to enhance the book's attractiveness, to highlight its organization and to arouse the user's interest.

Whether a teacher will use a particular textbook at all will depend upon policy decisions at the school, competing texts, etc. In addition, some criteria that a teacher might use include:

(a) is the content up-to-date?
(b) are major concepts of the discipline emphasised?
(c) is the print and general layout attractive?
(d) can it be adapted to students of different ability?
(e) are there opportunities to develop creativity?
(f) are there opportunities to educate for national values?
(g) is the level of the target student population specified?
(h) is the language difficult?
(i) what is the price of the textbook?
(j) is the teacher free to choose and initiate teaching strategies?
(k) is a teachers' guide included?
(l) can the teacher use it without special training?

(m)   do the materials contain suggestions for homework?
(n)   will it require a lot of preparation time?

Checklists to Evaluate Textbooks

Comprehensive checklists have been developed recently which enable persons to evaluate textbooks in *isolation* or *in actual use* in classrooms. The former involves teachers in far less time and can be undertaken in any location and with little if any disruption to other persons. By contrast, an examination of curriculum materials *in use* requires not only a prior analysis of the contents but also permissions and other administrative procedures to allow researchers to enter classrooms so that teachers and students can be observed in action (and often interviewed afterwards on specific topics relating to the implementation of a curriculum). There are obviously many more demands implicit in the second option, including the need for lengthy periods of time by the researcher for observation and interviews, and for obtaining cooperation from school personnel.

To be of *practical use* to teachers a checklist scheme must:

(a)   be relatively simple to apply and economical in its use of time;
(b)   be sufficiently broad and flexible so that it can be applied to different subject areas;
(c)   be comprehensive in coverage so that it exposes the structure used by the developer of the curriculum materials;
(d)   enables decisions to be made about two or more competing sets of curriculum materials;
(e)   have a logical format which enables the evaluative details to be communicated readily to others.

Some examples of checklists which have been developed include those by Eraut (1975), Piper (1976) and Gall (1981). The example included in table 7.1 is based upon Gall (1981). For each dimension, reviewers of a text give a rating on a five point continuum using the adjectives as listed in table 7.1. Having completed this checklist, a reviewer would have a very comprehensive picture of a textbook but clearly it is a time-consuming activity.

In some countries (and states within countries) textbooks are an important part of the publishing industry. In some states in the USA textbooks have to be approved by state agencies and it is quite possible that a few selected books are approved for adoption to a huge number of school boards and thence to students. It is a million dollar industry, especially in the enormous markets of California and Texas and consequently economics and politics are involved. Textbook companies try to avoid controversial issues and content which might deter 'mainstream' education systems from accepting their products. Apple (1986) points out that a number of approved texts deliberately avoid issues of class, race and gender, so as to maintain high volume sales.

Table 7.1:   Inventory of evaluative criteria stated as adjectives

Publication and Cost

Analytic Dimension	Bipolar Adjectives
1 Authors	Expert ... Unqualified
2 Cost	Expensive ... Cheap
3 Development History	Well funded ... Poorly funded
4 Edition	Current ... Earlier (in the sense of, 'an earlier edition')
5 Publication Date	Recent ... Old
6 Publisher	Reputable ... Unreliable
7 Purchase Procedures	Easy ... Difficult
8 Quantity	Sufficient ... Insufficient
9 Special Requirements	Easy (to satisfy) ... Cumbersome (difficult to satisfy)
10 Teacher Training	Simple ... Complex

Physical Properties

Analytic Dimension	Bipolar Adjectives
11 Aesthetic Appeal	Beautiful ... Ugly
12 Components	Few ... Many
13 Consumables	Few ... Many
14 Durability	Sturdy ... Flimsy
15 Media	Appropriate ... Inappropriate
16 Quality	Fine ... Poor
17 Safety	Safe ... Dangerous

Content

Analytic Dimension	Bipolar Adjectives
18 Approach	Sound ... Weak
19 Instructional Objectives	Clear ... Unclear
20 Instructional Objectives — Types	Classified clearly ... Classified unclearly
21 Issues Orientation	Sensitive to alternative views ... Onesided
22 Multiculturalism	Multicultural ... Ethnocentric
23 Scope and Sequence	Appropriate ... Overly broad/narrow
24 Sex Roles	Unstereotyped ... Stereotyped
25 Time-boundedness	Current ... Dated

Instructional Properties

Analytic Dimension	Bipolar Adjectives
26 Assessment Devices	Helpful ... Not helpful
27 Comprehensibility	Clear ... Unclear
35 Motivational Properties	Exciting ... Dull
36 Prerequisites	Clear ... Unclear
37 Readability	Comprehensible ... Incomprehensible
38 Role of Student	Active ... Passive
39 Role of Teacher	Active ... Passive

(After Gall, 1981)

Reflections and Issues

1 If you were able to plan the ideal text for your subject area:

   (a) Work out five or six major priorities you would have.
   (b) Provide a brief outline of your table of contents.
   (c) What are some major issues/problems that you would need to consider?

2 Textbook publishers have the power to stimulate and shape demand and to constrain the choices available to the consumer (Lorimer and Keeney, 1989).

Discuss.

3 Of the many kinds of text available to the modern reader, the school textbook holds a unique and significant social function: to represent to each generation of students an officially sanctioned, authorised version of human knowledge and culture (De Castell *et al.*, 1989).

Do you agree with this point of view?
What are the implications for the classroom teacher?

References

APPLE, M. (1986) *Teachers & Texts*, New York, Routledge and Kegan Paul.
APPLE, M. (1989) 'The Political Economy of Text Publishing', in S. DE CASTELL *et al.* (Eds) *Language, Authority and Criticism: Readings on the School Textbook*, London, Falmer Press.
DE CASTELL, S., LUKE, A. and LUKE, C. (Eds) (1989) *Language, Authority and Criticism: Readings on the School Textbook*, London, Falmer Press.
ERAUT, M. (1975) *The Analysis of Curriculum Materials*, Brighton, University of Sussex Press.
GALL, M.D. (1981) *Handbook for Evaluating and Selecting Curriculum Materials*, Boston, Allyn and Bacon.
LORIMER, R. and KEENEY, P. (1989) 'Defining the Curriculum: The Role of the Multinational Textbook in Canada', in S. DE CASTELL *et al.* (Eds) *Language, Authority and Criticism: Readings on the School Textbook*, London, Falmer Press.
MARSH, C.J. (1986) *Curriculum: An Analytical Introduction*, Sydney, Ian Novak.
PIPER, K. (1976) *Evaluation in the Social Sciences for Secondary Schools: Teachers' Handbook*, Canberra, A.G.P.S.

Chapter 8

Leadership and the School Principal

The position of school principal is certainly an exacting one to uphold. So many different groups and individuals have expectations about what the school principal should do and should achieve.

- Parents and community members expect a public-minded, highly principled person who is open to outside initiatives and who will communicate information regularly to them.
- Teachers expect their school principal to be an instructional leader and a supporter of curriculum initiatives and to be very visible and active around the school buildings.
- Students expect a sympathetic counsellor and the final arbiter on matters of justice, discipline and penalties, but above all, an inspirational, charismatic figurehead.
- State department officials and senior regional officers expect school principals to be thorough, reliable and efficient and capable of implementing and monitoring departmental policies and not to be overly influenced by vocal minority groups.

In total, these beliefs about the role of the school principal contain obvious conflicts and ambiguities. A common expectation from many of these groups however, is that the principal demonstrates *leadership*.

Leadership Qualities

Leadership qualities are especially important in attempting school improvement ventures. The principal is a key agent for change in any such ventures. He/she needs to demonstrate leadership in the following domains:

- curriculum and instruction
- performance and development of students
- professional/personal performance of staff
- administration/organization

Table 8.1: Domains in which the principal is expected to demonstrate leadership

Curriculum and instruction
• reviewing or revising an existing subject
• influencing specific teaching methods
• introducing new subjects/units

Academic performance of students
• influencing achievement standards in all subjects
• encouraging high attainments by students in accordance with their abilities
• monitoring tests and examinations in specific subjects

Non-academic development of students
• managing or controlling student behaviour
• influencing student welfare/attitudes
• influencing students' extracurricular activities

Professional/personal performance of staff
• influencing the performance of teachers
• influencing the performance of administrators
• influencing induction of newly graduated teachers
• influencing the performance of student teachers
• supporting teacher welfare and their personal development

Administration/organization
• influencing schedule of teaching
• influencing student enrolment priorities
• influencing student decisions
• influencing operational efficiency

School facilities
• managing use of buildings, grounds and furnishings
• initiating changes to improve instruction
• initiating changes to improve aesthetics

External relations
• maintaining regular communication with school board members
• maintaining regular communication with regional and state education department officials
• providing positive public relations with the local community

(After Rutherford and Huling-Austin, 1984; Coulson, 1987; Griffin, 1990)

• school facilities
• external relations (see table 8.1 for more detailed descriptions)

Principal Styles

Ideally, a school principal should be a competent leader in all the domains listed in table 8.1. However, the reality of the school day, with its constant interruptions can put a principal under considerable stress. Typically, a principal will adopt a particular *leadership style* which emphasises certain domains and downgrades others. This is his/her coping mechanism and it is quite understandable. Three styles that are commonly reported in the literature are *responders, managers,* and *initiators* (Leithwood and Montgomery, 1982; Hall and Rutherford, 1983).

A *responder* principal places a high emphasis upon maintaining good relations with the staff. He or she tends to delegate responsibilities, listens to others rather than initiating ideas, and is generally low key and not demanding. This style of principal provides help to teachers when they initiate the need for assistance. A responder principal doesn't anticipate crises in advance nor is very concerned about long-term goals.

By contrast, a *manager* principal concentrates on getting tasks achieved, rather than placing such a heavy emphasis upon personal relationships. Such a principal likes to have an orderly, well-organized approach and have established procedures for all routine tasks. The manager principal likes to be available to teachers when needed. To ensure that he or she is available to teachers during school hours, the manager principal puts in long hours before and after school to complete all the necessary administrative tasks. A manager principal is prepared to intervene directly with staff over school improvement matters. He or she may prefer to use face-to-face contact with staff but will also use written memoranda quite regularly. The *initiator* principal has other characteristics which distinguish him or her from a responder principal and, to a lesser extent, from a manager principal. The initiator principal tends to be very secure and confident, tending to be businesslike in relations with staff. This style of principal makes his or her expectations very clear to all staff, and these are typically couched in terms of activities that are initiated to provide a better learning environment for students. The emphasis is very much upon student outcomes and how these might be raised to even higher levels (see table 8.2).

Each of these three principal 'styles' enable school improvement activities to develop and prosper, yet it might appear that the 'initiator' style is especially successful. If this is the case, it raises some interesting questions:

(a) Does it mean, therefore, that only initiator-style persons should be appointed as school principals?
(b) Does it indicate that a principal will adopt a particular leadership style and that he or she cannot change it over successive years, even with the assistance of training programmes?

Traditionally, in-service programmes for principals usually provide periods of one to three days, repeated at intervals of half a year or a year. They tend to focus on issues deemed to be important to principals, such as managing financial systems or resolving conflicts between school council members. They do not normally examine the total role of principal or, more importantly, examine leadership styles. However, some new programmes have been developed, especially in the USA and Canada, which do attempt to provide individualized training.

The Leithwood *et al.* (1984) programme outlined in table 8.3 is especially interesting as it makes the assumption that principal effectiveness is a continuous process which can be enhanced through training rather than a per-

Table 8.2:   Three different styles of principal

Responders

- They see their role as mainly administrative
- They allow teachers and others to take the lead in decision-making
- They perceive teachers as professionals and so don't interfere with their instructional role
- They strive for strong personal relationships with staff
- They make decisions in terms of immediate issues
- They do not speak about long-term goals and plans
- They are flexible and willing to make changes at short notice to solve immediate problems

Managers

- They provide basic support for all their staff
- They keep teachers informed about decisions
- They are sensitive to teacher needs
- They will defend their teachers from unreasonable requests from external colleagues
- They do not typically initiate change but will follow it through if it is given a high priority by others and especially if it is initiated by head office personnel

Initiators

- They have clear, decisive long-range policies and goals for their schools
- They work very hard to translate their goals into actual practice
- They make decisions in terms of what is best for students, not necessarily what is easiest or whether it makes their teachers happy
- They have strong expectations for students, teachers and themselves
- They are prepared to seize the lead and will make things happen, so long as it is in the best interests of their school
- They will reinterpret, if necessary, central and regional programmes and policies to suit the needs of their school

Source: Hall and Rutherford, 1983, pp. 6–7.

Table 8.3:   A training programme based on the principal profile

Stages	Decision-making	Goals	Strategies
1 Administrator	Relies on autocratic forms of decision-making	To 'run a smooth ship'	Delegating authority Reacting rather than planning ahead
2 Humanitarian	Makes decisions in favour of staff preferences Values a happy school	To provide a friendly, happy environment	Building and maintaining good interpersonal relationships
3 Programme manager	Attempts to involve staff in decision-making Is consistent in decision-making criteria	To define personal beliefs about what constitutes good programmes To meet the needs of students	Requiring staff to use goal setting and planning Striving to manage time effectively
4 Systematic problem-solver	Works to get staff involved in decision-making Uses different forms of decision-making as appropriate	To be aware of, knowledgeable about and committed to the full set of educational goals	Using many strategies Setting priorities Active involvement in programme decision-making

Source: Leithwood, Stanley and Montgomery, 1984, pp. 60–1.

sonality characteristic which some have and some have not. Based on studies of school principals in Canada, they defined four stages which they maintain are part of the continuum through which all principals progress, from *administrator* to *humanitarian* to *programme manager* to *systematic problem-solver*. The ultimate purpose of the training programme is to train principals to become *systematic problem-solvers*. The systematic problem-solvers, according to Leithwood *et al.* (1984) rely largely on informal forms of authority, they involve their teachers extensively in school decision-making and they establish systematic procedures continually monitoring and refining them as needed.

Reflections and Issues

1   Effective principals have a clear vision of goals and are strongly oriented to those goals (Smith and Andrews, 1989).

In your experience, are these major factors?
If not, what do you consider are more important factors?

2   Principals as dynamic change agents are still very rate — probably fewer than one in ten. Is this simply a function of training, selection and support on the job or do we have the wrong conception of the role of the principal? (Fullan, 1988, pp. 7–8)

3   We now know quite a lot (in research terms) about the roles and tasks of school leaders ... but little about what are 'better schools' or what we mean by 'effective leadership performance' (Bolam, 1987, pp. 100–1).

What do you understand by these latter terms?

4   We need to move away from the notion of how the principal can become master implementer of multiple policies and programmes. What is needed is to reframe the question. What does a reasonable leader do, faced with impossible tasks? (Fullan, 1988, p. 12).
Is it more productive to consider schools as operating in a non-rational world — with complex, contradictory happenings occurring daily?
What realistic priorities should a 'reasonable' leader select?

5   Changes in teaching occur not as a consequence of administrative fiat or intervention, but because teachers can see that systematically examining what they do enables them to uncover alternative ways (Smyth, 1986, p. 41).

What are the implications of this stance to leadership activities by a school principal?

6   Principals have recently come under increasing pressure from deteriorating financial situations, falling enrolments, rapid social change and the more controlling and constraining

character of central and local government policies (Coulson, 1990, p. 17).

How have these pressures affected the leadership activities of principals in your experience?

7 Leadership is and must be oriented toward social change, change which is transformative in degree (Foster, 1989, p. 52).

To what extent is this a major concern for school principals? What impediments may limit this as an option?

References

BOLAM, R. (1987) 'Management Development: A Response from the UK Perspective', in HOPKINS, D. (Ed.) *Improving the Quality of Schooling*, London, Falmer Press.

COULSON, A.A. (1987) 'Recruitment and Management Development for Primary Headship', in SOUTHWORTH, G. (Ed.) *Readings in Primary School Management*, London, Falmer Press.

COULSON, A.A. (1990) 'The Managerial Work of Primary Head Teachers', in SOUTHWORTH, G. and LOFTHOUSE, B. *The Study of Primary Education, A Source Book, Volume 3, School Organization and Management*, London, Falmer Press.

FOSTER, W. (1989) 'Toward a Critical Practice of Leadership', in SMYTH, J. (Ed.) *Critical Perspectives of Educational Leadership*, London, Falmer Press.

FULLAN, M.G. (1988) *What's Worth Fighting for in the Principalship?*, Toronto, Ontario Teachers Federation.

GRIFFIN, G.A. (1990) 'Leadership for Curriculum Improvement: The School Administrator's Role', in LIEBERMAN, A. (Ed.) *Schools as Collaborative Cultures, Creating the Future Now*, London, Falmer Press.

HALL, G.E. and RUTHERFORD, W.L. (1983) *Three Change Facilitator Styles: How Principals Affect Improvement Efforts*, Austin, Research and Development Center for Teacher Education, University of Texas.

LEITHWOOD, K.A. and MONTGOMERY, D.J. (1982) 'The Role of the Elementary School Principal in Program Improvement', *Review of Educational Research*, **52**, 3.

LEITHWOOD, K.A., STANLEY, K. and MONTGOMERY, D.J. (1984) 'Training Principals for School Improvement', *Education and Urban Society*, **17**, 1.

RUTHERFORD, W.L. and HULING-AUSTIN, L. (1984) 'Changes in High Schools: What is Happening, What is Wanted', paper presented at the Annual Conference of the American Educational Research Association, New Orleans.

SMITH, W.F. and ANDREWS, R.L. (1989) *Instructional Leadership: How Principals Make a Difference*, Alexandria, ASCD.

SMYTH, W.J. (1986) *Leadership and Pedagogy*, Geelong, Deakin University Press.

Chapter 9

Teacher Appraisal

Appraisal is part of the everyday life of a school. Teachers appraise students for a number of reasons and do so informally through observations and conversations, and formally by the use of various written tests. Teachers form views about each other, based largely upon informal happenings. *Teacher appraisal* is more formalized and systematic and, in fact, it is often defined as 'a systematic and overt appraisal of the work of teachers' (Thomas, 1988, p. 21).

The term 'teacher appraisal' can either conjure up comments of a positive nature related to sound planning and professional development or it can bring forth cries of indignation, unfair searchings for teacher weaknesses. Put simply, teacher appraisal schemes tend to focus on:

(a) *Formative* appraisal concerned with professional development, the improvement of practice by identifying strengths, weaknesses, needs and interests.
(b) *Summative* appraisal concerned with the selection, promotion, redeployment and dismissal of teachers (Turner and Clift, 1988, p. 59).

It is when the latter purpose is given special prominence that teacher reactions tend to be decidedly negative, even hostile.

Why, What and Who

Why Do Teacher Appraisals?

Various reasons are advanced such as those listed by Marland (1987):

(a) knowing ourselves — teachers need to obtain feedback about what they are actually doing compared with what they think they are doing.
(b) curriculum planning — part of the curriculum planning cycle must

include evaluation and appraisal. The appraisal component provides a powerful incentive to undertake thorough planning.

(c) general school planning — for schools to be involved in sound decision-making they need to have in-school appraisal schemes to decide which policies and activities are worthwhile.

(d) professional development — appraisal provides a teacher with feedback so that he/she can develop professionally — adjusting, improving, keeping abreast of new ideas. It can help to identify specific in-service needs.

(e) claim for resources — to justify claims we might make for resources, administrators almost invariably require appraisals of how teachers use the resources.

(f) accountability — the community and parents in particular want more details and evidence that schools and teachers are accomplishing what they profess they are doing. This can also involve removing incompetent teachers.

What Should Be Appraised?

Teacher appraisals typically focus upon:

(a) behaviour of the teacher — detailed observations of what a teacher does in the classroom and in related settings.

(b) behaviour of the teacher working with colleagues and in teams — observing the context of the school and how the procedures enhance or limit a teacher's actions.

(c) behaviours and experiences of students — the activities they are engaged in, their interactions with each other and with the teacher.

(d) outcomes of students — details obtained from informal (for example, observations) and formal (for example, written tests) techniques.

Who Should Appraise?

(a) peer appraisal — for example by pairs of teachers of equal rank or seniority.

(b) superior-subordinate appraisal — typically by principals/headteachers appraising their teachers.

(c) outsider appraisal — for example, by teachers or Headteachers from another school, or by specialist evaluators.

(d) appraisal by lay people — for example, by school council members or governors.

(e) self-appraisal — this can be undertaken by the use of check-lists and self reports.

There is also the matter of deciding whether appraisals should be *closed* (people being appraised do not see any written report or grade) or *open* (people being appraised do see any reports; Wragg, 1987).

Criteria and Methods

Criteria Used in an Appraisal

Methods for appraising teachers have to be based upon specific criteria or qualities. There is no unequivocal research evidence on what 'effective teaching' really means. It is possible to list important qualities of effective teachers such as subject knowledge, empathy, communication skills, but it is not possible to produce a definitive list of priorities which should apply to all teachers.

Job descriptions for teachers working in particular schools are an important first step for appraisers and appraisees. They provide the criteria for any subsequent appraisals and can be readily understood by all parties. As a minimum, each job description should include components relating to *planning, interactive* and *review* phases of teaching.

Methods of Appraisal

(a) classroom observation — using open-ended descriptions or check-lists.
(b) sitting in — on other activities such as interviewing parents, task force meetings.
(c) interviews — open-ended or structured; two-way to allow interviewee to ask questions.
(d) analysis of work-samples — viewing notebooks, records of work.
(e) self-appraisal forms — structured or open-ended.
(f) assessment of students — analysis of student results in key subjects.
(g) questionnaire completed by the person being appraised.
(h) student feedback — using total class discussions, small groups, or questionnaire.

Self-Appraisal

Ideally, all teachers should be committed to self-monitoring their teaching and the consequences of their actions. Various check lists are available which serve as a framework for reflection (see table 9.1).

Self-appraisal reflections need to be carried out regularly and systematically if they are to be of any value. Teachers must be committed to act upon deficiencies they discover from such reflections. Self-appraisal enables

Table 9.1: An example of a self-appraisal check list

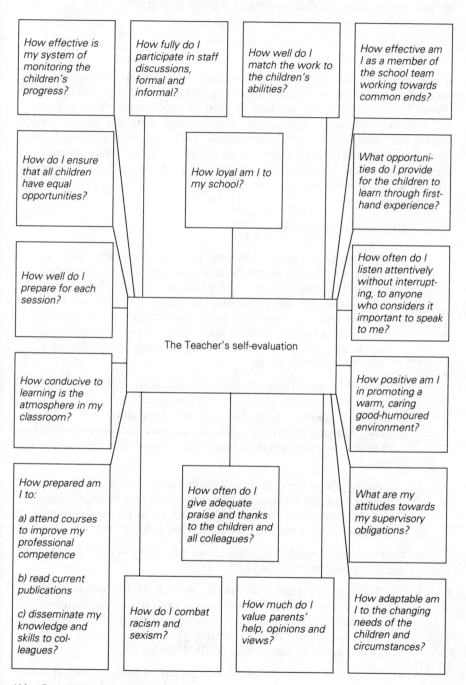

How effective is my system of monitoring the children's progress?

How fully do I participate in staff discussions, formal and informal?

How well do I match the work to the children's abilities?

How effective am I as a member of the school team working towards common ends?

How do I ensure that all children have equal opportunities?

How loyal am I to my school?

What opportunities do I provide for the children to learn through first-hand experience?

How well do I prepare for each session?

How often do I listen attentively without interrupting, to anyone who considers it important to speak to me?

The Teacher's self-evaluation

How conducive to learning is the atmosphere in my classroom?

How positive am I in promoting a warm, caring good-humoured environment?

How prepared am I to:

a) attend courses to improve my professional competence

b) read current publications

c) disseminate my knowledge and skills to colleagues?

How often do I give adequate praise and thanks to the children and all colleagues?

What are my attitudes towards my supervisory obligations?

How do I combat racism and sexism?

How much do I value parents' help, opinions and views?

How adaptable am I to the changing needs of the children and circumstances?

(After Day, Whitaker and Wren, 1987)

teachers to become empowered, to develop their self-motivation and creativity and yet to maintain their trust and dignity (see module 6).

Aftercare

If appraisal is to be credible then a carefully planned series of events must occur after appraisals have been undertaken and processed. Teacher appraisals should be able to pinpoint teachers in need of professional development.

Carefully planned professional development activities (for example, workshops, seminars) need to be scheduled. There may be a need for follow-up support for individual teachers in the form of regular visits, informal or formal discussions. Considerable resources may be needed to provide the level of support required.

Reflections and Issues

1   It must be recognized that the process of appraisal will in-
        volve a shift in perceptions, roles and activities. It will mean
        that private assumptions and practices must be shared with
        and opened up for questioning by others ... Thus the pro-
        cess of appraisal is unlikely to be comfortable — even where
        extensive negotiations have taken place, contracts have been
        made and forms of confidentiality ensured (Day, Whitaker
        and Wren, 1987, p. 19).

What are the benefits of doing appraisals if the problems loom so large? Can any of the problems be minimized?

2   If properly conducted, teacher-appraisal procedures can be in the interests of many individual teachers, students, parents and education authorities. In your experience can there be positive effects of teacher appraisals?

3   An appraisal procedure will have value only if it appraises
        aspects of the teacher's performance and competence which
        there is reason to believe tend to result in favourable pupil
        outcomes of a specified kind (Byrne, 1987, p. 40).

Can we make sound judgments about what is valid data? If not, what are some alternative solutions?

4   Schemes for teacher appraisal, written in the language of
        business (for example, performance indicators), implemented
        in traditionally hierarchical contexts, without the necessary
        accompaniment of experienced process facilitators, stand
        little chance of succeeding (Hall, 1990, p. 66).

Does this quotation mirror your experiences with teacher appraisal schemes? Are there any advantages in having such unilateral initiatives? How feasible is it to introduce a scheme using process facilitators?

5   Opposition from teachers and unions about systems of teacher appraisal in the UK are fundamental issues about power (Elliott, 1989).

Is it concern about how the central government is legitimating teacher appraisal? Is it a wider concern about power at work in educational systems? What can teachers do to ensure that the positive elements of appraisal can be retained without accepting the coercive, standardizing elements?

References

BYRNE, C. (1987) 'Can Teachers Be Validly Appraised?', in BUNNELL, S. (Ed.) *Teacher Appraisal in Practice*, London, Heinemann Educational.

DAY, C., WHITAKER, P. and WREN, D. (1987) *Appraisal and Professional Development in the Primary School*, Milton Keynes, Open University Press.

ELLIOTT, J. (1989) 'Knowledge, Power and Teacher Appraisal', in CARR, W. (Ed.) *Quality and Teaching*, London, Falmer Press.

HALL, S.H. (1990) 'Accounting for Teachers' Work: The Need for a Multifaceted Approach', *Curriculum Perspectives*, **10**, 4.

MARLAND, M. (1987) 'Appraisal and Evaluation: Chimera, Fantasy or Practicality?', in BUNNELL, S. (Ed.) *Teacher Appraisal in Practice*, London, Heinemann Educational.

SIMONS, H. and ELLIOTT, J. (Eds) (1989) *Rethinking Appraisal and Assessment*, Milton Keynes, Open University Press.

STIGGINS, R.J. and DUKE, D. (1988) *The Case for Commitment to Teacher Growth: Research on Teacher Evaluation*, Albany, State University of New York.

THOMAS, N. (1988) 'The Appraisal of Teachers', in BELL, L. (Ed.) *Appraising Teachers in Schools*, London, Routledge, Chapman and Hall.

TURNER, G. and CLIFT, P. (1988) *Studies in Teacher Appraisal*, London, Falmer Press.

WRAGG, E.C. (1987) *Teacher Appraisal: A Practical Guide*, London, Macmillan Education.

Part 3

Curriculum Planning and Development

Chapter 10

Curriculum Frameworks

Characteristics

A school curriculum typically consists of a number of subjects to be taught. The actual number varies between primary schools and secondary schools. Over recent years school personnel have been under pressure to teach additional subjects and topics such as road safety, AIDS education, sex education as well as 'new' fields of study such as Sociology, Law, and Psychology. In an endeavour to rationalize and to control the number of subjects taught, education systems in many countries have resorted to the use of *curriculum frameworks*.

A curriculum framework can be defined as a group of related subjects which fit together according to a pre-determined set of criteria to appropriately cover an area of study. Each curriculum framework provides a structure for designing subjects and a rationale and policy context for subsequent curriculum development of these subjects. Examples of curriculum frameworks include *Science* (including, for example, Biology, Chemistry, Physics, Geology) and *Commerce* (including Accounting, Office Studies, Economics, Computing).

Another definition of curriculum frameworks is that they are guides which have been explicitly designed and written to assist school communities of teachers, students and parents in their curriculum decision-making about K-10 programmes (Kerr, 1989). It should be noted that curriculum frameworks can assist in the review and development of curricula by schools and system-level personnel. That is, there is an important control element involved too.

A curriculum framework document usually includes

(a) a rationale or platform,
(b) scope and parameters of the curriculum area,
(c) broad goals and purposes of subjects within the curriculum area,
(d) guidelines for course design,
(e) content,
(f) teaching and learning principles,

(g) guidelines for evaluation of subjects,
(h) criteria for accreditation and certification of subjects,
(i) future developments for the area.

Hardy (1990) argues that the rationale or platform for a curriculum framework is of major importance — a statement of the values, principles and assumptions which have guided those who produced the framework.

A comprehensive and well developed curriculum framework should contain the following features:

(a) strong links between theory and practice;
(b) up-to-date and relevant information about pedagogy, learning and resources;
(c) is evocative and inspiring to teachers — they become impressed by its potential as a curriculum area.

Impact of curriculum frameworks upon teachers:

(a) frameworks provide greater coherence across subjects and across the grade levels K-12 — they demonstrate the commonalities between subjects within a framework and enable content and skills to be sequenced across grade levels.
(b) frameworks encourage teachers to evaluate the total learning environment — teachers need to consider the effectiveness of the taught curriculum, and their teaching effectiveness as well as student performances.
(c) frameworks enable curriculum boundaries to be reconsidered and sometimes redefined — they highlight the changing emphases and the evolving boundaries of subjects.
(d) frameworks encourage teachers to reconsider their packaging and delivery of subjects — it enables them to develop new emphases (for example, vocational, recreational) and career pathways.
(e) frameworks enable relatively low status subjects to be given a more prominent place in the school programme because equal status is given to all frameworks.

Advantages and Disadvantages

Some Advantages of Using Curriculum Frameworks

(a) students have access to a broader education by being able to select from a number of curriculum frameworks rather than a narrow range of traditional subjects.
(b) the curriculum will be more coherent and orderly because the framework for each curriculum area is arranged sequentially, usual-

ly from kindergarten to secondary levels and priorities are established for each level.

(c) high quality curriculum development is likely to occur because planning criteria and standards apply consistently across all curriculum frameworks.

(d) there are opportunities for curriculum frameworks to include subjects which are highly prescriptive and those that allow considerable flexibility and variation at the school level.

(e) new content areas and skills can be easily accommodated in curriculum frameworks including various multi-disciplinary and inter-disciplinary variations.

(f) curriculum frameworks developed at a state or regional level have the potential to become accepted as national frameworks.

(g) there are opportunities to incorporate desirable skills into each framework such as communication and language skills, numeracy skills, problem-solving skills.

Some Disadvantages of Using Curriculum Frameworks

(a) if frameworks become too detailed they can become very directive for teachers.

(b) they can become an instrument of compliance and used as a means of control by central education authorities.

Examples from the UK, Australia and Canada

In the United Kingdom a national curriculum framework was established under the Education Reform Act of 1988. The national curriculum consists of three *core* subjects (Mathematics, English and Science) and seven *foundation* subjects (History, Geography, Technology, Music, Art, Physical Education, Modern Foreign Language). For each subject, programmes of study have been developed which cover a range of knowledge, skills and understandings. Some of the subjects reflect the traditional academic subject boundaries (for example, Mathematics) whereas others are used as a broad area or framework (for example, Technology). These subjects are intended to comprise 70 per cent of the total school time and students are expected to study all core and foundation subjects.

A tightly prescribed structure has been organized whereby *attainment targets* (specifying up to 10 levels of attainment, covering the ages 5–16) have been established for each subject; assessment activities have been planned for four *key stages* at ages 5–7; 7–11; 11–14 and 14–16; and *standard assessment tasks* (SATs) have been designed for each key stage.

In the state of Victoria, Australia, forty-four curriculum frameworks have been established for students in Years 11 and 12. Each framework consists of four semester-length units which enables a student to study the curriculum area for the full two years of the Victorian Certificate of education. Examples of frameworks range from traditional ones such as English and History to relatively new groupings such as Australian Studies, Technological Design and Development, Materials and Technology, Contemporary Society, and Texts and Traditions.

Teachers involved in teaching in a specific curriculum framework are provided with a *study design* which outlines principles and aims, content, assessment procedures, work requirements and criteria for the award of grades and *development support materials* which provide details of content and teaching approaches which might be used. Common assessment tasks (CATs), similar to the standard assessment tasks (SATs) being developed in the UK, have been designed for all units.

To graduate with a Victorian Certificate of Education, students are required to study four English units, two Australian Studies units, two Arts or Humanities units, four Mathematics, Science or Technology units.

In British Columbia, Canada, new curriculum frameworks have been developed spanning the twelve years of schooling. Four frameworks consisting of the *Humanities* (English, Social Studies, French as a Second Language, Health); *Sciences* (Mathematics, Science, Environment and Technology); *Practical Arts* (Physical Education, Industrial Education, Business Education) and *Fine Arts* (Music, Visual Arts, Theatre and Dance) comprise a common curriculum.

At Years 11 and 12, students are required to complete twenty common curriculum units, a work experience unit, and twenty-eight credits in one of five programmes: College/University Preparation programme; Exploration programme (social and lifestyle issues, information management skills); Community-School Partnership programme (locally developed career preparation programme); Provincial Career Preparation programme (preparation for study in particular career fields such as communications media or metal fabrication); Provincial Pre-Apprenticeship programme (apprenticeship trade areas). The programmes at Years 11 and 12 have been designed to cater for the increasing number of students staying on at high school who do not have the capacity or the motivation to undertake college and university studies —

> In view of the new social and economic realities, all students, regardless of their immediate plans following school, will need to develop a flexibility and versatility undreamed of by previous generations (Ministry of Education, 1989, p. 6).

Reflections and Issues

1   Frameworks improve the quality of curriculum by assisting in the evaluation of existing curriculum and helping to revise and develop curriculum (Hardy, 1990, p. 5).

In what ways is this likely to occur?

2   Curriculum frameworks enable new subjects to be included and for them to have a legitimate place in the school programme. Do you agree? Use some examples to illustrate your answer.

3   Schools should operate within the general guidelines of central office personnel — curriculum frameworks enable this to occur.

Discuss.

4   Curriculum frameworks provide opportunities for an education system to include new subjects to suit a country's present and future social and economic needs.

To what extent can this occur? Give examples of where such initiatives have been successful.

5   The National Curriculum will equip students with the knowledge, skills and understanding that they need for adult life and employment (Baker, Secretary of State, in Cooper, 1990, p. 144).

Do you agree? What are some likely problems?

6   The National Curriculum reflects a broad political consensus that there is a common set of educational experiences that all young people should have in order to participate successfully in the larger social and economic community — it begins to bring Britain into line with its European Community neighbours (Guthrie and Pierce, 1990, p. 193).

To what extent is a common curriculum desirable and achievable? Is it inevitable that Britain should mirror education developments in continental Europe?

7   There has been an almost total lack of argument for the National Curriculum, both in general terms and in detail. (Wiegand and Rayner, 1989).

Why do you think the foundation subjects were selected for special attention in the framework?
What could have been some alternative ways of organizing the curriculum?
What opportunities are there for themes and for interdisciplinary work?

8   Control of the curriculum in the UK is supposedly in the hands of various groups including the government, parents, governors, employers, teachers (Flude and Hammer, 1990).

What influence have these groups had on the development of the National Curriculum and its implementation?

9   By direct and indirect means, the State contributes to formulation of the socially shared understandings that serve to standardize and control education (Cornbleth, 1990, p. 119).

Analyze how the UK government has developed means to provide a standard framework for all students.

References

COOPER, B.S. (1990) 'Local School Reform in Great Britain and the United States: Points of Comparison — Points of Departure', *Educational Review*, **42**, 2.

CORNBLETH, C. (1990) *Curriculum in Context*, London, Falmer Press.

FLUDE, M. and HAMMER, M. (Eds) (1990) *The Education Reform Act: 1988*, London, Falmer Press.

GUTHRIE, J.W. and PIERCE, L.C. (1990) 'The International Economy and National Education Reform: The Comparison of Education Reforms in the United States and Great Britain', *Oxford Review of Education*, **16**, 2.

HARDY, T. (1990) 'Curriculum Frameworks in the ACT: The Case of Could, Should or Must?', *Curriculum Perspectives*, **10**, 4.

KERR, D. (1989) 'Principles Underlying the Dissemination Implementation of Curriculum Frameworks', unpublished paper, Curriculum Section, ACT Schools Authority.

MINISTRY OF EDUCATION (1989) *Enabling Learners: Year 2000: A Curriculum and Assessment Framework for the Future*, Victoria, British Columbia, Ministry of Education.

WIEGAND, P. and RAYNER, M. (Eds) (1989) *Curriculum Progress 5–16: School Subjects and the National Curriculum Debate*, London, Falmer Press.

Chapter 11

Situational Analysis/Needs Assessment

Various curriculum writers refer to *needs* as a basis for curriculum planning. For example, Hilda Taba's (1962) model includes *diagnosis of needs* as the initial phase. She maintained that teachers need to diagnose the level of thinking of their students before embarking upon any curriculum activity.

During the 1970s, especially in the USA, *needs assessment* and *needs analysis* became popular terms. These terms refer to a process by which educational needs are defined and priorities are set. The process has been highlighted by those curriculum writers who favour a technology approach to curriculum planning.

Situational Analysis Factors

Advocates of school-based curriculum development in the 1970s, especially in the UK and Australia, produced their own variant of needs assessment which they termed *situational analysis*. For example, Reynolds and Skilbeck (1976) produced a situational analysis model of curriculum development. These authors were strongly opposed to technological solutions to curriculum planning — they considered that teacher-planners must consider the culture of the school and the needs of the major players.

Situational analysis really refers to two important concepts, namely the 'situation' and 'analysis'. The situation is the initial state in which the learner finds himself/herself. It is up to the teacher to find out about the initial states of their students and interpret what this means in terms of curriculum planning. Reynolds and Skilbeck (1976) argue that this process is really a cultural analysis and involves the teacher in reviewing *external* (broader contextual issues) and *internal* (immediate school environment) factors (see table 11.1). These authors suggest that many teachers may make this analysis intuitively and rapidly but there are advantages in working through the elements systematically and in a group setting with outside advisers.

Situational analysis can also be considered as the recognition of some school problem which then becomes a springboard for curriculum development. Soliman *et al.* (1981) takes this stance when she argues that situational

Table 11.1:   *Situational analysis factors*

(a)   *External factors to the school*
1   Changes and trends in society which indicate tasks for schools — e.g. industrial development, political directives, cultural movements, ideological shifts.
2   Expectations and requirements of parents and employers.
3   Community assumptions and values, including patterns of adult-child relations.
4   The changing nature of the subject disciplines.
5   The potential contribution of teacher support systems including teachers' centres, colleges of education and universities.
6   Actual and anticipated flow of resources into the school.

(b)   *Internal factors to the school*
1   Pupils, their aptitudes, abilities, attitudes, values and defined educational needs.
2   Teachers, their values, attitudes, skills, knowledge, experience and special strengths and weaknesses.
3   School ethos and political structures, common assumptions and expectations including traditions, power distribution.
4   Material resources, including plant, equipment and learning materials.
5   Perceived and felt problems and shortcomings in existing curriculum.

(After Reynolds and Skilbeck, 1976, p. 114)

analysis is about becoming aware of a school problem, identifying factors which bear upon the problem, and making priorities to solve or limit the problem. She maintains that

- information for problem illumination comes from a variety of sources, for example, students, teachers and parents.
- the scope of the planning has to be limited.
- time is an important factor.
- skills in information gathering (for example, questionnaire preparation) are necessary.

Soliman *et al.* (1981) have developed a *Situational analysis checklist* which covers such factors as

- societal and cultural values and expectations,
- resources and finances,
- educational system requirements,
- content,
- forms of knowledge,
- internal factors,
- learning processes.

She has also developed a number of useful techniques for collecting data (table 11.2). As indicated in table 11.2, various groups can be involved in collecting survey data, or being participants in meetings.

Table 11.2: *Situational analysis techniques*

Techniques	Who might be involved?
Surveys	

• questionnaires e.g., school climate
• interviews
• checklists
• inventory of skills
• written submissions
• subjective judgments
• literature
   learning theory
   other projects
• documents e.g., school or Department of
   Education
	Staff, parents, students, community (e.g.,
	churches, chambers of commerce, feeder
	schools), social workers, support agencies
	(e.g., universities, CAE's, TAFE's), delegated
	staff, consultant, school psychologist, P and C
	Association.

Meetings	
• brainstorming • discussions • nominal group technique (NGT)	Staff, small staff groups, parents, teachers, community groups, department officers.
Tests	
• norm referenced • criterion referenced • diagnostic	Students, staff, school psychologist, feeder schools, consultant.

(After Soliman et al., 1981, p. 15)

A major problem highlighted by Soliman *et al.* is that the data collected for situational analysis is only of value if it is *used*. Sometimes staff may perceive the data to be threatening to them personally and will take steps to subvert the process. On occasion, the decision-making groups may opt to take decisions which ignore the findings of the data. They may even fail to communicate the data findings to all staff.

Notwithstanding, situational analysis provides an ideal springboard for developing a new curriculum. It also enables curriculum developers to take local community factors into consideration.

Needs Assessment Procedures

Various writers, especially some US writers, extol the virtues of *needs assessment*, typically in terms of its value as a preliminary step in curriculum development. Needs assessment enables educational needs to be defined and priorities set. It is also a very valuable vehicle for bringing together parents, students, teachers and citizens to discuss alternative educational goals. English and Kaufman (1975, pp. 3–4) define needs assessment as

81

Table 11.3: Steps involved in needs assessment

1	Preparing — making decisions about resources available, time allotted, who will participate.
2	Stating of goals — experts are requested to supply a list of goals.
3	Goal validation — different groups from the community accept those goals which they consider are appropriate.
4	Goal priorities — a sample of different groups rank the goals in order of importance.
5	Goal translation — statements of goals are converted into instructional objectives.
6	Testing — instruments are selected and administered to ascertain current levels of student performance, to learn whether student achievement meets the desired, defined levels.
7	Collating the data — organizing the data into appropriate tables, graphs and charts.
8	Developing need statements — compiling a list of needs — gaps in student performance between what is desired and what is performed.
9	Ranking the need statements — according to the amount of difference between desired and actual levels.
10	Publishing list of gap statements.

(After Oliva, 1988, pp. 250–1)

a tool which formally harvests the gaps between *current* results (or outcomes, products) and *required* or desired results, places these gaps in priority order, and selects those gaps (needs) of the highest priority for action, usually through the implementation of a new or existing curriculum or management process.

Needs assessment activities can occur within a single school community or across a region or local education authority. The scale of the activity will depend upon the magnitude of the task/change being considered. It is evident from table 11.3 that needs assessments are typically on a much larger scale than situational analysis activities.

Needs assessment using the steps indicated in table 11.3 is very comprehensive and technical. Many would argue that such an approach is unnecessarily complicated for obtaining diagnostic data about students and the school community. It stresses systems level technology-oriented factors. Although there are advantages in using this approach (see table 11.4) there are also disadvantages (see table 11.5).

Reflections and Issues

1 Those who regard needs assessment as nothing more than a scientific information gathering procedure see it as a way to avoid ethical issues by justifying the curriculum merely on the basis of the popularity of certain goals and the magnitude of the discrepancy between where learners *are* and where learners *should be* with respect to these popular goals (McNeil, 1985, p. 97).

Discuss.

Table 11.4: *Advantages of using needs assessment*

1 It is a fair and objective way of deciding upon priorities for curriculum development.
2 It can lead to innovative and creative priorities and solutions.
3 It can be a very efficient procedure.
4 It is a valuable technique for getting different groups to discuss issues and to agree upon shared values and mutual support.

Table 11.5: *Disadvantages of using needs assessment*

1 It is often difficult to pinpoint actual needs.
2 There is an undue emphasis upon *how* to satisfy needs and little on *should* it be done.
3 In many circumstances, less costly and informal methods are likely to be more useful.
4 The approach gives a high priority to a technological/systems approach to curriculum development.

2   The need for conducting a situational analysis is a fundamental precept of curriculum development. Developers commencing their task should ask: 'What do we know about the context — the students, teachers, school environment — of this curriculum and why is it needed?' (Print, 1987, p. 82). Do you agree? Explain why these are important questions to ask.

3   Needs assessment is one of the most frequently used ways for justifying curriculum goals and objectives (McNeil, 1985, p. 93).

In your teaching experience has this been the case?
Consider some advantages and disadvantages of needs assessment in your teaching area.

4 Because schools are so complex and differ so much from each other, it is critical that each school staff determines via situational analysis what curricula are most appropriate for their school. Do you support this approach? What are some possible problems associated with this point of view?

References

ENGLISH, F.W. and KAUFMAN, R.A. (1975) *Needs Assessment: A Focus for Curriculum Development*, Alexandria, VA, ASCD.
McNEIL, J.D. (1985) *Curriculum: A Comprehensive Introduction*, Boston, Little Brown and Co.
OLIVA, P.F. (1988) *Developing the Curriculum*, Glenview, Scott, Foresman and Co.
PRINT, M. (1987) *Curriculum Development and Design*, Sydney, Allen and Unwin.
REYNOLDS, J. and SKILBECK, M. (1976) *Culture in the Classroom*, London, Open Books.

SOLIMAN, I., DAWES, L., GOUGH, J., and MAXWELL, T. (1981) *A Model for School-Based Curriculum Development*, Canberra, CDC.

TABA, H. (1962) *Curriculum Development: Theory and Practice*, New York, Harcourt, Brace and World.

WALKER, D. (1990) *Fundamentals of Curriculum*, New York, Harcourt Brace Jovanovich.

Chapter 12

Aims, Goals and Objectives

Characteristics and Examples

Aims

(a) are broadly phrased in statements;
(b) are long term;
(c) generally apply to systems rather than individual schools.
(d) An example would be 'Students should achieve high levels of literacy and numeracy'.

Goals

(a) are more precise statements of curriculum intent;
(b) are medium to long term;
(c) are directed to student achievement.
(d) An example would be 'Students will study important figures in Australian History'.

Objectives

(a) are specific statements;
(b) are short term;
(c) are usually expressed in terms of learner behaviours;
(d) are often devised by teachers.
(e) An example would be 'Students will be able to mark on a map of the United Kingdom, the location of three resources used in the motor vehicle industry'.

Eisner (1979) defines *aims* as

general statements that proclaim to the world the values that some group holds for an educational program ... these statements form a kind of educational manifesto ... (p. 116).

Goals are more specific statements which give details of intent. They represent the purposes of a particular course or unit of instruction. These goals, in turn, justify particular learning *objectives* which can be defined as specific statements of what students are to be able to do after having experienced an instructional unit or a portion of one (Eisner, 1979, p. 117). As shown in figure 12.1, the terms are closely interrelated.

Criteria for Use

Aims

Aims, because of their open-ended nature, will never be completely achieved. According to Wringe (1988), aims may be pursued ruthlessly or prudently and in a spirit of compromise and consideration for the interests of others.

Aims provide general guidelines for teachers — they are not dreamy visions of a distant state. They can be modest or they can be ambitious.

Some examples of aims of education include:

- mastery of basic facts and theories in fundamental subjects,
- cultivation of personal talents and interests,
- development of democratic attitudes,
- good study skills and work habits.

Goals

Many writers agree on common goals for schooling such as Academic, Vocational, Social and Personal, but they disagree on the emphasis to be given to each in a school curriculum.

Academic goals
Academic goals consist of two sub-categories, a mastery of basic skills and fundamental processes and intellectual development. Students who are not proficient in basic skills will be severely restricted in their abilities to function in our society. The sub-category of intellectual development contains many elements including problem-solving skills, an ability to use and evaluate knowledge, an adequate fund of knowledge from major disciplines, and a positive attitude toward intellectual activity.

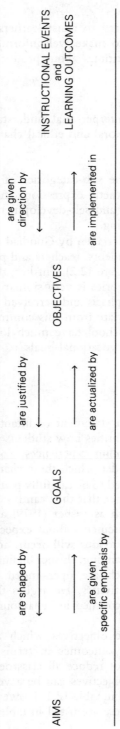

Figure 12.1: Relationships between educational aims, goals, objectives and instruction

(After Brookover et al., 1980)

AIMS

are shaped by

are given
specific emphasis by

GOALS

are justified by

are actualized by

OBJECTIVES

are given
direction by

are implemented in

INSTRUCTIONAL EVENTS
and
LEARNING OUTCOMES

Vocational goals
Vocational goals are geared to assist learners make decisions about career options and to be able to make well-informed choices. They also include developing habits and attitudes about productive participation in economic life.

Social, civic and cultural goals
Sub-categories include interpersonal understandings, citizenship participation, enculturation and moral and ethical character.

Personal goals
Personal goals include the sub-categories of emotional and physical well-being, creativity and aesthetic expression, and self-realization. These goals emphasize self-awareness and self-development — all the aspects of what it means to be a human being.

In a major study undertaken by Goodlad (1984), he noted that academic goals are perceived by students, teachers and parents as the major goals at all levels of schooling (see figure 12.2). Further, the distribution of emphasis for the other three goal categories is very similar for teachers and parents, both in terms of preferred emphasis and perceived actual practices. It is only the student results which deviate from this common pattern, to the extent that students at senior high school have much lower preferences for academic goals, preferring instead, vocational goals.

Objectives

Objectives are typically a statement of intent about anticipated changes in learners. An objective identifies how students should change their behaviour as a result of certain learning experiences. Sometimes objectives also make explicit the conditions under which these changes will occur.

Objectives are designed to be carefully planned specifications for a unit or topic but there is the danger that they can become too precise and inflexible. For example, writers such as Eisner (1979) argue that *behavioural objectives* which require explicit statements about expected student behaviour, conditions under which the behaviour will occur, acceptable standard of performance — are far too demanding. Eisner maintains that there is a place for *expressive* objectives which are open-ended statements about the consequences of curriculum activities. He argues that creative or value-oriented objectives should not be couched in behavioural terms.

Instructional objectives are objectives which are relatively specific, which describe desired learning outcomes in terms of student activities or behaviours but which do not reduce all classroom activities to behaviouristic outcomes. Instructional objectives can be a very valuable tool to the classroom teacher, as indicated in table 12.1. However there are some caveats that need to be heeded and these are listed in table 12.2.

Figure 12.2: Comparison between perceived and preferred goal emphasis (social, academic, personal and vocational) for students, teachers and parents

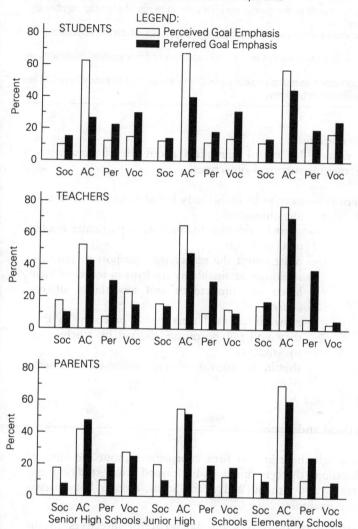

(After J. I. Goodlad, 1984, p. 64)

Table 12.1: Some reasons for using instructional objectives

1 They help teachers focus upon their real intentions.
2 They provide a clear direction for teachers in terms of what is to be taught.
3 They assist teachers in selecting relevant content, methods, assessment, resources.
4 They can be communicated easily to parents and students.
5 They enable a teacher to judge the quality of his/her teaching.
6 They enable a teacher to provide assessment procedures which are directly related to objectives.

Table 12.2: Some problems in using instructional objectives

---

1 It is not possible to specify all the outcomes for a class in terms of a limited number of instructional objectives.
2 Unintended outcomes cannot be accommodated in objectives which are specified in advance.
3 Specifying only some objectives can lead to the exclusion of other equally important areas of teaching.
4 They are more conducive to some subject areas (for example, mathematics, science) but not others (for example, art, poetry).

Criteria for effective objectives

The following criteria are useful reminders about the characteristics and qualities of effective instructional objectives.

comprehensiveness — have to be sufficiently broad to include all learning outcomes.

suitability — must be relevant to students at particular grades or class levels.

validity — must reflect the reality they purport to reflect.

feasibility — should be attainable by students in terms of their levels of competency and availability of re-sources.

specificity — must be phrased clearly and precisely so that they will not be misunderstood by teachers or by students.

compatibility — should be consistent with other stated objec-tives.

Reflections and Issues

1   Although there are no firm conclusions about the aims of education, there is much to be learned from studying and thinking about them (Walker and Soltis, 1986, p. 83). Discuss using examples.

2   Instructional objectives can be powerful directives in the teaching process (Conner and Lofthouse, 1990).

Discuss.

3   When specific skills or competencies are appropriate, such objectives can be formulated, but one should not feel com-pelled to abandon educational aims that cannot be reduced to measurable forms of predictable performance (Eisner, 1979, p. 98). Do you agree? Give examples to support your stance.

4   [Objectives] appear to stand for an excessive interest in efficiency, an undue and misplaced zeal for things rather than

process or experience ... they seem to portray little heaps of knowledge, rather than an integrating structure or matrix (Davies, 1976, p. 67).

Critically analyze this statement.

5   The school sets out deliberately to devise the right environment for children, to allow them to be themselves and to develop in the way and at the pace appropriate to them. It tries to equalise opportunities and to compensate for handicaps. It lays special stress on individual discovery, on first hand experience and on opportunities for creative work. It insists that knowledge does not fall into neatly separate compartments and that work and play are not opposite but complementary. A child brought up in such an atmosphere at all stages of his education has some hope of becoming a balanced and mature adult and of being able to live in, to contribute to, and to look critically at the society of which he forms a part (Central Advisory Council for Education, 1967, p. 187).

The goals and aims included in this statement are wide-ranging. In your opinion, are they desirable? Are they complementary to each other or contradictory? Are some more attainable than others?

6   The Education Reform Act in the UK was introduced for a number of reasons but especially to strengthen the rights of parents — to provide parent power in a market place of schools that are made more accountable to their consumers will improve educational standards (Flude and Hammer, 1990).

How might parent choice affect the goals and aims of schools? Is it likely that this will lead to different school priorities?

7   White (1990, p. 109) poses three basic questions about school aims:

Who should decide on aims?
What should the aims be?
What aims currently inform practice?

Provide answers in the light of your teaching experiences.

References

BROOKOVER, W.B. *et al.* (1980) *Measuring and Attaining the Goals of Education*, Washington DC, ASCD.

CENTRAL ADVISORY COUNCIL FOR EDUCATION (1967) *Children and Their Primary Schools*, London, HMSO.

CONNER, C. and LOFTHOUSE, B. (1990) *The Study of Primary Education, A Source Book, Volume 1, Perspectives*, London, Falmer Press.

DAVIES, I.K. (1976) *Objectives in Curriculum Design*, London, McGraw Hill.
EISNER, E.W. (1979) *The Educational Imagination*, New York, Macmillan.
FLUDE, M. and HAMMER, M. (Eds) (1990) *The Education Reform Act, 1988*, London, Falmer Press.
GOODLAD, J.I. (1984) *A Place Called School*, New York, McGraw Hill.
WALKER, D.F. and SOLTIS, J.F. (1986) *Curriculum and Aims*, New York, Teachers College Press.
WHITE, J. (1990) 'Who Should Decide?', in LOFTHOUSE, B., *The Study of Primary Education, A Source Book, Volume 2, The Curriculum*, London, Falmer Press.
WRINGE, C. (1988) *Understanding Educational Aims*, London, Unwin Hyman.

Chapter 13

Selection of Method

A teacher has to make many decisions about methods, about the *how* of teaching. To a certain extent, some of these decisions may be made for teachers by others via official syllabus documents, teacher guides, textbooks, but it is the teacher who is the ultimate implementer. He/she orchestrates the score which is finally played to the audience (the students).

It is useful to separate out two aspects of method, namely:

(a) methods of imparting content;
(b) methods of organizing the content.

Methods of Imparting Content

Teachers tend to use conventional methods that are very familiar to them, perhaps even ones that were commonly used on them when they were students at school. Research evidence (for example, Davidson *et al.*, 1982; Jones *et al.*, 1987) indicates that teachers use a small number of methods, typically teacher talk, question and answer and textbook assignments. There are, of course, a variety of methods available and it is important that teachers are aware of the range and are willing to experiment with a wide cross-section of them. Reasons why a variety should be used by teachers include:

(a) Not all students learn efficiently by the same methods and so there is always a risk of discriminating against certain students.
(b) Not all methods interest students equally.
(c) No single method is better than another for all types of content.
(d) Not all methods provide for attainment of a particular set of in-structional objectives.

It is possible to separate out several major groups of methods based upon the assumptions associated with each:

Table 13.1: Some major methods of imparting content

Method	Characteristics	Advantages/Disadvantages	Emphasis
Teacher talks, mini lectures, demonstrations	Verbal presentations by teacher to the whole class	Advantages 1 Can provide stimulating introduction to a topic; 2 Especially useful in some subjects, for example, literature. Disadvantages 1 Pupils required to passively listen; 2 Assumes all pupils interested in the topic and can concentrate for the length of time required.	behaviour-control/rational
Discussion, questioning, recitation	Questions and answers relating to assigned materials, usually pages in a workbook or textbook	Advantages 1 Enables teacher to judge whether pupils have understood the topic. Disadvantages 1 Teacher dominates the activity; 2 Students tend to regurgitate facts; 3 Emphasis upon acquiring knowledge.	behaviour-control/rational

Practice drills	Repetition of a skill until mastery has been reached	*Advantages* 1 Emphasis upon attaining skills *Disadvantages* 1 May become boring and counter-productive	behaviour-control
Problem-solving, inquiry, discovery, inductive learning	Pupils engage in collecting data, formulating hypotheses to solve problems and issues	*Advantages* 1 Active pupil participation; 2 Develops pupil initiative and organizing skills. *Disadvantages* 1 May require provision of wide range of resources; 2 May be time consuming to reach certain levels of cognitive understandings.	discovery-learning
Role-playing, games, simulation games	Pupils take on specific roles and act out near real-life situations	*Advantages* 1 Develops values and attitudes; 2 Powerful tool to develop empathy toward people and places. *Disadvantages* 1 Sometimes difficult to operate in a traditional classroom; 2 Time-consuming.	discovery-learning

Table 13.2: *Groupings of teaching methods*

Methods	Groupings
Assignments Programmed learning Textbooks	Behaviour-control
Contract learning Data pools Debates Excursions Games and simulations Group work Inquiry or research Role playing Surveys	Discovery-learning group
Discussion Interviews Reports	Rational group

(After Davidson et al., *1982)*

behaviour-control group — stimulus–response view of teaching
discovery-learning group — emphasis on the self-directed activity of the student
rational group — emphasis is on teaching as rational discussion

In table 13.1, five common methods are described in some detail, which can be associated with these three groupings. Some indication of the relative advantages and disadvantages of each are given. In table 13.2, a more extensive list is included, based upon Davidson *et al.* (1982). However it is also possible to categorize these into the three groupings listed above.

Methods of Organizing Content

How subject matter is organized for teaching and learning depends very much on one's philosophy of what counts as important knowledge. The terms *scope* and *sequence* are useful bases for initiating the discussion.

Scope and Sequence

Scope refers to the extent and arrangement of curriculum elements that can occur across topics or subjects while *sequence* refers to the organization over a period of time, in some cases, a number of years. Scope is sometimes termed *horizontal organization* while sequence is termed *vertical organization*.

Scope — Some Characteristics

(a) The scope of a curriculum gradually expands at higher levels of schooling.
(b) The scope of a curriculum changes from level to level as some elements are reduced or deleted (for example, specific lessons on handwriting) while others are added (for example, lessons on physics).
(c) An important decision for the scope of any curriculum is the breadth of coverage and the depth of coverage.
(d) The scope of a curriculum also has to consider common processes/skills which should occur in all subjects.

In terms of scope or horizontal organization a number of approaches have been advocated by educators over the decades, including:

organizing by subjects	— specially selected, important subjects are taught separately
organizing by activity	— student's own experience is the starting point for planning
organizing by core	— organized on basis of social problems
organizing by correlation	— elements from various separate subjects are correlated and interrelated
organizing in broad fields	— subject areas are correlated and fused into broad fields of study
organizing around persistent life forms	— content is organized into major societal problems or life situations

The first two listed are described in more detail below:

Organizing by separate subjects

(a) All subject matter is classified into separate subjects or disciplines.
(b) There is usually a hierarchy of subjects with some being more important than others.
(c) Each subject is studied independently of the others.
(d) Mastery of content sets the standard for each subject and hence influences how it is taught (mainly expository teaching) and how it is assessed (formal, written examinations, based upon textbook study).

Advantages

(i) backed by tradition;
(ii) provides disciplined knowledge and trains students in special systems of thought;
(iii) source material is readily available.

Disadvantages

    (i)   can create compartmentalization and rigidity;
   (ii)   can neglect individual interests;
 (iii)   excessive concern for acquiring specific facts.

An example The foundation subjects which comprise the recently introduced National Curriculum in the UK are predominantly the traditional disciplines (the core subjects: mathematics, science and English and other foundation subjects: history, geography, technology, music, art, physical education, modern foreign language). Lawton (1989) argues that important areas of learning are neglected such as political understanding, economic awareness, moral development and many other cross-curricular themes.

Organizing by Activity

  (a)   Student's needs and interests determine the curriculum.
  (b)   Content is not pre-planned or pre-organized.
  (c)   Students use problem-solving methods and set their own tasks.
  (d)   Skills and knowledge are acquired as they are needed.
  (e)   There are no subjects as such.

Advantages

    (i)   concentrates upon the felt needs and interests of learners;
   (ii)   learning begins with primary experiences;
 (iii)   is very flexible;
 (iv)   is very suited to young children.

Disadvantages

    (i)   is difficult to order in terms of sequence and continuity;
   (ii)   requires abundant resources and equipment;
 (iii)   there are difficulties in centring the curriculum exclusively on the interests or activities of students.

An example Learning stations in junior primary schools (for example, a Language Arts station) are typically partitioned off areas of the classroom containing a range of resources (charts, books, concrete objects) and where children can work on various activities — either entirely by themselves, or in informal groups or working on teacher-directed tasks. The emphasis is on natural, spontaneous development by children (Conner and Lofthouse, 1990).

Sequence

Sequence is concerned with the order in which content is taught and what is to follow what other learning content. Some traditional ways of establishing sequence include:

(a) going from the simple to the complex (for example, foreign languages);
(b) movement from whole to part (for example, geography);
(c) chronological ordering of events (for example, history);
(d) movement from the present into the past;
(e) concentric movement, spiralling of concepts (for example, based on developmental psychology);
(f) movement from concrete experiences to concepts.

A major design problem associated with sequence is to ensure that *cumulative* and *continuous learning* occurs as students progress through the curriculum.

Reflections and Issues

1   Good methods of teaching must be grounded in what is known about learning — in particular achieving a balance between what the students bring to learning and what the content goals are (Jones *et al.*, 1987, p. 161).

How can this balance be achieved? Give examples.

2   The principal design problem associated with *scope* is the difficulty of *integrating* the variety of learnings that students undergo at a particular level of the curriculum (Zais, 1976, p. 440).

Explain why this is a major problem for curriculum developers.
3 Provide answers for each of the following questions:
    (a) How can balanced curriculum development be assured?
    (b) How can there be continuous growth from year to year without undesirable repetition or undesirable gaps in learning?
    (c) How can desirable depth of knowledge be assured?
    (d) How can there be guarantees that choices of problems are not trivial and do not represent transitory interests rather than basic concerns? (Stratemeyer *et al.*, 1957)

4 According to Dadds and Lofthouse (1990) there is little to discriminate between different teaching methods yet a common trait of suc-

cessful teachers is that they have frequent interactions with their students. Is this an important factor? Give reasons for your answer.

5 Without learning a body of knowledge, pupils will flounder. They cannot master a discrete subject; and they will not — without sure, detailed knowledge and a framework — have the substance on which to reflect, or a basis on which to develop analytical powers (Lofthouse, 1990, p. 23).

Discuss.

6 Students are not failing because of the curriculum. Students can learn almost any subject matter when they are taught with methods and approaches responsive to their learning style strengths (Dunn, 1990, p. 15).

Do you support the view that students have dominant learning styles? Should students be 'matched' with resources that suit their learning styles?

7 Teachers use different methods of teaching for a number of reasons but predominantly because of perceived rewards, workloads and risks (Naeslund, 1990).

Consider whether the major methods listed in table 13.1 would enhance or reduce the impact of these three factors.

8 Teaching cannot simply consist of telling. It must enlist the pupil's own active participation since what gets processed gets learned (Tomlinson and Quinton, 1986).

What strategies can a teacher use to encourage more active pupil participation?

9 Some teachers perceive the 1988 Education Reform Act in the UK as setting up constraints and controls which will stifle teacher initiative and inspiration. Others see it as improving educational standards and extending opportunities for pupils and parents (Woods, 1990).

What do you consider to be the likely effects upon their teaching methods?

References

CONNER, C. and LOFTHOUSE, B. (1990) *The Study of Primary Education: A Source Book, Vol. 1, Perspectives*, London, Falmer Press.

DADDS, M. and LOFTHOUSE, B. (1990) *The Study of Primary Education: A Source Book, Vol. 4, Classroom and Teaching Studies*, London, Falmer Press.

DAVIDSON, A.J., ROWLAND, M.L. and SHERRY, M.F. (1982) *Strategies and Methods*, Melbourne, Victorian Commercial Teachers Association.

DUNN, R. (1990) 'Rita Dunn Answers Questions on Learning Styles', *Educational Leadership*, **48**, 2.

JONES, B.F. *et al.* (Eds) (1987) *Strategic Teaching and Learning: Cognitive Instruction in the Content Areas*, Alexandria, Virginia, ASCD.

LAWTON, D. (1989) *Education, Culture and the National Curriculum*, London, Hodder and Staughton.

LOFTHOUSE, B. (1990) *The Study of Primary Education: A Source Book, Vol. 2, The Curriculum*, London, Falmer Press.

NAESLUND, L. (1990) 'Teacher Styles', in DAY, C., POPE, M., DENICOLO, P. (Eds) *Insight into Teachers' Thinking and Practice*, London, Falmer Press.

STRATEMEYER, F.B. *et al.* (1957) *Developing a Curriculum for Modern Living*, 2nd edn, New York, Teachers College Press.

TOMLINSON, P. and QUINTON, M. (1986) *Values Across the Curriculum*, London, Falmer Press.

WOODS, P. (1990) *Teacher Skills and Strategies*, London, Falmer Press.

ZAIS, R.S. (1976) *Curriculum: Principles and Foundations*, New York, Thomas Y. Crowell Co.

Chapter 14

Assessment, Grading and Testing

Characteristics and Issues

Assessment is the term typically used to describe the activities undertaken by a teacher to obtain information about the knowledge, skills and attitudes of students. Activities can involve the collection of *formal* assessment data (for example, by the use of objective tests) or the use of *informal* data (for example, by the use of observation checklists). Teachers typically assign a *grade* or mark (numerical score, letter grade, descriptive ranking) for work undertaken by students such as a project or a written test.

Assessment is usually undertaken because of five major reasons:

(a) it is necessary to grade students in terms of their levels of achievement;

(b) it is necessary to select students for admission into a course or institution;

(c) it is used to provide diagnostic information to students/parents about aspects that a student has failed to learn;

(d) it is provided to help students make choices about future activities (for example, assessment results that guide a student about aptitudes for various career routes);

(e) it is used to predict how well a student will perform in particular areas.

Diagnosis for many teachers is the most important reason for assessing students. The information enables a teacher and the student to identify learning difficulties and to overcome them. If the assessment is undertaken systematically for a number of students in a class, it can also be used to identify teacher deficiencies in teaching or deficiencies in curriculum materials such as a textbook.

It is also the case that many groups such as employers, parents and students are mainly interested in assessment because it indicates levels of achievement. For example, parents are interested in term tests and reports; universities and employers are interested in examination scores.

Tests typically refer to materials that are used to assess students' work and which are amenable to grading. All tests should have a high degree of *validity* and *reliability*. Validity refers to the extent to which the test items are representative of the knowledge, skills or values areas being assessed. Reliability refers to the consistency with which items in a test measure the same thing. It is likely that teacher–made tests are not planned as carefully as standardized tests and so their levels of validity and reliability are likely to be much lower. *Standardized* tests are centrally developed and usually long periods of time are taken to develop items that discriminate adequately and have high levels of validity and reliability. However, a standardized test might not suit the teacher's instructional purposes to the extent that their own test might do so. Both types of tests have their uses in particular circumstances.

The term *evaluation* is often used synonymously with the term *assessment* but there are important distinctions. Evaluation subsumes assessment. It is an omnibus term which describes all the kinds of data which are collected about schooling including data about students' behaviour, teachers' planning and instruction, and the curriculum materials used. It is possible to do an evaluation of a teacher and his/her classroom, although more commonly evaluations of the total school are undertaken.

Assessment is typically described as being *criterion-referenced* or *norm-referenced*. Criterion-referenced assessment involves collecting information about an individual with reference to particular tasks or criteria. There are no absolute standards for individuals as such — each task has a number of criteria or competencies to be attained if the person is to be successful. An example might be a test of jumping skills in physical education. Norm-referenced assessment involves comparing the performance of an individual or group with others considered to be in the same category, such as on intelligence quotients (IQs) for particular age levels.

There are many different forms of assessment that can be used by teachers. The chart in table 14.1 distinguishes between those that might be used as a *summative* assessment (at the end of a course of study), or as a *formative* assessment (used to help a student at some stage during a unit or course), or as a *diagnostic* assessment (used to ascertain a student's deficiencies prior to commencing a unit or course).

Commonly Used Techniques

A number of the forms of assessment included in table 14.1 are commonly used (for example, objective tests and essay tests), but some others may need some explanation.

Interest Inventories

Knowledge of the student's interests helps the teacher plan the level of detail to be developed in other topics and to decide whether other topics should be

Table 14.1: Commonly used assessment techniques

Diagnostic Evaluation	Formative Evaluation	Summative Evaluation
Checklists	*Checklists*	Checklists
Rating Scales	*Rating Scales*	Rating Scales
Interest Inventories		
Projective Techniques		
Attitude Scales	Attitude Scales	Attitude Scales
Content Analysis	Content Analysis	*Content Analysis*
Semantic Differentials		*Semantic Differentials*
Objective Tests	Objective Tests	*Objective Tests*
Essay Tests	Essay Tests	*Essay Tests*
Standardized Tests		*Standardized Tests*
Interviews	Interviews	*Interviews*

(Categories in italics indicate the evaluation phase at which the technique is most frequently used.)

Table 14.2: Rating scales for skills development

Name

Date

Skill Being Taught

		1	2	3	4
1	understood the steps involved	Unsatisfactory	Fair	Good	Excellent
2	willing to be involved	Unsatisfactory	Fair	Good	Excellent
3	mastered each sub-skill in turn	Unsatisfactory	Fair	Good	Excellent
4	completed the skills activity	Unsatisfactory	Fair	Good	Excellent

deleted. An inventory is usually a set of five or six questions which can be asked orally of students or written answers can be elicited.

Rating Scales

Rating scales have a wide range of uses during the teaching of a unit. For example, it is possible to use a rating scale with a whole class, one small group, or selected individuals. Typically, students are rated on a 4- or 5-point scale such as the example included in table 14.2.

Semantic Differential

The semantic differential can be used to provide useful information about student attitudes, either as a single measurement or on a 'pre–post' basis. This instrument provides information about the intensity of a student's attitude by

Table 14.3: *Semantic differential example*

	1	2	3	4	5	6	7	
good						x		bad
strong					x			weak
ugly	x							beautiful
happy							x	sad
wanted					x			unwanted
familiar			x					unfamiliar
expected	x							unexpected
fast			x					slow

allocating a number for this intensity along the semantic space continuum. An example is provided in table 14.3. For further details about this instrument see Marsh (1980, pp. 112–3).

Reflections and Issues

1   Everyone who teaches has a professional obligation to assess performance.

Discuss.

2 Some common problems mentioned about various forms of assessment include:

> Students are fearful of external examinations. Many teachers are chary of external examinations. They fear they will reveal the inadequacies of some students, some schools and some teachers.

> Internal assessment permits teacher bias against individual students whom they dislike.

Discuss.

3   Without the enhanced professional training and experience of today's teachers new forms of examination would have been impossible (Kingdon and Stobart, 1988).

What assumptions need to be about teachers' training and experience? Are there problem areas still to be resolved?

4   There is evidence that carefully planned programmes of formative assessment can have a wide range of positive impacts on learning and teaching (Nuttall, 1986).

Give examples to illustrate this statement.

References

KINGDON, M. and STOBART, G. (1988) *GCSE Examined*, London, Falmer Press.
MARSH, C.J. (1980) *Curriculum Process in the Primary School*, Sydney, Ian Novak.
NUTTALL, D.L. (Ed.) (1986) *Assessing Educational Achievement*, London, Falmer Press.

Chapter 15

Tyler's Model of Planning

Tyler's model first appeared in 1949 in his book *Basic Principles of Curriculum and Instruction*. The model is still widely used in many countries because of its commonsense and clarity. It is sometimes called the 'objectives', 'rational', or 'means-end' model (see Grundy, 1987, pp. 27–28; Eisner, 1979).

Planning Steps

Tyler's model states *how* to build a curriculum. He argues that there are really four principles or 'big questions' that curriculum makers have to ask (see figure 15.1).

The first question to ask is 'What educational purposes do you seek to attain?' Many would argue that this is a logical and first step to take. Only when you have decided what you want to teach can you select and organize your content and teaching activities. However, do you select as your criteria what *students* need to know, or what *society* thinks should be taught or what *subject specialists* consider is important to their academic discipline? Tyler maintains that all three sources are important and must be considered. What you finally select as your purposes or objectives will be shaped by your *educational philosophy* and the *psychological* principles which you consider are important to classroom teaching. Tyler suggests that philosophy and psychology should be used as screens to sieve off the important objectives (see figure 15.2).

The second question is 'How can learning experiences be selected which are likely to be useful in attaining these objectives?' It is important to note that Tyler was referring to more than just 'content', although subsequent writers have simplified it to just that term. Tyler was concerned about students getting the learning experiences they needed to satisfy the intentions (objectives) of the curriculum. Further, he felt that students should be aware of the behaviours expected of them from undertaking these learning experiences. They should have the opportunity to practise the desired behaviours. Examples of learning experiences might include equipment set up as an experiment, slide-tape materials, readings from books, teacher talks.

Figure 15.1: Ralph Tyler's principles

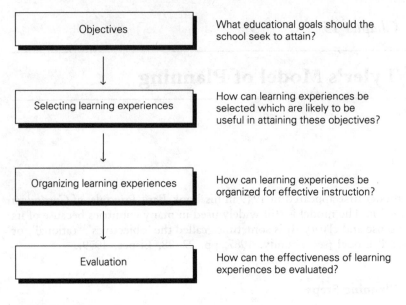

Objectives	What educational goals should the school seek to attain?
Selecting learning experiences	How can learning experiences be selected which are likely to be useful in attaining these objectives?
Organizing learning experiences	How can learning experiences be organized for effective instruction?
Evaluation	How can the effectiveness of learning experiences be evaluated?

(After Tyler, 1949, p. 1)

Figure 15.2: Tyler rationale for curriculum

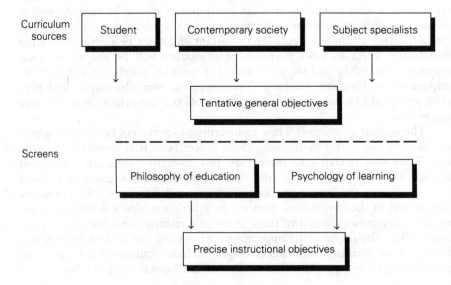

Curriculum sources: Student — Contemporary society — Subject specialists

Tentative general objectives

Screens: Philosophy of education — Psychology of learning

Precise instructional objectives

The third question is 'How can learning experiences be organized for effective instruction?' Tyler felt that a teacher had to be efficient and effective in organizing his/her forms of instruction. He suggested that learning experiences should build upon earlier activities (*vertical organization* or *spiral development*) and that there should be an interrelating or integrating of learning experiences across subjects (*horizontal organization*).

He thought that it was important to identify major *concepts*, *skills* and *values* which could be sequenced again and again in different units in the one subject and across different subjects. Students had to experience the continuity of this organization and to consciously attempt to integrate terms into their individual levels of understanding.

The fourth question is 'How can the effectiveness of learning experiences be evaluated?' Tyler considered that it was essential to see whether the learning experiences actually achieved the intended purposes (objectives). That is, did the 'means' produce the desired 'ends'? He considered that student data should be collected at various stages in the teaching of a unit and not just at the end of a unit (summative evaluation). Although he did describe some informal methods of evaluating students (for example, observations, work samples) he was mainly interested in devising valid and reliable written tests which could be targeted directly to specific instructional objectives.

Advantages and Disadvantages

Advantages of the Tyler Model

(a) It can be applied to any subject and any level of teaching.
(b) It provides a set of procedures which are very easy to follow and which appear to be most logical and rational.
(c) At the time the model was first published (1940s) it broke new ground by emphasizing 'student behaviours' and 'learning experiences'. The guidelines for evaluation were also far more comprehensive than others available in the 1940s. (See also Marsh and Stafford, 1988, p. 9.)

Disadvantages of the Tyler Model

(a) No explicit guidelines are given about why certain objectives should be chosen over others.
(b) Research evidence on teacher thinking and teacher planning indicates that few teachers use objectives as their initial planning point; neither do they use a set series of steps.
(c) Tyler is only concerned about evaluating intended instructional objectives. He ignores the unintended learnings which invariably occur.

(d) The separation of the four steps tends to under-estimate the inter-relationships which occur in any curriculum planning activity.

(e) The model overemphasizes measurable outcomes both in terms of what is set down as an objective and what is evaluated. (See also Grundy, 1987, p. 27; Eisner, 1979).

Reflections and Issues

1 Why is the Tyler model so popular and so widely quoted in books on curriculum?

2 If you were to rewrite the Tyler model for the 1990s which elements would you add or delete?

3 Does the Tyler model have more application to some school subjects than others? Give examples and reasons for your answer.

4 If teaching is so unpredictable is it folly to attempt to produce a model at all? Are there common aspects of teaching situations which can be included in a model? Give details.

5 To what extent is the Tyler model value-free? Do you see this as an advantage or a disadvantage? Give reasons for your answers.

6 The Tyler model uses 'metaphors of "construction" and "building". These are indicators of a technical, product centred approach to curriculum' (Grundy, 1987, p. 28). Do you agree? Develop an argument for or against this stance.

7 Schools persist in using curriculum models grounded in technical rationality (for example, Tyler's model) because it fits well with the bureaucratic organization of schools (Olson, 1989).

Is this the major reason? Consider other reasons why schools might support or reject the Tyler approach.

8 The real world of teaching is messy, indeterminate and problematic situations arise because of conflicting values (Carr, 1989, p. 9).

To what extent is the Tyler model able to include procedures that accommodate these situations?

9 The use of technical/rational administrative solutions to complex social issues in schools of equity, access, is wrong-headed, superficial and fundamentally flawed (Smyth, 1989).

Critically analyse this statement.

10 Comment on the following statements made by Cornbleth (1990 pp. 13–23).

The procedural steps of curriculum development suggest

that curriculum is composed of discrete components (p. 14).

... technocratic conceptions and rational management models of curriculum development are negatively perceived in use and often abandoned ... (p. 15).

There also is evidence that the curriculum products produced under the umbrella of these models are not widely used or used as intended by their developers (p. 15).

A technocratic approach seems to be apolitical and nonideological (p. 16).

References

CARR, W. (Ed.) (1989) *Quality in Teaching*, London, Falmer Press.
CORNBLETH, C. (1990) *Curriculum in Context*, London, Falmer Press.
EISNER, E.W. (1979) *The Educational Imagination*, New York, Macmillan.
GRUNDY, S. (1987) *Curriculum: Product or Praxis?*, London, Falmer Press.
MARSH, C.J. and STAFFORD, K. (1988) *Curriculum Practices and Issues,* (2nd edn), Sydney, McGraw Hill.
OLSON, J. (1989) 'The Persistance of Technical Rationality', in MILBURN, G., GOODSON, I.F. and CLARK, R.J. (Eds) *Re-Interpreting Curriculum Research: Images and Arguments*, London, Falmer Press.
SMYTH, J. (Ed.) (1989) *Critical Perspectives on Educational Leadership*, London, Falmer Press.
TYLER, R.W. (1949) *Basic Principles of Curriculum and Instruction*, Chicago, University of Chicago Press.

Chapter 16

Walker's Deliberative Approach to Planning

Walker (1972) was especially interested in how curriculum planners *actually* went about their task, rather than following Tyler's advice about how they *should* go about the task. He had an excellent opportunity to find out when he was appointed as participant observer and evaluator for the Kettering Art Project during the late 1960s in California. For a period of three years he meticulously recorded the actions, arguments and decisions of the project team. By analyzing transcripts of their meetings and other data, Walker was able to isolate important components in the curriculum development process. During the 1960s and 1970s a number of major, national curriculum projects were in operation and so he was able to compare his findings from the Kettering Art Project with several other projects. He developed his concepts into a process framework which he termed a *naturalistic model*.

Naturalistic Model

Walker used the term 'naturalistic' because he wanted to portray how curriculum planning actually occurs in practice, compared with other approaches which prescribe how curriculum planning should occur. His three-step sequence of *platform–deliberation–design* has since been used at various levels of curriculum development including small-scale projects with pre-service teachers (Roby, 1983) and with in-service teachers (Kennedy, 1984) as well as in large-scale programmes (Orpwood, 1981). This model is illustrated in figure 16.1.

Platform

Walker suggests that any individuals who come together as a group to undertake curriculum development activities approach the task with certain beliefs and values. They will have certain perceptions of the task, ideas about

Figure 16.1:   *Walker's naturalistic model*

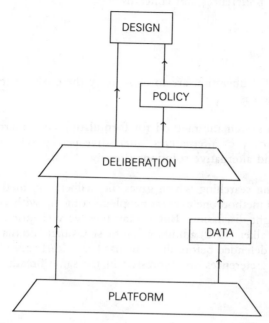

(After Walker, 1972)

what the chief problems are, assertions about what should be prescribed and certain commitments which they are prepared to pursue and argue about. The preliminary step is therefore to get everyone to join in, to talk, discuss and even argue about what the platform is or should be. Walker uses the term 'platform' because it provides a bench mark or basis for the future discussions.

Walker suggests that a platform typically consists of various *conceptions* (beliefs about what exists and about what is possible), *theories* (beliefs about relations held between existing entities); and *aims* (beliefs about what is desirable) that are relatively well formulated and thought out. But in addition, there will exist less carefully thought out notions which he terms *images* (indicating something is desirable without specifying what) and *procedures* (indicating courses of action without specifying why they are desirable) (see figure 16.1).

Walker's model does not make it quite clear when platform activities cease and deliberation activities commence. As he did not intend his model to be a linear algorithm, this might be expected. Presumably, deliberation refers to the ongoing pursuit of particular ideas and policies, as distinct from the platform stage at which individuals are more concerned about establishing their immediate preferences and concerns.

Deliberation

The purposes of deliberation are to clear away the clashes between alternatives. Deliberation is

> essentially a systematic method for formulating and entertaining an adequate variety of alternatives, alternative perceptions, alternative problems and alternative solutions (Pereira, 1983).

It is the on-going searching which gives the deliberation method its unique qualities. In this method one expects people to come up with viable solutions through forthright discussion. But it may be a very chaotic and frustrating experience as Walker (1972) admits when he states that 'alternatives are often formulated and defended before the issue has been clearly stated. Feelings run high. Personal preferences are expressed in the same breath with reasoned arguments.'

Design

The deliberative phase leads finally into some decisions for action. The *explicit design* consists of all discussions made after the alternatives have been sorted out and the most defensible solutions found. The *implicit design* consists of those courses of action taken automatically without considering alternatives. Walker argues that the design phase of a curriculum development project typically contains these explicit and implicit elements and that decisions are influenced as much by personal preferences as they are by rational discussion. The culminating activity for the design phase is the production of specific teaching materials.

Advantages and Disadvantages

Advantages of the Model

(a) It appears to portray quite accurately what actually happens during curriculum planning.
(b) It places emphasis upon the need for planners to spend a considerable amount of time initially on dialogue — to react to different 'platforms' and to undertake 'deliberation'.
(c) It highlights the divergent thrusts and arguments that can occur within any curriculum planning team.

Disadvantages of the Model

(a) It appears to be an accurate reflection of what occurs in large-scale curriculum projects but it may not be appropriate for small-scale, school-based curriculum planning activities.
(b) It assumes that considerable blocks of time are available for participants to establish a platform and to undertake deliberation.
(c) It assumes that curriculum planners are enthusiastic and articulate proponents of a specific curriculum area.
(d) It is not appropriate for curriculum planning activities which are routine and non-problematic.

Reflections and Issues

1 The naturalistic model explodes the myth that curriculum planning must commence with objectives. Do you support this statement? Are there additional caveats to consider?
2 What are the characteristics of good curriculum planning? What priorities would you give to such matters as:

sequenced learning experiences,
comprehensive goals and objectives, or
group deliberation?

3 Deliberation just masks people's preferences in high-sounding phrases.

Reflect on your experiences in curriculum planning teams and on this basis argue for or against the statement.

References

KENNEDY, K. (1984) 'Lesson From a Curriculum Development Project', *Curriculum Perspectives*, **4**, 1.
ORPWOOD, G.W.F. (1981) 'The Logic of Curriculum Policy Deliberation: An Analytic Study from Science Education', unpublished doctoral dissertation, University of Toronto.
ROBY, T.W. (1983) 'Habits Impeding Deliberation', paper presented at the Annual Conference of the American Educational Research Association, New Orleans.
PEREIRA, P. (1983) 'Perception and the Practical Arts', paper presented at the Annual Conference of the American Educational Research Association, San Francisco.
WALKER, D.F. (1972) 'A Naturalistic Model for Curriculum Development', *School Review*, **80**, 1.

Chapter 17

Teachers as Researchers/
Action Research

Over the decades various writers have argued that teachers should do their own classroom research. Various terms have been used such as 'teachers as researchers' and 'action research'. Advocates of these approaches suggest that teachers must use the results of their own inquiries to change and improve their practices.

Action Research Processes

Action research can be defined as

> a way of thinking and systematically assessing what is happening in a classroom or school, implementing action to improve or change a situation or behaviour, monitoring and evaluating the effects of the action with a view to continuing improvement (Thomson, 1988, p. 3).

Kemmis and McTaggart (1984, p. 6) describe action research

> as a method for practitioners to live with the complexity of real experience, while at the same time, striving for concrete improvement.

Interest in action research has become very marked over several periods in the twentieth century but especially during the 1940s due to the work of Kurt Lewin (1948) with his social science research in the USA; Stenhouse's (1975) emphasis upon the teacher as researcher in his Humanities Project in the UK; Elliott and Adelman's (1976) Ford Teaching Project in the UK in the 1970s and 1980s whereby teachers developed inquiry skills; and Kemmis and McTaggart's (1984) and colleagues' on-going research at Deakin University in Australia during the 1980s and into the 1990s.

Making a Start with Action Research

Kemmis and McTaggart (1984, pp. 18–19) suggest that participants in action research should commence by addressing questions such as:

What is happening now?
In what sense is this problematic?
What can I do about it?

and then go on to consider:

How important is the issue to me?
How important is it to my students?
What opportunities are there to explore the area?
What are the constraints of my situation?

Examples of Action Research

1 How can we collaborate to improve student assessment?
2 How can we improve parent-teacher nights?
3 How can I give more emphasis to inquiry teaching?

Action research can be conducted entirely by individual teachers but it is more usual for small groups of teachers to do it. Frequently, an *external facilitator* is invited to enhance the processes. There is some evidence that without ongoing support from facilitators, teachers find it difficult to sustain their action research (Ebbutt and Partington, 1982). The external facilitator can act as a 'sounding board', as a 'critical friend'. He/she can be of considerable value in:

(a) providing a wider perspective
(b) asking participants to clarify ideas
(c) giving individuals support when needed.

Nevertheless, the vital aspect is that teachers within the group take responsibility for researching solutions to their problems.

To do action research a person must undertake four fundamental processes or 'moments':

(a) To develop a *plan* of action to improve what is already happening:
● it must be forward looking.
● it must be strategic in that risks have to be taken.
(b) To *act* to implement the plan:
● it is deliberate and controlled.
● it takes place in real time and encounters real constraints.
● it may involve some negotiations and compromises.

(c) To *observe* the effects of action in the context in which it occurs
  - it is planned.
  - it provides the basis for critical self-reflection.
  - it must be open-minded.

(d) To *reflect* on these effects as a basis for further planning and a succession of cycles
  - it recalls action.
  - it comprehends the issues and circumstances.
  - it judges whether the effects were desirable (Kemmis and McTaggart, 1984).

Figure 17.1 illustrates these processes whereby participants undertake a field of action, develop a specific plan, implement it and reflect upon it.

Writers have indicated that 'action research' is an umbrella term for a number of approaches. Grundy (1982) suggests that there are three major sub-types of action research:

Technical Action Research

- directed by a person or persons with special expertise,
- the aim is to obtain more efficient practices as perceived by the directors,
- the activities are product-centred,
- operates within existing values and constraints.

Practical Action Research

- directed by the group,
- the aim is to develop new practices,
- the activities are process-oriented,
- personal wisdom is used to guide action.

Emancipatory Action Research

- directed by the group,
- the aim is to develop new practices and/or change the constraints,
- involves a shared radical consciousness.

Tripp (1987) suggests that emancipatory action research is very rare because it can only occur in circumstances where a critical mass of radical participants can work together over a considerable period of time.

Figure 17.1: The action research spiral

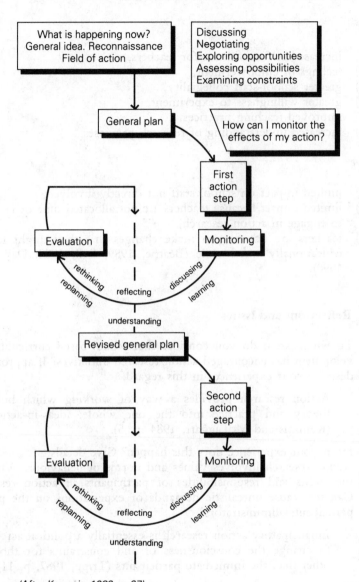

(After Kemmis, 1982, p. 27)

The Impact of Action Research on Schools

Positive

(a) increased self-confidence for teachers,
(b) feelings of empowerment,
(c) greater school-staff collegiality,
(d) greater willingness to experiment,
(e) improved teaching practices,
(f) increased understanding of research processes.

Negative

(a) limited impact on school staff not directly involved,
(b) limited impact because teachers are not allocated time or resources to engage in action research,
(c) teachers are not free to make changes that they might feel are educationally worthwhile (Beattie, 1989; Bell, 1988; Day *et al.*, · 1990).

Reflections and Issues

1   To what extent do you consider that school-based curriculum development has encouraged action research initiatives? If appropriate, describe your experiences in this regard.

2   Action research provides a way of working which links theory and practice into the one whole: ideas-in-action (Kemmis and McTaggart, 1984, p. 5).

From your experience does this happen? Give details.
3   Action research involves values and norms of behaviour. What are the rights and responsibilities of participants in action research? Can this cause unrealistic demands or expectations on the part of participants/administrators?

4   Emancipatory action research is essentially a political act — to change the consciousness of and constraints for those other than the immediate participants (Tripp, 1987, p. 11).

To what extent can action research transform practices, understandings and situations?

5   One of the characteristics of action research is that it is research which people get on with and do quickly ... Academics are watchers of the world: teachers are actors in it. Teachers make decisions and search for 'right' decisions (Bassey, 1990, p. 161).

Comment upon how action research differs from traditional academic research. What are its strengths and limitations over academic research?

6   Action research stands or falls by its demonstrable relevance to the practical ethic of education, as well as whether it is reliable, valid and refutable as a methodology (Adelman, 1989, p. 177).

Have published studies demonstrated the relevance of action research? Is it difficult to prove the quality (reliability, validity) of action research? What solutions can you offer to this dilemma?

7   Action research provides the necessary link between self-evaluation and professional development (Winter, 1989, p. 10).

Explain why reflection and self-evaluation are so important to action research. Should action research lead to actual changes in practice? If so, does this provide professional development for teachers?

8   ... to place the teachers' classroom practice at the centre of the action for action researchers is to put the most exposed and problematic aspect of the teachers' world at the centre of scrutiny and negotiation (Goodson, 1991, p. 141).

Do you agree that it could be undesirable to start a collaborative mode of research from a study of classroom practice? Are teachers sensitive to these studies? Are there advantages which outweigh the possibility of exposing teacher vulnerability?

References

ADELMAN, C. (1989) 'The Practical Ethic Takes Priority over Methodology', in CARR, W. (Ed.) *Quality in Teaching*, London, Falmer Press.

BASSEY, M. (1990) 'Action Research in Action', in DADDS, M. and LOFTHOUSE, B., *The Study of Primary Education, A Source Book, Volume 4, Classroom and Teaching Studies*, London, Falmer Press.

BEATTIE, C. (1989) 'Action Research: A Practice in Need of Theory?', in MILBURN, G., GOODSON, I.F. and CLARK, R.J. (Eds) *Re-Interpreting Curriculum Research: Images and Arguments*, London, Falmer Press.

BELL, G.H. (1988) 'Action Inquiry', in NIAS, J. and GROUNDWATER-SMITH, S. (Eds) *The Enquiring Teacher: Supporting and Sustaining Teacher Research*, London, Falmer Press.

CARR, W. and KEMMIS, S. (1986) *Becoming Critical: Knowing Through Action Research*, Geelong, Deakin University Press.

DAY, C., POPE, M. and DENICOLO, P. (Eds) (1990) *Insight into Teachers' Thinking and Practice*, London, Falmer Press.

EBBUTT, D. and PARTINGTON, D. (1982) 'Self-Monitoring by Teachers', in BOLAM, R. (Ed.) *School Focussed In-Service Training*, London, Heinemann.

ELLIOTT, J. and ADELMAN, C. (1976) *Classroom Action Research*, Ford Teaching Project Unit 2, Norwich, University of East Anglia.

GOODSON, I.F. (1991) 'Teachers' Lives and Educational Research', in GOODSON, I.F. and WALKER, R., *Biography, Identity and Schooling: Episodes in Educational Research*, London, Falmer Press.

GRUNDY, S. (1982) 'Three Modes of Action Research', *Curriculum Perspectives*, 2, 3.

KEMMIS, S. (1982) 'Research Approaches and Methods: Action Research', in ANDERSON, D. and BLAKERS, C. (Eds) *Transition from School An Exploration of Research and Policy*, Canberra, ANU Press.

KEMMIS, S. and McTAGGART, R. (1984) *The Action Research Planner*, Geelong, Deakin University.

LEWIN, K. (1948) *Resolving Social Conflicts*, New York, Harper and Row.

STENHOUSE, L. (1975) *An Introduction to Curriculum Research and Development*, London, Heinemann.

THOMSON, M. (1988) 'The Action Research Spiral as a Model of Curriculum Change', unpublished paper, Perth, Murdoch University.

TRIPP, D.H. (1987) 'Action Research and Professional Development', in HUGHES, P. (Ed.) *Better Teachers for Better Schools*, Melbourne, Australian College of Education.

WINTER, R. (1989) *Learning from Experience: Principles and Practice in Action-Research*, London, Falmer Press.

Chapter 18

Centrally-Based Curriculum Development

Centrally-based curriculum development refers to head office personnel in an educational system making decisions about *what* is to be taught, and often *how* it is to be taught and *how* it is to be assessed. The personnel who make these curriculum decisions were, up until recent years, senior administrators or senior academics/project directors, but are now, increasingly, politicians.

The reasons for these personnel being given responsibility for curriculum planning include:

(a) They are specialists/experts.
(b) They have senior status.
(c) They have access to a wide range of knowledge and information.
(d) They have access to considerable funds.

Notwithstanding, questions need to be asked such as:

Should they be given control?
Should they have the power to make these choices?
Is it desirable for *superordinate* groups to make decisions for subordinate groups, as illustrated in figure 18.1?

Characteristics

Large scale curriculum projects are typically developed centrally. Many of these were produced in the 1970s in the USA, the UK and Australia and include such examples as BSCS Biology (USA), Nuffield Science (UK) and Australian Science Education Project (Australia). These large scale projects can be identified by the following characteristics:

(a) They are often undertaken by large teams of curriculum workers, often hired because of specific expertise, and working full-time on a project for several years.

Figure 18.1:   An authority model for a state education system

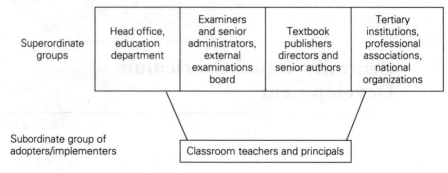

| Superordinate groups | Head office, education department | Examiners and senior administrators, external examinations board | Textbook publishers directors and senior authors | Tertiary institutions, professional associations, national organizations |

Subordinate group of adopters/implementers — Classroom teachers and principals

(After Marsh and Huberman, 1984)

(b) Project needs are carefully assessed through surveys and question-naires.

(c) Development activities are allocated to specialist teams, with all products being regularly reviewed and piloted as part of an elaborate, systematic series of procedures.

(d) Final products are made available to schools by the developing agencies, or are published by commercial publishers, in any case with elaborate procedures for the communication of information, for advertising, and for training intending consumers.

They are often termed *generic* because their locus of operation is large-scale, at the state, national, and in some cases, international levels.

Politically-contrived curriculum development can also be large-scale and generic. For example, in the United Kingdom the passing of the Education Acts in 1986 and 1988 have created a national curriculum consisting of:

three core and seven foundation subjects,
prescribed allocations of time per subject,
prescribed content and attainment targets for each subject,
prescribed testing at key stages (ages 7, 9, 11 and 14) (Flude and Hammer, 1990).

This national curriculum is administered by two agencies newly created by the government, namely the National Curriculum Council (NCC) and the Schools Educational Assessment Council (SEAC). All LEA administered schools will follow the national curriculum.

Hargreaves and Reynolds (1989) describe how centralized control of education in the UK over the last decade has occurred by:

(a) controlling the curriculum — creation of a national curriculum.

(b) strengthening the place of public examinations and testing through the new GCSE examinations and benchmark testing at ages 7, 11 and 14.

(c) strengthening the control of the preparation of teachers and professional development through the Council for the Accreditation of Teacher Education.

In Canada, provinces control curriculum centrally by the use of detailed curriculum guidelines, subject testing and secondary school graduation requirements. In Australia, states and territories control curriculum centrally by the use of curriculum frameworks, and in some states, by the use of common assessment tasks and testing.

Advantages and Disadvantages

Major Advantages of Centrally-Based Curriculum Development

Centrally-based curriculum development:

(a) provides a uniform delivery system.
  - promotes uniformity;
  - encourages standardization of curricula;
  - enhances equity in allocation and distribution of scarce resources.
(b) saves time.
  - avoids detailed analysis of the needs of individual schools;
  - is efficient and easy to manage;
  - saves time, energy and funds.
(c) ensures continuity.
  - policies can be maintained over a number of years;
  - students and parents can be assured that policies will be the same even if students move schools.
(d) concentrates expertise.
  - enables teams of experts to be used;
  - enables sufficient funds to be provided to produce quality materials.
(e) provides 'tighter coupling' between the school and the system.
  - central office can control activities in individual schools;
  - central office can require schools to reach certain goals, (after Johnston, 1990).

Major Disadvantages of Centrally-Based Curriculum Development

Centrally-based curriculum development:

(a) provides little teacher initiative.
  - teachers are mere technicians;
  - no scope for teacher involvement in planning.

   (b)   often lack implementation strategies.
- insufficient attention is given to implementation strategies at the school level;
- central office personnel not involved in monitoring implementation.

   (c)   increases standardization.
- can lead to narrow goals;
- assumes that schools are more alike than dissimilar.

   (d)   depends on rational model.
- assumes that school personnel will want to implement policies developed centrally (after Johnston, 1990).

Most education systems have adopted various compromise positions between the extremes of total centralized curriculum development and total school-based curriculum development. The compromises also appear to be cyclical as witnessed by moves to decentralization and devolution and then to centralization in the United Kingdom and Canada over the last few years. The changes of stance are often politically motivated but also driven by changing preferences for particular educational philosophies.

Reflections and Issues

1   Top-down strategies can never succeed because they assume passive recipients and rational adopters.

Critically analyze this statement.

2   Top-down strategies are effective when:
   (a)   the content of the reform is targeted at all students;
   (b)   there are external pressures such as testing;
   (c)   textbooks support the reform;
   (d)   the roles of state, district and school are complementary (Marsh and Bowman, 1987).

Do you accept these variables as being crucial? To what extent to these variables come together in educational settings with which you are familiar?

3   Administrative decisiveness bordering on coercion, but intelligently and supportively exercised, may be the surest path to significant school improvement (Huberman, 1986).

Do you accept this stance of 'assistance-rich enforcement'? Consider situations where it could work or fail.

4   In the United Kingdom, power has flown away from children, professionals (teachers, teacher trainers, etc.) and LEAs to bureaucrats and politicians at the centre. Control and ownership will, therefore, largely fall to whatever group or

groups (for example, industry and commerce) that can persuade the centre to advance what they take to be their interests (Hartnett and Naish, 1990).

Do you accept this statement? Provide points to support or reject the quotation.

References

FLUDE, M. and HAMMER, M. (1990) *The Education Reform Act, 1988: Its Origins and Implications*, London, Falmer Press.

HARGREAVES, A. and REYNOLDS, D. (1989) *Education Policies: Controversies and Critiques*, London, Falmer Press.

HARTNETT, A. and NAISH, M. (1990) The Sleep of Reason Breeds Monsters: The Birth of a Statutory Curriculum in England and Wales, *Journal of Curriculum Studies*, **22**, 1.

HUBERMAN, M. (1986) 'Rethinking the Quest for School Improvement: Some Findings from the DESSI Study', in LIEBERMANN, A (Ed.) *Rethinking School Improvement: Research, Craft and Concept*, New York, Teachers College Press.

JOHNSTON, V.A. (1990) 'Exchange Your Reality — An Evaluation of the Implementation of a Journey in Faith', unpublished doctoral dissertation, Macquarie University.

MARSH, C.J. and HUBERMAN, M. (1984) 'Disseminating Curricula: A Look From the Top Down', *Journal of Curriculum Studies*, **16**, 1.

MARSH, D.D. and BOWMAN, G.A. (1987) 'Top-Down Versus Bottom-Up Reform in Secondary Schools', unpublished paper, University of California, Los Angeles.

Chapter 19

School-Based Curriculum Development

In many Western countries during the last two decades the term *School-Based Curriculum Development* (SBCD) has been used as a rallying cry for various innovatory educational practices. There have been variations in terms used such as 'school-focused' rather than 'school-based' and 'curriculum decision-making' rather than 'curriculum development'. Further, some would argue that SBCD is a slogan, while others prefer to conceptualize it as a method or technique. These variations need to be considered in gaining a sound appreciation of the concept.

Types and Characteristics

Definitions of SBCD reflect, to a large degree, the predispositions of the respective authors. For example, Skilbeck (1984) defines SBCD as:

> the planning, design, implementation and evaluation of a programme of students' learnings by the educational institution of which those students are members (p. 2).

This definition in itself may seem quite acceptable but in accompanying descriptions, Skilbeck is emphasizing particular aspects such as:

- shared decision-making between teachers and students;
- that SBCD is internal and organic to the institution;
- that it involves a network of relationships with various groups;
- that it is characterized by a definite pattern of values, norms, procedures and roles.

Harrison (1981) perceives SBCD as:

- a combination of participants' intended curriculum (a progressively-modifiable plan);

128

- their operational curriculum (what actually happens to the person/s);
- their perceived curriculum (their perceived situation and outcomes).

She maintains that these three phases of curriculum interact, as an interlocking set, bringing about continuous evaluation and decision-making, for progressive modification of the curriculum.

A literal definition of 'school-based' might imply that all educational decisions are made at the school level. Apart from independent and 'alternative' schools operating as separate entities, it is highly unlikely that this situation pertains to systemic schools (for example, government schools, schools in a school district). The term 'school-focused' is a weaker interpretation in that it suggests that decision-making, at whatever level it occurs and by whom, is undertaken in terms of the interests and needs of school communities. This latter term could apply to a whole range of highly centralized decision-making activities. Expressed along a continuum, 'school-based' is closer to the extreme of individual schools being responsible for all curriculum decisions, whereas 'school-focused' could be represented as a middle position between the centralized and decentralized extremes.

The term 'curriculum development' has wide connotations and is used to describe the various curriculum processes of planning, designing and producing, associated with the completion of a particular set of materials. It can also include teaching activities associated with the implementation and evaluation of a set of materials. One might ascribe such elaborate activities to a well-funded curriculum project team, but the scale and range of these activities could well be beyond the scope of individual school communities. As a result, the term 'curriculum-making' is preferred because it signifies a less grandiose range of activities for school personnel. Walton (1978) makes a further distinction when he suggests that SBCD may typically involve *creating* new products or processes but that it can also involve *selecting* from available commercial materials and making various adaptations. The latter two processes, of course, require less time and funds and a lower level of commitment from participants. Yet it can be argued that SBCD tasks should be embarked upon only if they are manageable and can be achieved within a relatively short space of time. Certainly adaptations and selections are more manageable activities than creating new materials but they raise, in turn, problems of ownership and internalization.

There are many variations of SBCD. Any classification system for SBCD needs to include *type of activity* (creation, adaptation, selection of curriculum materials) on one axis; *people involved* (individual teachers, pairs of teachers, groups, whole staff) on another axis, and a *'time commitment'* dimension on a third axis. It is possible to construct a three-dimensional model using these three dimensions, as illustrated in figure 19.1.

Taking an example from the matrix in figure 19.1, a typical SBCD activity might be the adaptation of a primary science workbook by a small group of teachers as part of a short-term plan to upgrade their teaching of science in the upper primary grades. A more ambitious undertaking based upon the matrix cells in figure 19.1 could be the creation of new materials for

Figure 19.1:   A matrix of SBCD variations

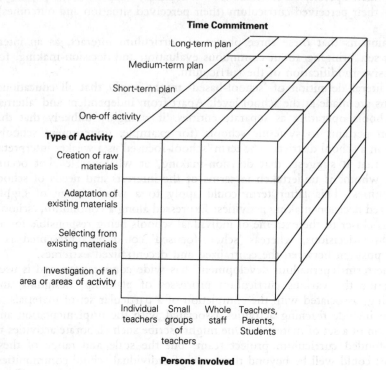

(*After Marsh* et al., *1990*)

a local community unit by a team of teachers, parents and students as a long-term plan to be completed over a period of one calendar year.

SBCD has been accepted very readily in Australia and the United Kingdom, but to a lesser extent in Canada and the USA. Cultural traditions in different countries have either facilitated or impeded its acceptance, but major reasons which are advocated for accepting SBCD in education systems include:

(a)   'Top-down' modes of curriculum development do not work (see module 18).

(b)   SBCD allows schools to have increased autonomy.

(c)   Schools need to be responsive to their environment and this requires the freedom, opportunity, responsibility and resources to determine and direct their affairs.

(d)   Schools are best fitted to plan and design the curriculum, and to construct the teaching and learning of specific programmes.

(e)   Teacher self-actualization, motivation and sense of achievement are integrally bound up with curriculum decision-making which is the staple of teachers' professional lives (see module 6).

(f) The school is a more stable and enduring institution for curriculum development than regional and national bodies.

Problems that Participants can Experience with SBCD

At a superficial level it is possible to list a number of problems that teachers and principals experience in undertaking SBCD activities. Common ones include:

(a) lack of time — to plan, to reflect, to develop curricula;
(b) lack of expertise — knowledge, understandings, skills;
(c) lack of finance — for materials, for teacher relief days;
(d) externally imposed restriction — by employers, parents;
(e) a threatening school climate — numerous resistors, lack of effective leadership.

These problems should not be underrated as they are very real and are often given as the reasons why particular SBCD activities have been abandoned. However, it can be argued that there are more deeply-rooted problems about SBCD which need to be considered and these include:

(a) If curriculum policy (planning) and action decisions (implementation) are both devolved to schools, teachers cannot cope with both tasks without considerably more funds for professional development and relief teacher assistance.
(b) There are considerable numbers of teachers who are not interested in SBCD, seeing their role as confined to teaching curricula devised by others.
(c) Sometimes powerful lobby groups can bring about changes at the local level which produce curricula that are lacking in breadth, or are biased and outdated.

Reflections and Issues

1 Is SBCD little more than a slogan? Is it merely powerful rhetoric which doesn't reflect what typically happens in schools? Discuss, using examples from schools you have visited or experienced recently.
2 To be successful with SBCD, participants (teachers, parents and students) need to have decision-making and group process skills. In your experience, do they have these skills? Where can they turn to receive training in these skills?
3   Self-evaluations by schools are often a valuable means of demonstrating the need for SBCD activities (Simons, 1987).

Consider some reasons why a school might undertake an evaluation. What activities would you suggest would be necessary to encourage SBCD follow-up activities?

4   Active SBCD participation is critical — teachers must be empowered to reflect on their own practices and to become curriculum reformers, rather than defenders of the *status quo* (Marsh *et al.*, 1990).

Do you agree? To what extent is it occurring in your school, region, country?

5   If SBCD is to be successfully engaged in, the leadership question has to be faced. Can a single person, acting as head teacher or principal, manage an environment in which apparently contradictory purposes have to be pursued (Reid, 1987)?

Do you see this as a major problem? Give examples to support your answer.

6 Fielding (1989) used the following terms to highlight key aspects of SBCD from the viewpoint of participants:

   conversation
   confrontation and experimentation
   consolidation and compromise
   communication

Do you consider these to be important components/processes of SBCD? Use examples from personal experience to support or reject these concepts.

7   The development of schools grows from within and therefore teachers, parents and students should work continuously and actively towards their own improvement (Holly and Southworth, 1990).

Do you support this stance? Are there major reasons why SBCD should be promoted?

8   The involvement of teachers in a 'generative' role is both a valuing of their capacities to (actively) evaluate and design as well as to deliver the curriculum and a recognition of their resistance to (passively) implementing other people's ideas (Day, Pope and Denicolo, 1990, p. 213).

Elaborate upon why these factors are of critical importance to teachers and to SBCD.

References

DAY, C., POPE, M., DENICOLO, P. (Eds) (1990) *Insight into Teachers' Thinking and Practice*, London, Falmer Press.

FIELDING, G. (1989) 'Describing Curriculum Development from the Inside Out', *Journal of Curriculum and Supervision*, 4, 2.

HARRISON, M. (1981) 'School-Based Curriculum Decision Making: A Personal Viewpoint', *Curriculum Perspectives*, 2, 1.

HOLLY, P.J. and SOUTHWORTH, G.W. (1990) 'Characteristics of School Development Plans', in SOUTHWORTH, G. and LOFTHOUSE, B., *The Study of Primary Education, A Source Book, Volume 3, School Organization and Management*, London, Falmer Press.

MARSH, C.J., DAY, C., HANNAY, L., McCUTCHEON, G. (1990) *Reconceptualizing School-Based Curriculum Development*, London, Falmer Press.

SABAR, N., RUDDUCK, J. and REID, W. (Eds) (1987) *Partnership and Autonomy in School-Based Curriculum Development*, Sheffield, University of Sheffield Press.

SIMONS, H. (1987) *Getting to Know Schools in a Democracy*, London, Falmer Press.

SKILBECK, M. (1984) *School-Based Curriculum Development*, London, Harper and Row.

WALTON, J. (1978) 'School-Based Curriculum Development in Australia' in WALTON, J. and MORGAN, R. (Eds) *Some Perspectives on School-Based Curriculum Development*, Armidale, University of New England Press.

Part 4

Curriculum Management

Chapter 20

Innovation and Planned Change

The second half of this century is an era in which *change* has become a familiar term. In fact, one frequently used phrase implies that the only permanent feature of our time is change.

There is hardly any social institution which would escape the process of change, and education is no exception. Formal education in schools over the last five decades has been marked by significant and frequent changes in its aims and objectives, its content, teaching strategies, methods of student assessment, provisions, and the level of funding. Not always have the changes led to something better — some innovations have been disappointing and brought about yet another turn in the search for the 'best' education.

Curriculum change is a generic term which subsumes a whole family of concepts such as 'innovation', 'development' and 'adoption'. It can be either *planned* or *unplanned* (unintentional, spontaneous, accidental movements or shifts). The curriculum literature tends to focus upon 'planned change', which, for Lippit *et al.* (1958), is

> the conscious, deliberate and collaborative effort to improve the operations of human systems ... through the utilisation of valid knowledge.

Phases of Planned Change

Most curriculum writers now agree that there are four basic phases in the process of educational change:

Orientation/Needs Phase

Dissatisfaction, concern, or need is felt and expressed by one or more individuals who seek answers to such dominant questions as:

What is the problem that is concerning me (us)?
How and why has it arisen?
Is it important enough to rectify?
Do I (do we) want to take the necessary steps to overcome the problem?

Initiation/Adoption Phase

A person (or a group of persons) initiates and promotes a certain programme
or activity. Dominant questions of this phase are:

What should I (we) do?
What will it look like?
What will it mean for me (us)?

Implementation/Initial Use Phase

Attempts are made by teachers to use the programme or activity and this can
have varied results from a success to a disastrous failure. Dominant questions
for the teacher at this phase include:

How do I do it?
Will I ever get it to work smoothly?
To whom can I turn to get assistance?
Am I doing what the practice requires?
What is the effect on the learner?

Institutionalization/Continuation Phase

The emphasis here is to ensure that structures and patterns of behaviour are
established so that the use of the innovation will be maintained over time.
The dominant questions for the school are:

How do I (we) make sure that the innovation will continue?
Who will take responsibilities to ensure the adequate operation of it?
(Loucks, 1983).

Although these four phases can be separated for purposes of analysis, in
practice they will merge imperceptibly into each other. There can be forward
and backward modifications between the phases (as indicated by the two-way
arrows in figure 20.1), and the time periods for each phase can vary
tremendously.

The *initiation/adoption* phase is often termed 'the front end' of an innovation (Roberts-Gray and Gray, 1983). It is the period when basic decisions are
made by external agencies and publishers for whom numbers of adopters

Figure 20.1: Educational change process

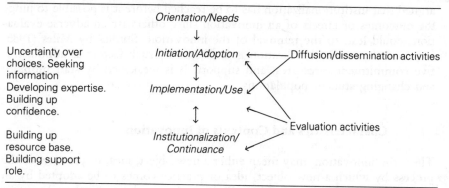

(After Fullan, 1982)

(and therefore sales) are of crucial importance. They can expect that schools and teachers will adopt a curriculum package only if it fulfils a special need for them, although there are other factors which can influence their decision. Fullan (1982) listed a number of factors which codetermine adoption rates, including existence and quality of related innovations, access to information, advocacy from central administrators, change agents, availability of federal or state funds, community pressures, and decrees by state governments.

The *implementation phase* has been defined as 'what an innovation consists of in practice' (Fullan and Pomfret, 1977). But this simple statement does not reveal the complex realities and problems associated with the phase. Leithwood's (1981) definition raised some of the complexities: 'Implementation is a reduction in the gap between current and preferred status.' The factors which seem to influence the effectiveness of implementation (Fullan and Pomfret, 1977) include:

- the characteristics of the innovation (for example, explicitness, complexity);
- the strategies available (for example, in-service training);
- the characteristics of the unit undertaking the implementation (for example, peer and authority relationships); and
- the characteristics of the macro-socio-political unit (for example, political complexity).

Whilst the answer to the question whether an innovation has been adopted is simply *yes* or *no*, the same cannot apply to implementation. There is a continuum of degrees of implementation ranging from major to minor adaptations through to a high fidelity of use level. The only definite point on the continuum is for non-implementation.

Institutionalization occurs when an innovation is supported in schools after an initial period of use (usually the first two years). The real test for continuance or disappearance of an innovation comes after external funds have been terminated or after consultant assistance has stopped. It can be argued that institutionalization has to be reached before it is possible to judge the outcomes or effects of an innovation since otherwise an adverse evaluation would lead to the removal of the innovation. Studies by Miles (1983) indicated that institutionalization is facilitated by such factors as administrative commitment, pressures, and support. It is weakened by staff mobility and changing student populations.

Characteristics and Contexts of Innovation

The term 'innovation' may mean either a new object, idea, or practice, or the process by which a new object, idea or practice comes to be adopted by an individual group or organization. Early studies in the curriculum literature (for example, Havelock, 1969; Rogers and Shoemaker, 1971) tended to view innovations as objects or events, similar to a new item of machinery for farmers or a new apothecary line. Much more emphasis is now placed upon innovation as a process, as evident in the following definition by Henderson (1985):

> Innovation process is the planned application of ends or means, new to the adopting educational system, and intended to improve the effectiveness and/or efficiency of the system.

This definition with its emphasis upon *intention* and *application* is indicating that innovation process is not only an awareness of alternatives but a definite intention to implement one or more of the alternatives. Many early studies of innovations tended to focus upon knowledge, awareness and adoption decisions (Mort, 1953; Rogers, 1962), but few penetrated the crucial area of implementation, to find out how teachers were actually using an innovation.

Henderson's definition also directs attention to *improving* the effectiveness of a system. Educators do not always agree with the contention that a change has to be an improvement to qualify as an 'innovation'. Whether an innovation is regarded as an improvement or not depends of course upon the judgment of the adopting agency or individual, as they will perceive an innovation in terms of their past experiences and aspirations. If it is 'new' to them, and different to what they have done before, then they will probably choose it because it is considered likely to bring about an improvement. Innovations are not objective and unchanging, but are constantly being changed and redefined as a result of experience. In other words, the initial perception of an innovation by teachers and other individuals or agencies may be that it is 'new' and an 'improvement' to what they were doing, but the final judgment of worth cannot be really known until some time later when they have become fully conversant with the innovation and how it might be applied to their situation.

The inclusion of the attribute 'improvement' in the concept of an innovative process emphasizes the political nature of curriculum innovations.

'Innovations' are initiated in school situations because certain authorities are not satisfied with particular directions or levels of learning and want to do something about it. The tremendous growth of studies in the US over the last decade on 'school improvement' and 'school effectiveness' are a sure sign of the political nature of innovations (Apple, 1982; see module 22).

Contexts of Innovations

Schools in which innovations are implemented can vary enormously in terms of staff interest and expertise, organizational structure, and resources. The staff will have their own special identity based upon their attributes, informal and formal values and norms, leadership traits and organizational climate. Students at a particular school will have certain characteristics in terms of socio-economic status, social orientation, norms, values and skills.

There are many examples in the literature of innovations that have not lasted in particular schools. Some typical reasons for failure include:

(a) originated by outside experts,
(b) difficult to manage,
(c) inadequate planning,
(d) not understood by teachers,
(e) parents did not understand (Lighthall and Allan, 1989; Clough *et al.*, 1989).

According to Vanterpool (1990), the characteristics of an innovation that predict a high probability of success are implicit in the following questions:

(a) Relative advantage (compared with what exists):
  ☐ Will it be more effective in improving learning?
  ☐ Will it conserve resources more efficiently?
  ☐ Will it have a positive impact on the total programme?
(b) Compatibility (consistent with values, experiences, needs):
  ☐ Will it fit well with other aspects of the programme?
  ☐ Will it be accepted?
(c) Testability (can be tried on an experimental basis):
  ☐ Has it been tested in schools like ours?
  ☐ Can it be pilot-tested?
  ☐ Can we use selected parts?
(d) Observability (can be seen in action):
  ☐ Can we see a live demonstration with children?
  ☐ Can we see a videotaped demonstration?
  ☐ Can we see variations in its application?
(e) Complexity (ease of use):
  ☐ Will teachers need special training?
  ☐ Will it add to teachers' paperwork?

Diffusion and Dissemination

Diffusion and dissemination activities are two crucial terms for understanding how innovations are communicated. Rogers (1983) defines *diffusion* as 'the spontaneous, unplanned spread of new ideas'. It involves a special type of communication between individuals and groups because the messages are concerned with 'new' ideas. Groups and individuals will often seek out further information about an innovation before they make a decision to adopt it or not. If they are unable to decide between several alternatives, the diffusion of information enables them to make an informed choice.

Information transfer is rarely a one-way process; most frequently it is effected by an exchange of ideas and information between individuals. Rogers (1983) is therefore correct in his assessment that diffusion activities typically involve a two-way communication of information. Information about an innovation can of course be diffused by different communication channels, from mass media to face-to-face exchange.

The term *dissemination* is often used synonymously with diffusion but it really has a narrower focus and applies to the specific procedures used to inform individuals or groups about an innovation and to gain their interest in it. The emphasis is upon goal-directed activities and upon the arousing of interest in the innovation among potential clients. Some writers (for example, Zaltmann *et al.*, 1977; and Rosenau, 1973) view dissemination very much like marketing activities. For other writers (Rudduck and Kelly, 1976; Barrow, 1984), curriculum dissemination occurs within a cultural framework. They maintain that change agents need to be aware of a school system's attitudes and administrative structure and to only use dissemination activities which are suited to these prevailing norms.

Change Agents and Strategies

Change Agents

Change agents appear essential to innovations because they provide the communication links between the developers and the clients. According to Rogers (1983), change agents will always be needed to facilitate the implementation of innovations because there 'is a social and technical chasm between the change agency and the client system'. This is clearly the case with regard to innovations in agriculture, industry and distribution; change agents with specialist technical knowledge are needed to communicate and persuade clients that an innovation is needed and should be adopted. However, in the field of education, change agents cannot be simply regarded as technical and social experts coming to schools only from outside. Certainly there are occasions when external specialists do fulfil an important information-giving role, but there are circumstances when internal teacher-change agents are required.

Since the 1970s there has been less interest in idealized types of change agents and more upon individuals who operate in particular educational roles, so as to understand more fully how the latter can influence levels of implementation within particular contexts. A number of studies have focused upon the *classroom teacher* and how he or she reacts to change. Hall *et al.* (1975), and Leithwood and Montgomery (1980) have developed stages to explain how classroom teachers adjust to an innovation at different time periods and how their behaviours, in turn, influence other teachers. Huberman and Crandall (1982), Feld (1981), and Larkin (1983) have completed studies recently on the change agent activities of the *superintendent* and central office administrators. Over the last decade there has been a surge of interest in the change agent activities of the *school principal* and how they can provide encouragement and incentives for curriculum change (Berman and McLaughlin, 1978; Emrick and Peterson, 1978; Rutherford *et al.*, 1983).

Change Strategies and Tactics

Strategy in the area of curriculum change means, reduced to the simplest form, a plan for replacing an existing programme by an innovation. Several such strategies have been proposed by education writers. A well-known set of strategies developed by Bennis, Benne, Chin and Corey (1976) are 'power-coercive', 'normative/re-educative' and 'empirical-rational'. They provide a general guide about typical behaviours but it is quite feasible that in a single setting, two or more of these strategies might be used.

Power-coercive strategies are based on the control of rewards and punishments and are relatively easy to apply. The recipients simply have to comply if they want to obtain the rewards offered but the motivation for complying is of course not meaningfully related to the innovation. That is, it is extrinsic in nature, and teachers on the receiving side will have no inner self-generated need for accepting and implementing an innovation (intrinsic motivation).

Normative/re-educative strategies refer to actions intended to manipulate recipients so that they see the situation differently. This can be achieved by biased messages, persuasive communication, and by training workshops. The recipients are trained or re-educated to appreciate the beneficial aspects of a particular innovation.

Empirical-rational strategies rely upon the recipients realizing that they should change to the new innovation in their best interests. The strategies rely upon providing detailed knowledge about the innovation by holding workshops, seminars and demonstrations.

Tactics are specific actions that are taken to reinforce the impact of a strategy. There are many possible tactics that might be used and some examples are included in figure 20.2, under the categories of *impersonal information, personal demonstration*, and *interpersonal field agents*. Each of these tactics can be rated on criteria such as relative cost, coverage, impact and user convenience. It can be noted that tactics such as direct mail can have a *high* coverage but a *low* impact whereas an on-site demonstration of an innovation

Figure 20.2: Tactics and their potential effects

IMPERSONAL Information	Rel. Cost of Implementation	Relative Coverage	Relative Impact	User Convenience	Feedback	Ideal for	Unsuited to	Incentives Required
Direct Mail	L	H	L	H	H	Installing or replacing visible, low-risk, familiar innovations	Complex innovations	Low price, ease of ordering, guarantee, bonus, etc.
Mass Media	L	H	L	M	L	Awareness, arousal	Complex, high-cost innovations	Stimulus to act on information (limited time, special introductory offer, etc.)
Printed Matter	L	M	L	H	L	Awareness, interest	Complex innovations requiring hands-on trial	Stimulus to act on information
Professional Association	L	M	M	M	M	Awareness of innovations, data on trials	Mass-market adoptions	Professional membership status, interaction with peers, prepaid travel to meetings

PERSONAL Demonstration

On-Site	M	L	M	H	H	Trial of high-risk innovations in large LEAs	Low-risk routine adoptions	Released time for observation, testimonials
Visitation	H	M	M	L	M	Demonstration of complex, high-risk innovations	Low-cost, routine adoptions	Released time, prepaid travel materials to take home, testimonials
Workshop	M	L	L	M	M	Hands-on trial	Persuasion of university personnel	Free registration, credit, materials to take home, snacks

INTERPERSONAL Field Agents

Non-Commercial	H	M	M	H	H	Implementing high-risk, unfamiliar, complex training or organizational innovations	Mass-market adoptions	Free consultation, technical assistance, targeted information retrieval system, etc.
Commercial	H	H	H	H	H	Installing high-markup, low-risk, consumable innovations	Low-markup, complex innovations	Free samples, entertainment, volume discounts, special deals, etc.

L = low M = medium H = high
(After Rosenau, 1973)

can have *low* coverage but a *moderate* impact and a *high* rating in terms of user convenience.

Reflections and Issues

1   Teachers are not prone to explore curriculum innovations because they guard jealously the privacy of their own class and their established procedures.

Do you agree with this statement? What strategies and tactics might be used to encourage teachers to try an innovation?

2   Culture and change are antithetical, in that change threatens the stability, predictability and comfort of the culture (Deal, 1987).

Is this the case? Describe some experiences you have had which support or refute this statement.

3   Adoption of innovations should not be left to chance. By identifying and managing several of the variables it is possible to increase the probability of successful matches between innovations and their schools.

Do you support this statement? Give details of important variables that need to be managed.

4   Schools cope with change in different ways. Miles (1981) suggests that teachers use *shallow coping strategies* (delays, avoidance, people-shuffling) or *deep coping strategies* (training and developing people, new roles and structures). Are deep coping strategies possible in present periods of financial constraint? Give examples.

5   Planned change implies intended action, a theory of value of what is important, and specific elements within a limited setting (Smith *et al.*, 1988).

Are these three aspects all important? Describe school situations of planned change which have been successful and unsuccessful. What criteria were used to make these judgments?

6   Curriculum change occurs in situations in which a certain amount of consonance and conflict will inevitably occur (Paris, 1989).

How might the histories, practices and ideologies of teachers and administrators cause conflicts? How might they be resolved?

7   Successful curriculum change and implementation depends upon an environment in which innovation is seen as a learning process — innovation of the school, rather than innovation in the school (Dalton, 1988).

How can these attitudes be fostered? What are some strategies which need to be considered?

References

APPLE, M.W. (1982) *Education and Power*, Boston, Routledge and Kegan Paul.

BARROW, R. (1984) *Giving Teaching Back to Teachers*, London, Wheatsheaf Books.

BENNIS, W.G., BENNE, K.D., CHIN, R., and COREY, K.E. (Eds) (1976) *The Planning of Change*, New York, Holt, Rinehard and Winston.

BERMAN, P. and McLAUGHLIN, M.W. (1978) *Federal Programs Supporting Educational Change Vol VIII: Implementing and Sustaining Innovations*, Santa Monica, California, Rand Corporation.

BOWMAN, P. and McLAUGHLIN, M.W. (1977) *Federal Programs Supporting Educational Change Vol VII: Factors Affecting Implementation and Continuation*, US Office of Education, Department of Health, Education and Welfare, Santa Monica, Rand Corporation.

CLOUGH, E., ASPINWALL, K. and GIBBS, B. (Eds) (1989) *Learning to Change: An LEA School-Focused Initiative*, London, Falmer Press.

DALTON, T. (1988) *The Challenge of Curriculum Innovation: A Study of Ideology and Practice*, London, Falmer Press.

DEAL, T.E. (1987) 'The Culture of Schools', in SHEIVE, L. and SCHOENHEIT, M. (Eds) *Leadership: Examining the Elusive*, Alexandria, Virginia, ASCD.

EMRICK, J. and PETERSON, S. (1978) *A Synthesis of Findings across Five Recent Studies in Educational Disseminaton and Change*, San Francisco, Far West Laboratory.

FELD, M.M. (1981) 'The Bureaucracy, The Superintendent and Change', *Education and Urban Society*, **13**, 4.

FULLAN, M. (1982) *The Meaning of Educational Change*, New York, Teachers College Press.

FULLAN, M. and POMFRET, A. (1977) 'Research on Curriculum and Instruction Implementation', *Review of Educational Research*, **47**, 2.

HALL, G.E., LOUCKS, S.F., RUTHERFORD, W.L. and NEWLOVE, B.W. (1975) 'Levels of Use of the Innovation: A Framework for Analyzing Innovation Adoption', *Journal of Teacher Education*, **26**, 1.

HAVELOCK, R.G. (1969) *A Guide to Innovation and Education*, Ann Arbor, Center for Research and Utilization of Knowledge.

HENDERSON, J.C. (1985) 'Organization Development and the Implementation of Planned Change', unpublished doctoral dissertation, Murdoch University.

HUBERMAN, M. and CRANDALL, D.P. (1982) *People, Policies and Practices: Examining the Chain of School Improvement, Vol IX: Implications for Action A Study of Dissemination Efforts Supporting School Improvement (DESSI)*, Andover, MA, The Network.

LARKIN, R.F. (1983) 'Achievement Directed Leadership: A Superintendent's Perspective', a paper presented at the Annual Conference of the American Research Association, Montreal.

LEITHWOOD, K.A. (1981) 'Managing the Implementation of Curriculum Innovations', *Knowledge: Creation, Diffusion, Utilization*, **2**, 3.

LEITHWOOD, K.A. and MONTGOMERY, D. (1980) 'A Procedure for Assessing the Nature and Degree of Programme Implementation', *Education Evaluation Review*, **4**, 2.

LIGHTHALL, F.F. and ALLAN, S.D. (1989) *Local Realities, Local Adaptations*, London, Falmer Press.

LIPPITT, R.O. *et al.* (1958) *The Dynamics of Planned Change*, New York, Harcourt Brace and Jovanovich.

LOUCKS, S.F. (1983) 'Defining Fidelity: A Cross-Study Analysis', paper presented at the Annual Conference of the American Educational Research Association, Montreal.

MILES, M.B. (1981) 'Mapping the Common Properties of Schools', in LEHMING, R. and CAIN, M. (Eds) *Improving Schools: Using What We Know*, Beverly Hills, California, Sage.

MILES, M.B. (1983) 'Unraveling the Mystery of Institutionalization', *Educational Leadership*, **41**, 3.

MORT, P.R. (1953) 'Educational Adaptability', *The School Executive*, **71**.

PARIS, C.L. (1989) 'Contexts of Curriculum Change: Conflict and Consonants', paper presented at the Annual Conference of the American Educational Research Association, San Francisco.

ROBERTS-GRAY, C. and GRAY, T. (1983) 'Implementing Innovations', *Knowledge: Creation, Diffusion, Utilization*, **5**, 2.

ROGERS, E.M. (1962) *Diffusion of Innovations*, New York, Free Press.

ROGERS, E.M. (1983) *Diffusion of Innovations*, 3rd edition, New York, Free Press.

ROGERS, E.M. and SHOEMAKER, F.F. (1971) *Communications of Innovations*, New York, Free Press.

ROSENAU, F.S. (1973) *Tactics for the Educational Change Agent*, San Francisco, Far West Laboratory.

RUDDUCK, J. and KELLY, P. (1976) *The Dissemination of Curriculum Development*, Windsor, NFER.

RUTHERFORD, W.F. *et al.* (1983) *Change Facilitators: In Search of Understanding Their Role*, Austin, University of Texas Research and Development Center for Teacher Education.

SMITH, L.M. *et al.* (1988) *Innovation and Change in Schooling: History, Politics and Agency*, London, Falmer Press.

VANTERPOOL, M. (1990) 'Innovations Aren't For Everyone', *Principal*, **69**, 4.

ZALTMANN, G. *et al.* (1977) *Dynamic Educational Change*, New York, Free Press.

Chapter 21

Managing the Curriculum: The Collaborative School Management Model

The curriculum is not merely a set of documents but a particular combination of formal and informal learning experiences that occur within a school. How the staff of a school work together and how they interact with students is of course of major importance. All teachers are involved to a certain extent in managing the curriculum but some have a far greater impact than others, such as the school principal and deputy principal.

Many school management models have been published in the literature. By focusing here on *one* example in some detail, it is anticipated that a number of the major issues will be highlighted for readers.

Phases of the CSM Model

The Collaborative School Management (CSM) approach was developed by Caldwell and Spinks (1986) in Australia and subsequently published in the UK in 1988. The model is now widely used in many countries including the UK, Canada, New Zealand and Australia.

The CSM approach appears to be very popular with school decision-makers because:

(a) the guidelines are clear-cut and practical
(b) they are directly linked to patterns of work in schools.

Management Teams — A Policy Group and Project Teams

The separation of tasks (and rules) for a *policy group* and for *project teams* is a vital aspect of the CSM approach (see table 21.1). It is an attempt to provide a task-oriented focus with a set of checks and balances to provide some degree of accountability.

The *policy group* need not be narrow and prescriptive (although this is an option), but it might more typically be a school council with a wide representation of parents and students as well as teachers. The policy group is

Table 21.1: Guidelines for establishing the Collaborative School Management (CSM) cycle

1 There are two different action groups. The *policy group* (e.g. School Council) sets the policies and the priorities. *The program teams* (e.g. the Mathematics team) prepare program plans and budgets which must be approved by the policy group.
2 The use of these teams enables teachers, principal, students and community to all be participants.
3 There is inevitably some overlap between the tasks of the policy group and those of the program teams. Some persons may be members of both groups.
4 There are strict maximum writing limits for each of the six phases. For example,
   Policy statement: 1 page (maximum)
   Program plan: 2 pages (maximum)
   Evaluation report: 1 page (maximum)
5 All planning and evaluation reports must be written in non-technical language which can be easily understood.
6 School communities should work on completing a small number (e.g. 3–5) of policy-making, program planning and budgeting activities each *calendar year*, with a systematic plan in subsequent years for the evaluation of existing programs.
7 Each school community should plan for a period of 3–5 years to complete most of their planned changes.

Source: Caldwell and Spinks, 1986, pp. 20–3.

required to make decisions about goals, identification of needs and policy-making guidelines and to share responsibility for evaluation activities. The task of the policy group is to shape the direction and range of activities for their school community.

By contrast, the task of the *project teams* (largely comprised of teachers) is to undertake evaluation. One of the checks is that their programme plans and budgets have to be approved by the policy group.

The Six Phases of CSM Which Operate as a Management Cycle

As illustrated in figure 21.1, the phases include:

(a) goal-setting and identification of needs,
(b) policy-making,
(c) planning of programmes,
(d) preparation and approval of programme budgets,
(e) implementing,
(f) evaluating.

Goal-setting and identification of needs

Goal-setting and needs identification is the typical starting-off point for the process, but it need not be, and any of the other five phases could be used as the entry point as depicted in figure 21.1.

Goals, according to Caldwell and Spinks, should not be concerned with particular outcomes, nor should they apply to a particular time period. They should merely be a statement of broad direction. An example cited by the

Figure 21.1:   Phases in the Collaborative School Management (CSM) cycle

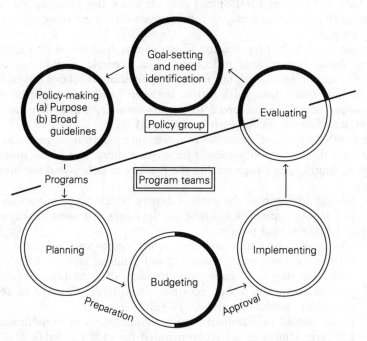

(Reproduced with permission from B.J. Caldwell and J. Spinks (1988) The Self-Managing School, *London, Falmer Press.)*

authors is: 'To provide a variety of opportunities for parental involvement in the activities of the school' (1988, p. 39). The authors suggest that formulating these goals will involve contestation by different individuals. Not all will agree upon particular goals about specific student outcomes or the provision of resources or the management of the school.

A related activity is *identifying needs*. The authors do not go into detail about this aspect but view it simply as the difference between 'what is' and 'what should be'. The authors tend to use quantitative examples (for example, teaching workloads) to illustrate needs and do not delve into discussions about why and how needs might vary between individuals and groups. They prefer to be practical, businesslike and target-oriented by suggesting that important questions to ask include:

- Is the discrepancy between 'what is' and 'what ought to be' large enough to warrant action?
- What harm will be done if the gap is not closed?
- How important is this need compared with others that may exist? (Caldwell and Spinks, 1986, p. 11)

Policy-making
The details that Caldwell and Spinks provide about this phase of the process are eminently practical and easy to follow, even if they are somewhat rational and prescriptive.

Policies need to be prepared for all issues that are viewed by participants as being more than routine procedures. For example, a policy is usually needed for school homework but not for supervision of school bus pick-ups. Caldwell and Spinks distinguish further between issues that might be viewed as *contentious* and those perceived to be *non-contentious*, and they provide a different set of strategies for each (see table 21.2).

The authors produce a number of interesting practical suggestions. They are adamant that each policy should be written down but be no more than *one page* in length. They suggest that the process of policy-making involves:

• Giving attention to the various desires which occur in various ways in a school community. These are the issues that must be shaped into a definite school policy.
• The first step is to search for policy alternatives — gathering information about legal, economic and political aspects of each issue.
• The next step is to communicate with all stake-holders (teachers, parents, students) about possible alternatives. Criteria to use are *desirability*, *workability* and *acceptability*.
• Issues should be classified as either contentious or non-contentious. Different strategies are recommended for each (see table 21.2).
• A timetable for policy-making must be established. Contentious issues: three to five policies per year. Non-contentious issues: up to four policies each month. A total of one to two years is needed for a school community to establish all policies required.

As indicated in table 21.2 the task for *non-contentious issues* is to have the writing of one-page written policies shared between various teachers and others with special expertise. Previously developed examples can provide a useful model and can save time for the persons involved. Draft policies should be pinned up on staff noticeboards (to avoid paper wars). Refined policies, in due course, must be submitted for approval to the policy group. Once adopted, policies must be made known to all the school community, preferably in a policy handbook.

For a *contentious issue* it is suggested that a working party of six to eight people should be formed (presumably nominated by the policy group or the school council). Information should be gathered from a wide range of individuals and groups, by informal conversations and by the use of surveys. Caldwell and Spinks insist that at least three options for each issue should be prepared (to incorporate and reflect the range of views) and submitted in due course to the policy group.

Table 21.2: *Preparing policies on non-contentious and contentious issues*

For non-contentious issues	For contentious issues
Document existing practice as follows: 1 Share the task of writing different policies among members of staff and others with expertise. 2 Provide a good example for policy-writers to follow: • one page long; • statement of purpose and broad guidelines included; • free of jargon. 3 Refine draft policies on the basis of critical reaction from those who have experience in or knowledge of the issue. 4 Submit refined policies to the policy group in batches for adoption or further refinement. 5 Disseminate policies regularly to all in the school community.	Prepare options as follows: 1 Set a maximum of 3–5 policies per year. 2 Appoint a working party for each issue. 3 Have a maximum of 6–8 people in each working party. 4 Appoint to the working party people with both stake *and* expertise. 5 The working party should gain information from a wide range of individuals and groups with expertise *or* stake. 6 Formulate at least three options to help build consensus. 7 Each option should be based on a good example as far as format is concerned. 8 Elements of consensus should be refined in a well-written statement. 9 Adopt a policy. 10 Disseminate the policy.

Source: *Caldwell and Spinks, 1986, p. 79.*

Planning and budgeting

After written policy statements have been produced it is then possible for the programme teams to develop plans for implementation. Caldwell and Spinks stress the need to make direct links between policies and programmes.

The programs can be concerned with simply the traditional subject divisions (for example, a Mathematics programme for Years 1–7 or Years 8–12), but there might also be cross-subject programmes (for example, Pastoral Care). It may be necessary in each school to have a few all-encompassing programmes and a number of specific ones (eight to twenty-five) in total for primary schools, thirty or more in total for secondary schools.

The authors stress that an economical use of time is a major consideration in writing up details of the programme plan and budget. This document should be no longer than two pages, and useful headings are:

• purpose,
• broad guidelines,
• plan for implementation,
• resources required (budget),
• evaluation,
• details of programme team members.

The first two headings provide a link with the policy document, in that they will have been taken directly from this source.

The plan for implementation establishes specific information about which groups of students will be involved, the staff involved, materials and equipment to be used, and other related matters. It might be argued that teachers do these activities as a matter of course. Caldwell and Spinks (1988) argue that being precise about this information using standardized headings, and completing the document at the same time each year, enables a much better integration of school management activities.

The authors suggest that the costs of all resources should be listed, including teaching services stated either as units of time or in salary-time costs. They argue that it is important for the wider school community to realize that the staff's time represents the major resource of any school.

The programme budget summary should identify expenditure amounts required for each programme in terms of teaching staff, travel, book materials and services. A total expenditure figure is then calculated, which has to be reconciled with resources available. The authors point out that 'deficits' are usually the order of the day, and so lower-priority programmes may have to be deleted. These decisions are typically made by the policy group or a finance committee. Regardless of who is involved in the reconciliation decisions, the policy group must give final approval to the budget.

Implementing

The implementing phase belongs squarely with the programme teams, because it is concerned with:

- learning,
- teaching,
- use of resources,
- supervision and day-to-day facilitation of each programme.

Caldwell and Spinks (1988) provide little specific information about the learning-teaching aspect except to assume that this belongs to the teachers, who have the appropriate professional training to do the task.

The authors pay more attention to the need for the principal or a member of each programme team nominated by the principal to *supervise* the implementation process. The supervisor in each team should take responsibility to ensure that policy guidelines are followed; materials and services are made available when needed; and to have control over the selection and ordering of materials and services.

The authors suggest that the school bursar or registrar can provide a lot of assistance in coordinating the supply of resources and providing accounting assistance.

Evaluating

Caldwell and Spinks provide more detailed comments on this final phase of their CSM cycle, although their focus is a rather limited interpretation of evaluation. They make three assumptions which guide all the evaluative activities:

1 The CSM details of policy statements and programmes are used to judge whether a programme has achieved its objectives or not.
2 The CSM details of programmes are used to judge how achievement levels were intended to occur, and if not, why not.
3 The CSM details can pinpoint which resources are being used and whether redistribution of certain resources should occur.

Caldwell and Spinks (1988) maintain that their CSM cycle facilitates and provides the direction for evaluative activities. It can also save teachers and administrators valuable time because a wealth of data is readily available via the various policy statements. Nevertheless, the authors suggest that other practical measures are needed, such as:

- Choose to evaluate only a few programmes in depth each year (for example, one-fifth).
- Each in-depth evaluation should be written up in a maximum of two pages and should use standard headings (success indicators, areas of concern, comments and recommendations).
- Each major evaluation should be carried out by a group including parents, programme team and others as appropriate.
- Other programmes in any one year should have minor evaluations; the report on each should be completed in a maximum of one page.
- Both major and minor evaluation reports must be presented to the policy group for review and possible future action.

Advantages and Disadvantages

Advantages of the CSM Model

(a) It is an eminently practical one, which does seem to work.
(b) It is possible to schedule the tasks over the school year to suit the routines of administrators, teachers and other members of the school community.
(c) The six phases that comprise the CSM cycle are logical and easy to follow.

Disadvantages of the CSM Model

(a) The separation of the policy group from the project teams could lead to undesirable hierarchical distinctions.
(b) The inclusion of students in the decision-making process is given minimal treatment.
(c) There appears to be an overemphasis on the financial aspects of school planning.

Reflections and Issues

1   Successful management of the curriculum depends upon the
        principal's capacity to maintain a purposeful concentration
        on the tasks in hand while at the same time providing sensi-
        tive and encouraging support to individuals (Day *et al.*, 1985,
        p. 122).

What are some problems in trying to achieve these ends?
How does the CSM model try to account for these ends?

2   A change to school-based management implies greater flex-
        ibility of decision-making, changes in role accountability
        (particularly for the principal) and the potential enhancement
        of school productivity (Brown, 1990, p. vii).

Do you consider that these are the major changes resulting from
school-based management?
Are these addressed adequately in the CSM model?

3   Brown (1990) cites two problems with the CSM model, namely:

    (a)   they do not address district decentralization; their focus is
          on the school in a decentralised district.
    (b)   the authors accept the model fully and optimistically leave
          the reader to surmise what difficulties might ensue with
          its adoption.

Comment on these and other problems you perceive with using the
CSM model.

4   The ability to handle conflict is a key factor in managerial
        success. Whenever we wish to make changes, there is poten-
        tial for conflict (Everard and Morris, 1986, p. 80).

To what extent does the CSM model accommodate conflict resolu-
tion?

5   The 1988 Education Reform Act in the UK has catapulted
        financial management to the top of the education manage-
        ment agenda (Levačić, 1989, p. 1).

Is financial management an integral and adequate part of the CSM
model? What shortcomings are there?

6   School-based management stems from a belief in the indi-
        vidual school as the fundamental decision-making unit with-
        in the educational system (Guthrie, 1986, p. 306).

Do you agree that the individual school should be considered as the
management base? What are some problems in making this assumption? How are these addressed in the CSM model?

7   In many schools the professional staff appear to go through the motions of collegiate management without integrating the full implications of the approach into everyday practice — a situation of innovation without change (Wallace, 1990, p. 110).

Is this a common occurrence in your experience?
Does the CSM model provide teachers with meaningful collegiate management?

8 Compare and contrast these two management perspectives about schools:

Organizations have clear boundaries, goals are specified. There has to be consensus between organizational members on operational goals if the organization is to function effectively (Hoyle, 1986; Glatter, *et al.*, 1988).

Conflict is present in all schools. Class relationships are vital in understanding why certain ideas and actions are contested. There will always be innovations and individuals opposing authority and resisting official influences (Bates, 1983; Watkins, 1983).

References

BATES, R. (1983) *Educational Administration and the Management of Knowledge*, Melbourne, Deakin University Press.

BROWN, D.J. (1990) *Decentralization and School-Based Management*, London, Falmer Press.

CALDWELL, B.J. and SPINKS, J. (1986) *Policy-Making and Planning for School Effectiveness*, Hobart, Education Department of Tasmania.

CALDWELL, B.J. and SPINKS, J.M. (1988) *The Self-Managing School*, London, Falmer Press.

DAY, C., JOHNSTON, D. and WHITAKER, P. (1985) *Managing Primary Schools*, London, Harper and Row.

EVERARD, K.B. and MORRIS, G. (1986) *Effective School Management*, London, Paul Chapman.

GLATTER, R. *et al.* (1988) *Understanding School Management*, London, Open University Press.

GUTHRIE, J.W. (1986) School-Based Management: The Next Needed Education Reform, *Phi Delta Kappan*, **25**, 3.

HOYLE, E. (1986) *The Politics of School Management*, London, Hodder and Stoughton.

LEVAČIĆ, R. (1989) *Financial Management in Education*, Milton Keynes, Open University Press.

WALLACE, M. (1990) 'Curriculum Management and Organization: the Collegiate Approach', in SOUTHWORTH, G. and LOFTHOUSE, B.; *The Study of Primary Education, A Source Book, Volume 3, School Organization and Management*, London, Falmer Press.

WATKINS, P. (1983) *Class, Control and Contestation in Educational Organization*, Melbourne, Deakin University Press.

Chapter 22

Effective Schools and School Improvement

Over recent years there have been two major orientations to how schools are operating and how they might be improved. The *school effectiveness* literature has tended to prescribe school characteristics which are associated with successful student outcomes. By contrast, the *school improvement* literature has concentrated upon school leadership and sustained efforts by all participants to change learning conditions.

School effectiveness studies tend to concentrate on quantitative measures and indicators that seem to be related to successful student achievements. School improvement studies have a broader focus and consider all major participants (especially students, teachers and parents) and tend to have a greater qualitative emphasis. Both approaches are concerned of course with producing better schools.

Effective Schools — Factors and Examples

Some Empirical Studies

Effective schools research has tended to focus on inner-city schools, especially in the USA but also in the UK. Major studies include those by Weber (1971), Edmonds (1979), MacKenzie (1983) and Mortimore and Sammons (1987).

As an example, Edmonds (1979) studied effective schools in the north-eastern quadrant of the USA. He defined an instructionally effective school as one that brings the children of the poor to those minimal masteries of basic school skills that now describe minimally successful pupil performance for the children of the middle class (Edmonds, 1979, p. 16). He isolated the following factors:

(a) strong administrative leadership;
(b) a climate of expectation for satisfactory student achievement;
(c) an orderly but not oppressive school climate;
(d) a focus on pupil acquisition of basic school skills;
(e) a system for continuous monitoring of pupil progress; and

Table 22.1:   Dimensions of effective schools and schooling

Core Elements	Facilitating Elements

Leadership

- Positive climate and overall atmosphere
- Goal-focused activities toward clear, attainable and relevant objectives
- Teacher-directed classroom management and decision-making
- In-service staff training for effective teaching

- Shared consensus on values and goals
- Long-range planning and coordination
- Stability and continuity of key staff
- District-level support for school improvement

Efficacy

- High and positive achievement expectations with a constant press for excellence
- Visible rewards for academic excellence and growth
- Cooperative activity and group interaction in the classroom
- Total staff involvement with school improvement
- Autonomy and flexibility to implement adaptive practices
- Appropriate levels of difficulty for learning tasks
- Teacher empathy, rapport, and personal interaction with students

- Emphasis on homework and study
- Positive accountability; acceptance of responsibility for learning outcomes
- Strategies to avoid nonpromotion of students
- De-emphasis of strict ability grouping; interaction with more accomplished peers

Efficiency

- Effective use of instructional time; amount and intensity of engagement in school learning
- Orderly and disciplined school and classroom environments
- Continuous diagnosis, evaluation, and feedback
- Well-structured classroom activities
- Instruction guided by content coverage
- Schoolwide emphasis on basic and higher order skills

- Opportunities for individualized work
- Number and variety of opportunities to learn

(After MacKenzie, 1983, p. 8)

(f) resources that can be focused on the fundamental learning objectives of the school.

MacKenzie (1983) synthesized a number of American studies and concluded that the three major core elements were leadership, efficacy and efficiency (see table 22.1). There were other factors that also seemed important which he termed as facilitating elements.

Mortimore and Sammons (1987) undertook a study of effective elementary schools in the Inner London Education Authority and concluded that variations can be accounted for by differences in school policies and

Table 22.2: Key factors of effectiveness in elementary schools in the Inner London Education Authority

1 Purposeful leadership of the staff by the principal — he/she understands the needs of the school and is actively involved.
2 Involvement of the assistant principal — assisting with policy decisions.
3 Involvement of teachers — teachers involved in curriculum planning.
4 Consistency among teachers — teachers follow school guidelines in the same way.
5 Structured sessions — school day has sufficient structure.
6 Intellectually challenging teaching — progress is greatest where students are stimulated and challenged.
7 Work-centred environment — a high level of industry in the classroom.
8 Limited focus within sessions — a focus upon one curriculum area at a time.
9 Maximum communication between teachers and students — students gain from having frequent communication with the teacher.
10 Record-keeping — an important aspect of teachers' planning and assessment.
11 Parental involvement — a positive influence upon students' progress and development.
12 Positive climate — a positive ethos is important.

(After Mortimore and Sammons, 1987)

practices within the control of the principal and teachers. For them, there are twelve key factors, as listed in table 22.2.

Effective schools have been described as vital environments where people matter. The interactions between students and teachers are meaningful. The checklists of important factors such as those in tables 22.1 and 22.2 are somewhat sterile in that they do not convey the vitality and ethos of such schools. As noted by Sunderland (1989, p. 20), 'only an ecological analysis of each unique school can begin to uncover the full range of its effectiveness and help to account for why it is so.'

It is also worth noting that effective schools do not continue to thrive — many falter over time due to changes in personnel or other external factors. Stedman (1987) argues that many of the factors included in the effective schools literature cannot be substantiated. Studies of 'effective' inner-city schools have demonstrated only moderate improvements in student achievements. Stedman also notes that some schools have only achieved success by teaching to the test, which has produced in turn such negative effects as increasing teacher frustration and burnout.

School Improvement Targets and Factors

School improvement involves a commitment, especially by teachers and students, to examine their current practices and routines to see whether these are appropriate for their present situation. This takes a lot of time, perseverance and a considerable amount of collaboration.

School improvement can refer to relatively minor changes where there is some change to the programme without any change in the basic goals and values; or it can refer to changes in the programme and in the existing goals and values, which, in total, could amount to considerable change. An individual school community can get involved in minor or major changes, but the costs in time and resources usually limit their opportunities to minor changes.

Major changes are often initiated by state education systems and by federal government agencies. In fact, the term 'school improvement' first came into prominence in the United States in the 1960s with reference to federal and state programmes for school improvement in specific areas such as bilingual education and science education. Many of these innovatory programmes included new subject matter and modes of instruction, unfamiliar to most teachers.

Which Individuals/Groups are the Targets for School Improvement?

The traditional target for most school improvement endeavours is of course the student. The emphasis is upon ensuring that students — the clients of schooling — attain their highest possible levels of understanding, skills and values development.

Teachers are also a major client group in any school improvement activity. Teachers involved in implementing new curricula will obviously need intensive, additional training. It cannot be assumed that a teacher will be able to adopt a new program and be proficient in its use without assistance and training. Even for minor changes it is crucial that teachers be given information about the new programme and, where necessary, additional training for using it.

Attention has been directed in recent years to another target, namely parents and community members. If the goal of the school improvement includes having a higher level of parent involvement, then this must be an important focus. Unless parents have had other professional experiences which have equipped them with the skills needed for school decision-making, special training sessions must be provided (see module 23).

What Factors Are Important in Bringing About School Improvement?

Studies of school improvement, especially major ones in the United States such as Rand (Berman and McLaughlin, 1977) and DESSI (Crandall *et al.*, 1983), indicate that many successful cases do occur. Factors that seem to be important in bringing about successful school improvements include:

People:

1   Change should be acknowledged as a process, not an event — any change requires time for teachers to participate in planning and decision-making.
2   Commitment by teachers to a new programme is important but not a prerequisite — it can often occur through the process of implementing it.

3   There are key individuals who can set the expectations and tone for school improvement and who maintain general support and assistance (for example, the school principal).

4   Teachers will be supportive if they perceive that the new programme fits within their overall framework of interests and if it helps them to be more effective in teaching their students.

5   Teachers will accept external assistance if it is seen to be personal and practical.

Characteristics of the innovation:

6   The innovation is more likely to be implemented if it has a relative advantage and if it is more complex than other programmes.

Resources:

7   External staff and finances are crucial to provide ongoing staff development support for a new programme — the staff development activities have to be task-specific and geared to teachers' concerns and skills (Clark *et al.*, 1984; Crandall, 1983).

These factors appear to represent some of the major reasons why teachers will be willing to embark upon school improvement programmes. There are many others, of course, resulting from different levels of schooling and subject areas. Nevertheless, the 'people' factors such as commitment, credible dynamic leaders, and opportunities for teachers to try out new practices are important ingredients for most school improvement programmes.

Reflections and Issues

1   School improvement is about building collaboration and cooperation between major stakeholders such as teachers, students and parents.

In your experience how important is it to facilitate collaboration and cooperation? What are some possible impediments?

2   The last decade of research into effective schools supports the view that attempts at educational change when imposed from outside the school has little impact (Ramsay and Clark, 1990, p. 206).

Do you agree that the school is the essential unit of change? To what extent are changes doomed to failure if they are introduced from outside?

3   We have learned a great deal from quantitative research on the determinants of school effectiveness (Murnane, 1981, p. 26).

Consider some of the lessons we have learnt.

4 School improvement is

about a group of individuals using what they know intelligently, taking responsibility for their actions within a collective enterprise and working hard, very hard, together towards a common goal (Hopkins, 1987, pp. 196–7).

Discuss.

5 The 1980s have witnessed a rapid growth in the effective schools movement and a subsequent growth in the body of literature dealing with schooling practices that influence student outcomes. How do you account for this surge of interest?

6   There are major problems which relate to inferring cause and effect in effective schools. What outcomes should we look for and what characteristics are we looking for that are common to effective schools? What is the best mix of these characteristics? (Sunderland, 1989, p. 16)

What do you consider are major problems?
Which outcomes and characteristics should be pursued?

References

BERMAN, P. and McLAUGHLIN, M.W. (1977) *Federal Programs Supporting Educational Change Vol VII: Factors Affecting Implementation and Continuation*, US Office of Education, Department of Health, Education and Welfare, Santa Monica, Rand Corporation.

CLARK, D.L., LOTTO, L.S. and ASTUTO, T.A. (1984) 'Effective Schools and School Improvement: A Comparative Analysis of Two Lines of Enquiry', *Educational Administration Quarterly*, **20**, 3.

CRANDALL, D. (1983) 'The Teacher's Role in School Improvement', *Educational Leadership*, **41**, 3.

CRANDALL, D. et al. (1983) *The Study of Dissemination Efforts Supporting School Improvement (DESSI)*, Andover, MA, The Network.

EDMONDS, R. (1979) 'Effective Schools for the Urban Poor', *Educational Leadership*, **37**, 1.

HOPKINS, D. (Ed.) (1987) *Improving the Quality of Schooling*, London, Falmer Press.

MacKENZIE, D. (1983) 'Research for School Improvement: An Appraisal of Some Recent Trends', *Educational Researcher*, **12**, 4.

MORTIMORE, P. and SAMMONS, P. (1987) 'New Evidence on Effective Elementary Schools', *Educational Leadership*, **45**, 1.

MURNANE, R.J. (1981) 'Interpreting the Evidence on School Effectiveness', *Teachers College Record*, **83**, 1.

RAMSAY, W. and CLARK, E.E. (1990) *New Ideas for Effective School Improvement: Vision, Social Capital, Evaluation*, London, Falmer Press.

STEDMAN, L.C. (1987) 'It's Time We Changed the Effective Schools Formula', *Phi Delta Kappan*, **69**, 3.

SUNDERLAND, R. (1989) 'School Effectiveness and School Improvement: An International Perspective', *The Educational Administrator*, **32**.

WEBER, G. (1971) 'Inner-City Children Can Be Taught to Read: Four Successful Schools', occasional paper No. 18, Washington, DC, Council for Basic Education.

Chapter 23

School Councils and Governing Bodies

Characteristics and Major Factors

It is often argued that schools as institutions within a democratic society should ensure that their decision-making processes are also democratic. School councils/boards/governing bodies have the potential for teachers and parents to work together.

School councils represent one opportunity for interaction between the stakeholders (teachers, students and parents). However, the formal meetings of a school council should not be viewed as the only or even the most important opportunity for interaction — there are many other informal opportunities. No outstanding type of governing body has yet been established. Various combinations of membership, functions and legal status have been initiated within and between countries.

There are a number of important questions which need to be raised about the actual operation and achievements of school councils/governing bodies (see table 23.1). For example, do school boards really practise democratic decision-making? Lutz (1980) argues that school council participation of parents from a local school community is very limited and sporadic; that few council members are closely involved in decision-making; and that few issues are ever made public and widely debated. It is certainly evident that for large schools it is extremely difficult for school board members to represent more than a few of the community interests. Many of the disadvantaged community groups are never represented. Yet it might be argued, in response to the question, that democracy means the freedom to participate or not to participate and that if individuals and groups feel strongly enough about an issue then they will participate vigorously.

Questions might also be raised whether school councils actually reduce conflicts between various interest groups or heighten the conflicts still more. Various writers such as Pettit (1980), Alexander (1985) and Schofield (1985) have highlighted conflicts between teacher and parent members. Is it possible that parent priorities (for example, school discipline, and literacy and numeracy) are likely to be different from the priorities expressed by teachers (for example, providing a caring atmosphere and building student self-esteem)?

Table 23.1: Some unanswered questions about school councils

1 Are school councils able to practise the democratic decision-making and not respond chiefly to special-interest groups? (Lutz, 1980, p. 453)
2 Does the establishment of school councils simply mean that decisions are made *nearer* to the people involved but not necessarily by them? (Manning, 1983, p. 59)
3 How can school council members understand and represent all sections of a local community if they tend to be better educated and more affluent than the majority of local citizens? (Lutz, 1980, p. 459)
4 Will school councils ever be able to represent effectively such disadvantaged groups as migrants, the unskilled, the unemployed and low income earners? (Pettit, 1980, p. 41)
5 Does parent participation in decision-making on school councils actually lead to higher levels of achievement of the students and stronger levels of home support for school activities? (Hunt, 1981, p. 36)
6 Do school councils really provide a structure for school principal, teachers and parents to co-exist harmoniously?
7 Do school councils ever get complete control over decision-making?

Decision-making at the school level with high levels of interaction between teachers, students and parents has varied over the decades within and between countries.

In the United Kingdom, parent participation in schools was recommended in the Plowden Report in 1967 but it has not been until the recent Education Acts of 1980, 1981, 1986 and 1988 that parents have been given more rights, namely:

- membership as equal partners on the school governing body,
- wider choice of schools for their children,
- the right to receive a report on their school annually.

However, parents have lost power over curriculum decision–making by the introduction of a National Curriculum which has been designed and will be assessed centrally (Deem, 1990; Sallis, 1990).

Within Australia parental participation has varied considerably between different categories of schools. For example, 'alternative' schools typically depend upon a participative democratic input from parents. The schools usually have a small number of enrolments and so it is practicable as well as desirable for everyone (teachers, students and parents) to have a say in the running of their school. Parent and community participation has also been a feature of many parish schools operating within Catholic education systems. The school boards/boards of management established at these schools make decisions about appointing staff and the principal, school buildings and control of finances, including the setting of school fees. For some alternative schools and Catholic parish schools, parent and community participation has been operative for many years and is not a recent phenomenon. However, it has been a recent innovation for state education systems. The Australian Capital Territory (ACT) Schools Authority system, established in 1973, created a school board for each school operating within its system. School boards were established in the state of Victoria in 1975 by act of parliament and parents and community members are actively involved in decision-making in that state.

In Canada, parents are involved in decision-making at the local school district level. In matters such as implementation of curricula and acquisition of financial resources, however, the scope and direction of their initiatives are influenced very considerably by provincial priorities.

Advantages and Disadvantages

Reasons Why Parents Should Be Active School Decision-Makers

1 The school environment can be greatly enriched if parents' skills, talents and interests are used along with teachers', in planning and implementing the school curriculum.
2 A student's level of learning at school will be increased if he/she is positively supported and reinforced by parents in the home environment.
3 Parents will have a greater understanding and appreciation of the complexities of schools if they have first-hand experience of it.
4 Parents have the legal and long-term responsibility of their children and therefore should have a say in decisions that affect their life chances.
5 It fosters the development of common purposes between teachers, parents and students.
6 By increasing the number of interest groups involved in education there is a greater likelihood that the interests of all students will be taken into account.
7 Shared decision-making will reduce the number of legal actions taken out by parents against the school.
8 There are greater opportunities for a school to develop a strong sense of identity.

Reasons Why Parents Should Not Be Active School Decision-Makers

1 Parent and community groups can interfere in what is seen as the teacher's professional responsibility.
2 Minority pressure groups can have a disproportionately powerful influence on decision making.
3 Inequalities will increase as participatory democracy tends to favour upper income, educated communities — a 'power hungry, articulate élite'.
4 Greater parent and community group participation in decision-making can lead to a decline in school standards.
5 Because many community bodies are very conservative it is less likely that schools will be innovative.

6 Few parents have the time to take an active and informed role in decision making.
7 School staff are sometimes reluctant or opposed to parent participation activities.
8 Matters involving confidentiality become complicated when the data have to be circulated to a wide range of decision-makers.
9 More open communication between parents and teachers can often lead to teachers being perpetually 'on call'.
10 Decisions about individual students are often made more complicated when teachers have additional information about and are in frequent contact with the parents of these students.

What is needed are new relationships and responsibilities between parents and teachers. To a certain extent new, positive attitudes will have to be forged, but it will also require skills training. Overcoming these deficiencies will require long-term processes as well as short-term expediencies, and the cost in time and extra personnel for training are very considerable.

Areas of Assistance Needed

(a) Knowledge of the educational system — few have a clear understanding of the bureaucratic structures and how various policies and procedures are initiated and implemented and how they affect the operations of their local schools.
(b) 'Drop-in centres' for parents are becoming a little more common in schools as school principals realize that it is a valuable strategy for getting them more involved in school activities.
(c) Special provisions need to be made to assist parents with language difficulties. Those staff with second-language expertise can be used on home visits. Community liaison officers can also be used with good effect to maintain regular home visits.
(d) Interpersonal and communication skills are of fundamental importance. Experienced parent participants need to be able to break down the apathy of other parents and to seek out their support by informal home visits, telephone calls and parent meetings. They have to be able to develop and demonstrate empathy for the needs of the apathetic or uninvolved parent and be able to devise ways of gradually wearing down that person's resistance.
(e) Being able to express oneself clearly to others takes a lot of practice and confidence. A parent may be willing at a first meeting to discuss matters informally to a small group over a cup of coffee, but it may take several months before she or he is willing to make a comment at a semi-formal meeting.

Reflections and Issues

1   It is an open question how far and in what ways it will be
     legitimate to involve parents in the many different functions
     of schools (Golby, 1989, p. 134).

What functions are legitimate in your opinion?
Give examples from your teaching experiences or readings.

2   What role should parents and community members play in school
    decision-making? For example, discuss your attitude about the fol-
    lowing:

    ● parent governors being members of a staff selection commit-
       tee.
    ● parent governors discussing a pupil suspension.

3   Parents and community members could rapidly constitute a
     large, powerful force in education. They have the potential
     influence to bring about change in schools: to cause changes
     in attitudes from politicians, administrators and teachers, and
     in the long term, changes in policy. (Beattie, 1985)

Is this an over-optimistic stance?
Consider some possible impediments to this occurring.

4   It is important that parent governors should be the choice of
     parents, people that parents feel they can approach with trust
     and confidence (Edwards and Redfern, 1988, p. 109).

Are there difficulties in getting representative governors?
What are some possible solutions?

5   The parent-teacher partnership is fundamental to effective
     learning in classrooms — teachers' professional training,
     knowledge and experience are complementary to those of
     parents (Allen, 1989, p. 14).

Discuss.

6   Parents are the school's best resource, its 'social capital' for
     making education possible. To take advantage of this re-
     source, however, a reconceptualization of the family as part
     of the school community is needed (Jackson and Cooper,
     1989, p. 284).

What changes of attitude are needed — for example, by administrators and teachers? How else might parents be encouraged to become
active decision-makers?

References

ALEXANDER, K. (1985) 'Political Intervention and Curricular Accountability', paper presented at the Annual Conference of the South Pacific Association of Teacher Educators, Hobart.

ALLEN, S. (1989) 'Parent Participation: Productive Partnerships', *The Australian Teacher*, **24**.

BEATTIE, N. (1985) *Professional Parents*, London, Falmer Press.

DEEM, R. (1990) 'The Reform of School-Governing Bodies: The Power of the Consumer over the Producer', in FLUDE, M. and HAMMER, M. (Eds) *The Education Reform Act: 1988: Its Origins and Implications*, London, Falmer Press.

EDWARDS, V. and REDFERN, A. (1988) *At Home and School: Parent Participation in Primary Education*, London, Routledge.

GOLBY, M. (1989) 'Parent Governorship in the New Order', in MACLEOD, F. (Ed.) *Parents and Schools: The Contemporary Challenge*, London, Falmer Press.

HUNT, J. (1981) 'The Curriculum and the Community', occasional paper No. 5, Canberra, Curriculum Development Centre.

JACKSON, B.L. and COOPER, B.S. (1989) 'Parent Choice and Empowerment: New Roles for Parents', *Urban Education*, **24**, 3.

LUTZ, F.W. (1980) 'Local School Board Decision-Making: A Political-Anthropological Analysis', *Education and Urban Society*, **12**, 4.

MACLEOD, F. (1989) *Parents and Schools: The Contemporary Challenge*, London, Falmer Press.

MANNING, J. (1983) 'The School Board: Tame Cat Accessory and Detour to Oblivion', *Curriculum Perspectives*, **4**, 2.

PETTIT, D. (1980) 'Strategies and Educational Change: The Victorian School Councils Debate', *School and Community News*, **4**, 1.

PUGH, G. and DE'ATH, E. (1984) *The Needs of Parents: Practice and Policy in Parent Education*, London, Macmillan.

SALLIS, J. (1990) 'Governors and Parents', in SOUTHWORTH, G. and LOFTHOUSE, B. *The Study of Primary Education. A Source Book, Vol. 3. School Organisation and Management*, London, Falmer Press.

SCHOFIELD, H. (1985) 'A Study of Educational Needs: The Conflicting Views of Parents and Teachers,' paper presented at the Annual Conference of the Australian Association for Research in Education, Hobart.

Chapter 24

School Evaluations/Reviews

The task of embarking upon a school-level evaluation is an ambitious undertaking, but extremely worthwhile. It assumes:

- a degree of openness,
- that schools need to present accounts of their work to the public,
- that teachers should be largely responsible for their evaluations but other groups should have access to the accounts.

Reasons for Undertaking Evaluations

Internal Factors

(a) a means of improving the learning opportunities of students;
(b) a means of staff establishing an understanding of their current position in relation to their aims and objectives;
(c) it allows staff to redefine, where applicable, their aims and objectives;
(d) a means of coordinating the total school effort better and increasing the expertise of the school community;
(e) a means of accounting to an external agent;

External Factors

(a) pressures from a head office in an education system to have a formal evaluation scheme (see Holly, 1987; Becher, 1990);
(b) new requirements in conditions of work schedules as negotiated between employers and unions (see Wilson *et al.*, 1989);
(c) new examination demands (for example, GCSE in the UK);
(d) falling rolls and school closure threats;
(e) release of national assessment data.

Some Principles for Undertaking School-Level Evaluations

Although different approaches have particular priorities it is possible to stipulate some common principles which are generally applicable:

(a) Teachers and others involved should see the evaluation as significant and worthwhile.

(b) The major purpose of any evaluation is to achieve internal school development and not to produce a formal report to satisfy accountability requirements.

(c) The evaluation process must be clearly explained to staff at the outset.

(d) Teachers have to be convinced that privacy in one's teaching, assessing and curriculum planning has to give way to open discussion and public documentation.

(e) Groups of teachers should work on aspects of the evaluation so that they collectively analyze issues and produce solutions to problems.

(f) Teachers should draw up realistic timetables so that the pace and momentum of the evaluation can be maintained.

(g) Demands made on time, money and skilled personnel should be realistic for a school.

(h) At each stage of the evaluation there should be a review of progress made.

(i) Outside experts should be brought in when needed to give advice (Simons, 1987; Day *et al.*, 1987; Lighthall and Allan, 1989).

Techniques for Collecting Evaluative Data

If major participant groups such as teachers, students and parents are involved in an evaluation, then the range of data sources needs to be quite extensive. However, the number of techniques depends on the scale of the evaluation and the time and resources available.

Examples of techniques include:

- interviews — with students, parents, teachers,
- checklists — of skills, behaviours, resources,
- portfolios — of students' work, of documents,
- individual files — of students' work,
- diaries — written by teachers, students, parents,
- anecdotal records — of students,
- logs — of meetings, lessons,
- questionnaires — of attitudes, opinions,
- audio tapes — of meetings, discussions,
- video tapes — of classrooms, a day in a school,
- slides/prints — of groups working, classrooms,
- time-on-task analysis — of students, teachers,

- external consultants/consultative panels — to collect data, lead meetings.

School-level evaluations need to address:

- curriculum matters — identifying, defining and solving curriculum problems;
- personal and interpersonal matters — changes needed by individual staff — to reflect upon present practices, challenge familiar assumptions, explore new ways, obtain mutual support for actions.

Various approaches or models for undertaking school-level evaluations have been published over recent years. Three examples are described below. It will be evident that the first two of these emphasize *curriculum* matters with only the last model concentrating upon *personal* and *interpersonal* aspects.

Examples

Example 1: Traditional Evaluation Model

Distinguishing features of the Traditional Evaluation Model are typically:

- There is an external panel involved.
- The principal initiates the evaluative activity and defines the range of activities.
- A formalized, linear system of procedures is used.
- Senior teachers and the principal play an active role; other teachers, parents and students play a passive role.

The Traditional Evaluation Model depends to a large extent upon the drive and initiative of the school principal. He or she typically selects the external panel, is a major force in determining the school's aims and objectives, and usually selects the senior staff to be the chairpersons for collecting the data and writing the sections of the school evaluation report (see figure 24.1).

The use of an external panel of eight to ten people is an important element of the model. Its members can comprise experts, citizens, teachers or principals from other schools. The panel provides an aura of objectivity and respectability about the evaluation process. It can play a major role in uncovering dysfunctions between reported and actual practices.

Stage 2 in the traditional Evaluation Model is the preparation of the evaluation report by the school. The aims and objectives must form the focus for all subsequent data collection. School personnel are given specific roles to play in the collection of data for the school evaluation report. There is preference for the collection of quantitative data. There is little emphasis

Figure 24.1:   Stages in the traditional evaluation model

---

1   Consideration of the school's written aims and objectives
This is an essential first stage.
(a)   The principal is responsible for preparing the written statement, but others may be involved.
(b)   Two major questions should be asked:
      How effectively are the aims and objectives stated?
      To what extent are the aims and objectives known and understood by the members of the school?

↓

---

2   Compilation of a detailed school evaluation report
(a)   The school itself compiles the report by responding to a series of questions and tasks enumerated in the *School Evaluation Manual for Australian Schools*.
(b)   A detailed account of current practice and an evaluation of current practice against stated aims and objectives can be up to twelve months.

↓

---

3   Assessment by the external panel
(a)   The panel of eight to ten people visits the school for four or five days.
(b)   The panel considers whether what is written in the school evaluation report is in accord with current practice in the school.
(c)   The panel produces its report (about three weeks after their visit).

↓

---

4   Follow-up
(a)   The school considers the recommendation in both reports and decides on recommendations that will be implemented and those that will not.
(b)   The decision as to the course of action lies with the principal and staff.

---

upon the processes of teaching; instead the emphasis is upon examining outcomes of the schools.

During the visit of the external panel, its members are heavily involved in collecting data and reconciling this information with the details included by staff in their school evaluation report.

The final stage is when a school 'follows up' the recommendations made by the panel. Quite rightly, the follow-up decisions are left entirely with the school community, but in practice this appears to be an area of weakness.

The widespread and continued use of this model indicates that it is successful, especially in the context of independent schools. As noted by Cumming (1986) there can be a number of advantages; the panel of outsiders can often expose weaknesses and strengths not recognizable by insiders; the use of a small panel on a specified task provides an efficient use of resources; members of the panel bring a wealth of experiences and insights which can aid a school; and the evaluations can, in due course, promote higher standards and increased efficiency for a school.

There are also many critics of the Traditional Evaluation Model. Robinson (1984) maintains that the benefits gained by a school are often disproportionate to the amount of effort involved and that school staff cannot identify and resolve important school problems unless the school climate encourages openness and a sharing of ideas. Straton (1979) criticizes the emphasis upon inputs to the educational enterprise (for example, physical plant and facilities) rather than upon processes and outcomes. He also suggests that the criteria used by the panel may not be those of the school community. Cumming (1986) is critical of the precision of this evaluation model and the undesirable aspects of parents, students and many of the teaching staff playing a relatively minor and passive role in the evaluation process.

Example 2: GRIDS Evaluation Model

The Guidelines for Review and Internal Development in Schools (GRIDS) model was the result of a project initiated by the Schools Council and developed collaboratively with fifteen primary schools in five LEAs. McMahon *et al.* (1984) consider that GRIDS was conceived as a means of achieving staff and curriculum development — the intention is that all staff at a school are consulted and involved in the evaluation process.

There are five stages in a cyclical development process, as indicated in figure 24.2.

(a) getting started — establishing the conditions for the review and development and appointing a coordinator;
(b) an initial review of work of the school in order to identify priority area(s) for specific review and development;
(c) specific review of the area(s) selected as priorities;
(d) development of the priority areas;
(e) assessment of what has been achieved and selection of further priority areas.

The intention is that one such cycle might be completed within a school year.

The GRIDS model has been widely used in schools in the UK. It provides a valuable do-it-yourself kit for schools wanting to embark upon self-evaluation. However, there have been critics of the model including Day *et al.* (1987) and Simons (1987) who consider that it is a 'top down' approach to school review and that it is too clinical. Holly (1984) suggests that GRIDS is mainly attractive to school managers and that it fails to engage teachers in evaluating the fundamental processes of teaching.

Example 3: Teacher-Oriented Evaluation Model

The St John's Girls High School evaluation, as reported by Adams (1985), illustrates a number of features of this model of evaluation. Adams saw the

Figure 24.2:   *The five stages of the institutional review and development process*

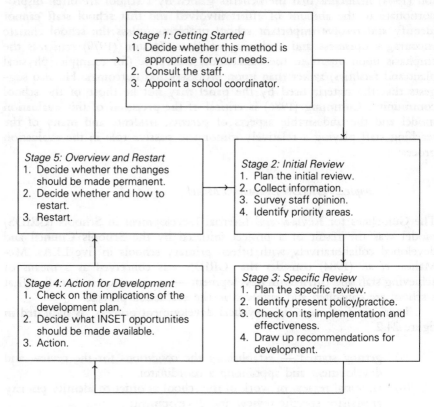

Stage 1: Getting Started
1. Decide whether this method is appropriate for your needs.
2. Consult the staff.
3. Appoint a school coordinator.

Stage 5: Overview and Restart
1. Decide whether the changes should be made permanent.
2. Decide whether and how to restart.
3. Restart.

Stage 2: Initial Review
1. Plan the initial review.
2. Collect information.
3. Survey staff opinion.
4. Identify priority areas.

Stage 4: Action for Development
1. Check on the implications of the development plan.
2. Decide what INSET opportunities should be made available.
3. Action.

Stage 3: Specific Review
1. Plan the specific review.
2. Identify present policy/practice.
3. Check on its implementation and effectiveness.
4. Draw up recommendations for development.

(Source: McMahon et al., 1984)

evaluation activities as being a school development exercise over a period of six years, with the process being far more important than the outcome.

Adams emphasizes the most important phase of the evaluation as being 'people preparation'. He uses the analogy of a space rocket (see figure 24.3) and its stages to indicate that 'preparing people' is 'by far the biggest and most cumbersome, consuming inordinate amounts of fuel, generating most friction and most liable to go wrong' (Adams, 1985, p. 31).

As indicated in figure 24.3, in stage 1 there are three tasks for each participant:

(a)   to empty oneself before being able to receive or share a common vision;

(b)   to search for the 'coat hanger' initiative which will facilitate sharing and excite the imagination;

(c)   to identify and sort out key personnel.

Figure 24.3: Teacher-oriented model of evaluation, using the analogy of a space rocket

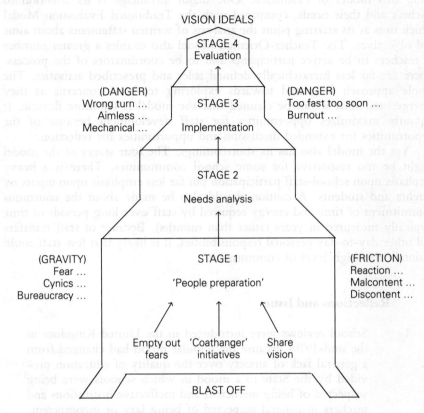

VISION IDEALS

STAGE 4
Evaluation

(DANGER)
Wrong turn ...
Aimless ...
Mechanical ...

STAGE 3
Implementation

(DANGER)
Too fast too soon ...
Burnout ...

STAGE 2
Needs analysis

(GRAVITY)
Fear ...
Cynics ...
Bureaucracy ...

STAGE 1
'People preparation'

(FRICTION)
Reaction ...
Malcontent ...
Discontent ...

Empty out
fears

'Coathanger'
initiatives

Share
vision

BLAST OFF

Source: after Adams, 1985a, p. 32

Adams (1985) noted that it took his staff two years to complete this first stage. Again using the analogy of the space rocket, he suggests that the deeper the consensus that can be achieved from the 'preparing people' stage, the more powerful will be the thrust given to the next stage of the process.

The second stage is the analysis of needs and structures in the school. At St John's Girls High school two consultants were used to facilitate the task of digging out and exposing real needs, compared with the visible, largely superficial ones. Student-free days enabled staff to have uninterrupted periods of time to sort out their major needs.

The implementation stage is usually the exciting and rewarding one for teachers. If a long, painstaking preparation period has occurred then teachers will be eagerly anticipating the actual trying out of new practices. But, effective implementation depends upon the provision of time, money and a great deal of encouragement to all the teachers concerned. Evaluation procedures, especially formal evaluation procedures, are very necessary to ensure that the earlier plans are achieved.

177

As noted by Cumming (1986), there are a number of advantages in using this model of evaluation. One major advantage is its attention to teachers and their needs, compared with the Traditional Evaluation Model which uses as its starting point the analysis of written statements about aims and objectives. The Teacher-Oriented Model also enables a greater number of teachers to be active participants and to be coordinators of the process. There are far less hierarchically defined roles and prescribed activities. The whole approach is geared towards exploring teachers' concerns as they emerge, and thus it can be claimed that the model is far more flexible. It certainly maximizes opportunities for staff development because of the opportunities for extended discussion and opportunities for reflection.

Yet the model also has its shortcomings. The four stages of the model might be too restrictive for some school communities. There is a heavy emphasis upon school-staff participation but far less emphasis upon inputs by parents and students. A caution should also be made about the enormous commitment of time and energy required by staff over long periods of time (typically measured in years rather than months). Because of staff transfers and other day-to-day personal responsibilities, it is likely that few staff could maintain this high level of commitment.

Reflections and Issues

1   School reviews were introduced in the United Kingdom in the mid-1970s because the popular mood had changed from a general lack of anxiety over the quality of education provided by the State to a mood in which schools were being suspected of being inefficient and ineffective institutions and teachers in general suspected of being lazy or incompetent, or both (Turner and Clift, 1988, p. 17).

Is this an accurate interpretation of school activities? What are some negative effects of this perception on current evaluation efforts?

2   In the last ten years we have witnessed a rapid growth in school self-evaluation models and practices.... What is least clear and most controversial in this range of activity is who has control of the process, who has access to any product that emerges and whose interests are served (Simons, 1987, pp. 219–20).

What groups do you consider are controlling school evaluation processes? Are you aware of successful evaluation efforts? What do you consider are some of the major inhibiting factors?

3   Evaluation can be a constructive process leading to stronger professionalism, but only if teachers grasp the opportunity for reflection and growth that it presents (Granheim et al., 1990, p. 1).

Do the evaluation models with which you are familiar allow teachers to 'reflect and grow'? What are some important safeguards you would propose to allow this to happen?

4   The relationship between LEAs and schools will be changed radically as the effects of the Education Reform Act begin to work through. (Clough *et al.*, 1989, p. 1)

The shift of power away from LEAs raises important questions about who will initiate or monitor school-level evaluations. Consider some likely scenarios in the decade of the 1990s.

References

ADAMS, M. (1985) 'A School Coping with Change: St John's Girls High School, Part 2 The Process of Development: People Preparation', *Curriculum Exchange*, **3**, 1.

BECHER, T. (1990) 'Approaches to Accountability at School Level', in LOFTHOUSE, B., *The Study of Primary Education, A Source Book, Vol. 2. The Curriculum*, London, Falmer Press.

CLOUGH, E., ASPINWALL, K. and GIBBS, B. (1989) *Learning to Change: An LEA School-Focused Initiative*, London, Falmer Press.

CUMMING, J. (1986) 'Evaluating Your Own School: A Guide to Action', occasional paper No. 13, Melbourne, Victorian Institute of Secondary Education.

DAY, C., WHITAKER, P. and WREN, D. (1987) *Appraisal and Professional Development in Primary Schools*, Milton Keynes, Open University Press.

GRANHEIM, M. *et al.* (1990) *Evaluation as Policy Making*, London, Jessica Kingsley Press.

HOLLY, P. (1984) 'The Institutionalization of Action-Research in Schools', *Cambridge Journal of Education*, **14**, 2.

HOLLY, P. (1987) 'Making It Count: Evaluation for the Developing Primary School', in SOUTHWORTH, G. (Ed.) *Readings in Primary School Management*, London, Falmer Press.

LIGHTHALL, F.F. and ALLAN, S.D. (1989) *Local Realities, Local Adaptations*, London, Falmer Press.

McMAHON, A. *et al.* (1984) *Guidelines for Review and Internal Development of Schools: Primary School Handbook*, London, Longman.

ROBINSON, V. (1984) 'School Reviews: A New Zealand Experience', in HOPKINS, D. and WIDEEN, M. (Eds) *Alternative Perspectives on School Improvement*, London, Falmer Press.

SIMONS, H. (1987) *Getting to Know Schools in a Democracy: The Politics and Process of Evaluation*, London, Falmer Press.

STRATON, R.G. (1979) *Curriculum Evaluation: Approaches and Planning*, Geelong, Deakin University.

TURNER, G. and CLIFT, P. (1988) *Studies in Teacher Appraisal*, London, Falmer Press.

WILSON, J.D., THOMSON, G., MILLWARD, R.E. and KEENAN, T. (Eds) (1989) *Assessment for Teacher Development*, London, Falmer Press.

Chapter 25

Curriculum Implementation

Curriculum starts as a plan. It only becomes a reality when teachers implement it with real students in a real classroom. Careful planning and development are obviously important, but they count for nothing unless teachers are aware of the product and have the skills to implement the curriculum in their classrooms.

The term *implementation* refers to the *actual use* of a curriculum/syllabus, or what it *consists of in practice* (Fullan and Pomfret, 1977). It is a critical phase in the cycle of planning and teaching a curriculum. *Adoption* of a curriculum refers to somebody's intentions to use it, be it a teacher or a head office official, but it does not indicate whether the curriculum is implemented or not.

Implementation refers to actual use, as outlined above, but there is also an important attitudinal element. In education systems where teachers and principals have the opportunity to choose among competing curriculum packages (i.e. acting as 'selectors') then attitudinal dispositions are clearly important. For example, if a teacher perceives that the current curriculum he/she is using is deficient in certain areas, then an alternative will be sought which overcomes these problems. Leithwood (1981) maintains that teachers will only become involved in implementing new curricula if they perceive a dysfunction — they have a desire to reduce the gap between current and preferred practices, with reference to their teaching in a particular subject.

But for many subjects, a revised or new curriculum is produced to be used by teachers in *all* schools in a school district and no choice is available. There is no opportunity for teachers to consider alternatives. Their task is to find out how to use the new curriculum as effectively as possible. In these circumstances, the dominant implementation questions for the teacher might be:

How do I do it?
Will I ever get it to work smoothly?
To whom can I turn to get assistance?
Am I doing what the practice requires?
What is the effect on the learner?

This emphasis on *how* to use a new curriculum is a major concern for teachers because as 'craft specialists' they gain most of their intrinsic satisfaction from being successful in using a particular approach and materials with their students. However, the implementation of any new curriculum will take a teacher a considerable period of time as he/she needs to become competent and confident in its use. It is only when a new curriculum is completely accepted by teachers in a school and the activities associated with it are a matter of routine, that the phase of *institutionalization* is said to have been reached.

There are two extreme views about curriculum implementation which often appear in academic writing and in the media, but which rarely, if ever, occur in practice. One view is that teachers have absolute powers over what will or will not be implemented in their classrooms. In reality, it is not possible for any individual teacher to have such wide powers. This view is inaccurate because it assumes that a teacher:

(a)   has the authority to introduce any new course or topics at any time without restrictions from the system, parents, or the community;
(b)   knows about and has access to the full range of knowledge, skills, and values associated with a particular topic or unit;
(c)   is in the position of spending the long periods of time needed to prepare student materials.

The other extreme view is that an external authority exercises complete prescription over what teachers do in their respective classrooms, and that it directs teachers in selecting and using particular topics or units in specified ways. The system is stereotyped as 'centrally planned' and characterized as being dictatorial, authoritarian and traditional. Some writers have commented adversely on such systems and singled out for attention the officious inspectors who visit schools to ensure that the official curricula are being taught as intended. Their criticism is directed at the bureaucratic obsession for uniformity, so that all schools are taught the same curricula at the same time.

A realistic view of curriculum implementation lies therefore between these two extremes. Some subjects in schools are considered to be important core areas and are given detailed treatment in syllabus documents. For these subjects, teachers may be expected to cover particular content and to follow a certain instructional sequence. The term used for this adherence to prescribed details is *fidelity of use*. Alternatively, there may be other subjects where teachers can exercise their creative flair and implement very special, individual versions of a curriculum. This is then termed *adaptation* or *process orientation*.

Factors Affecting Implementation

Several education experts have produced very useful insights about implementation and the relative success of it in schools. In the early 1980s Fullan

Table 25.1:   *Factors affecting implementation*

A   *Characteristics of the Change*
1   Need and relevance of the change
2   Clarity
3   Complexity
4   Quality and practicality of programme (materials etc.)

B   *Characteristics at the School District Level*
5   The history of innovative attempts
6   The adoption process
7   Central administrative support and involvement
8   Staff development (in-service) and participation
9   Time-line and information system (evaluation)
10   Board and community characteristics

C   *Characteristics at the School Level*
11   The principal
12   Teacher-teacher relations
13   Teacher characteristics and orientations

D   *Characteristics External to the Local System*
14   Role of government
15   External assistance

(After Fullan, 1982, p. 56)

(1982) produced a list of factors affecting implementation (see table 25.1) which is frequently quoted in the literature. These factors refer to the attributes of the innovation or change, characteristics of the school district, characteristics of the school as a unit, and factors external to the local school system. A wide-ranging list of factors is provided in table 25.2 based on experiences of a project developer (Parsons, 1987).

House (1979) uses three perspectives (technical, political and cultural) to explain how and why certain implementation practices have occurred over the decades. The *technical* perspective assumes that systematic planning and a rational approach can overcome typical teacher problems of lack of time and expertise. The *political* perspective recognizes that rational behaviour is limited in practice and that it is the balance of power among parties that determines whether curriculum implementation efforts will be successful or not. The *cultural* perspective emphasizes cultural transformation as a major factor in determining the success or otherwise of implementation endeavours. It is the deeply ingrained beliefs and values of stakeholders, which are socially shared and shaped, that ultimately affect what happens in classrooms.

Problems of Describing/Measuring Implementation

Attempts to describe the implementation of new curricula are fraught with all kinds of difficulties. For example, do you focus upon the curriculum materials, or what the teacher is doing, or what the students are doing? If the

Table 25.2: Some important factors in promoting successful implementation practices

1	The need for time — to experiment, for attitudes to change.
2	A technology for change — a phased plan of action is needed.
3	Recognizing school culture — awareness of situational conditions.
4	Incentives and rewards must be provided — time, resources, materials.
5	Sharing the burden in the workplace — to collaborate and to share.
6	Releasing energy for innovation — creating the right conditions.
7	A collaborative framework — the value of local collaborative groups.
8	Leadership — persons to coordinate and to lead.
9	Recognizing system level culture — awareness of overall policies.
10	The need for a political perspective — keeping visible with stakeholders.
11	The need to win allies — gaining legitimacy and support in a region and within schools.
12	Recognizing the role of individuals — commitment and charisma are essential qualities.

(After Parsons, 1987, pp. 220–4)

intention is to try to do all three things what criteria do you use to select out instances of each, since they are all occurring simultaneously in the classroom? Are there optimal times to examine how a curriculum is being implemented, such as after six months of operation, or a year, or even longer?

Trying to measure degrees of implementation is even more difficult than trying to describe it. Decisions have to be made about what kinds of data should be collected, such as observational data, document analysis or self-report data. Measurement data also tend to have a punitive air about them and so this can lead to concerns about who is doing the measuring and who is to receive the results.

Measuring Student Activities and Achievements

A major reason for producing a new curriculum is to provide better learning opportunities for students, such as higher achievement levels in terms of particular understandings, skills and values. Rarely is it possible, however, for measurements to be obtained on student achievements so that it can be stated unequivocally that a new curriculum is superior to the previous one, in terms of particular dimensions. There are so many confounding variables which affect student scores. A single test is unlikely to be suitable for use and to be able to provide valid and reliable comparable data between a new curriculum and the previous one.

Measuring Use of Curriculum Materials

In most teaching programs, curriculum materials figure prominently in the day-to-day activities undertaken by the teacher and students. In fact, surveys have revealed that school students can spend up to 80 per cent of their time engaged with particular curriculum materials (Cornbleth, 1990).

It is clearly important in any study of implementation to gather information about how curriculum materials are used. Some of the curriculum materials analysis schemes developed in the 1970s provide convenient criteria for evaluating curriculum materials (for example, Eraut *et al.*, 1975, Piper, 1976). However, these schemes are often very time consuming to complete and tend to emphasize the characteristics of the curriculum materials in isolation.

During the 1980s more attention has been paid to developing checklists which provide ratings of curriculum materials *in use* (for example, the Innovations Configuration developed by Hall and Loucks, 1978, and the Practice Profile developed by Loucks and Crandall, 1982).

Measuring Teacher Activities

Various methods have been used over the decades to measure teachers' implementation activities, ranging from formal visitations to observation checklists, questionnaires, interviews and self-report techniques. In the US, where implementation studies have been very extensively undertaken since the 1970s, observation checklists and rating scales are commonly used. In these studies, particular categories of behaviour are determined in advance and used as the basis for the checklist items and rating scales. Some methodological difficulties in using these instruments include the problem of achieving inter-rater reliability (Farrar *et al.*, 1980; Blakely *et al.*, 1983) and the potential problem of ignoring other classroom dimensions (Kimpston, 1983). Questionnaires have been used in a number of studies although they rely on self-report data and so doubts can arise over the authenticity of the responses.

Two Perspectives of Implementation

Fidelity of Implementation

Adherents of the fidelity perspective emphasize the importance of the innovation itself and assume that products which can be demonstrated to be exemplary and effective, will be readily accepted *in toto* by teachers in schools. Roitman and Mayer (1982) note that hard-line pro-fidelity adherents insist that innovations should be implemented with close correspondence to the validated models or else suffer the consequences of 'dilution', and hence reductions in outcome effectiveness.

In a fidelity perspective, a structured approach to implementation is recommended whereby teachers are given explicit instructions about how to teach a unit or course. The instructions to teachers are specified *a priori*, and this means, of course, little provision is made for the various school contexts in which the unit might be used. The basic assumptions are:

(a) Central planning and definition is necessary to eliminate the in-
efficiency that occurs when local users are left with leeway to define
an innovation.

(b) The less ambiguity and authority left to implementers, the greater
the fidelity.

(c) Evaluation is conducted to assess how closely implementation re-
sembles the plan for programme execution.

This orientation to implementation implies that the classroom teacher must
be thoroughly trained to use the new program or unit. It also appears that the
teacher's role is largely that of passive receiver, who will be willing to be
trained to use the new curriculum package and once having received this
training, will teach it at a high level of technical proficiency.

Undoubtedly some curriculum packages are suited to this, especially
where the content is complex and difficult to master and thereby requires
careful sequencing; in subjects where teachers may lack the necessary knowledge or skills; and in subjects or units where appropriate diagnostic and
achievement tests can be incorporated. Many of the nationally produced
projects in the 1960s and 1970s came under this category. For example, in the
Biological Sciences Curriculum Study Project (BSCS) the teacher's role was
tightly programmed.

Process Orientation

The alternative perspective to implementation is termed variously as 'adaptation', 'process' and 'mutual adaptation'. Adherents of this approach maintain
that differing organizational contexts and teacher needs will require on-site
modifications (Berman and McLaughlin, 1977; Lighthall and Allan, 1989).
They suggest that all innovations become modified during the process of
implementation and that this is vital, if it is to achieve the outcomes desired
by the users.

The term 'mutual adaptation' was first used by Dalin and McLaughlin
(1975) to describe the adaptation process whereby adjustments are made to
the innovation itself and to the institutional setting. The term came into
popular use in the 1970s especially due to the emphasis given to it in studies
in the USA.

'Mutual adaptation' has been reified in the literature as *the* desirable
consensual modification between developers and users and possibly the most
effective way of ensuring successful implementation. For example, Mac-
Donald and Walker (1976) maintain that implementation really involves
'negotiation' and that there are trade-offs in meaning between curriculum
developers and teachers. Farrar *et al.* (1980) and Rudduck (1976) take a
cultural interpretation of what happens when curricula are implemented in
classrooms. For example, Farrar *et al.* use the term 'evolution' to characterize
the process by which a curriculum package, although appearing as a well-

defined blueprint, is perceived by classroom practitioners as a malleable entity to be adapted.

Curriculum Alignment

Curriculum alignment is a term which has figured prominently over recent years and represents a strategy by states and school districts in the USA to produce more effective schools. It can be likened to an updated version of the fidelity perspective. In simple terms, it is a process of ensuring maximum congruency between the written, the taught and the tested curricula.

As noted by Glatthorn (1987) the arguments for curriculum alignment are very convincing. If the written curriculum has been developed by a number of specialists and represents an informed consensus at the district level, then it should be followed closely by teachers. This depends, of course, upon the incentives provided and if a district does not provide any, then it is quite feasible that the taught curriculum could vary widely from the written curriculum. This is where district frameworks, textbook committees and district/state tests can be used to provide a closer alignment with the written curriculum.

Frameworks are official documents which establish general areas/themes and sometimes specific topics to be covered. Textbook committees, especially at state levels, can have an enormous influence if they prescribe areas of content that will be acceptable from commercial publishers — they are an important leverage point within the educational system (Brandt, 1989). Standardized tests, like any assessment measure, can also be a very powerful influence in persuading teachers what to teach.

Although curriculum alignment is supported by many educators as being desirable and soundly-based, the process does have its detractors. Some critics suggest that curriculum alignment is an invidious device to reduce teacher autonomy and creativity. Others note that it gives far too much power to tests and leads to teachers teaching for the test only. A middle position could be that curriculum alignment is a desirable practice for those subjects which are seen to be core areas and involve mastery but that it should not apply to electives or enrichment subjects.

Curriculum alignment as a process has been developed more enthusiastically in some states than others. Not unexpectedly, California has been in the forefront of this movement and has used curriculum alignment extensively in an endeavour to achieve better implementation levels and consequently higher student achievement standards.

Reflections and Issues

1 Some common implementation problems according to Clough *et al.* (1989) include the following:

    (a)   too little time for teachers to plan for and learn new skills and practices.

    (b)   too many competing demands make successful implementation impossible.

    (c)   failure to understand and take into account site specific differences among schools.

Explain why these could be major problems.
What solutions would you offer?

2   For a new curriculum project to be fully implemented there are four core changes required of a teacher — changes in class groupings and organization, materials, practices and behaviours, and in beliefs and understandings (Fullan, 1989, p. 8).

Do you agree with these four core changes?
Give examples to illustrate their importance.
Alternatively, put forward other more important factors.

3   Because implementation takes place in a fluid setting, implementation problems are never 'solved'. Rather they evolve ... new issues, new requirements, new considerations emerge as the process unfolds (McLaughlin, 1987, p. 174).

What are the implications of this statement to implementing new curricula in schools? What implementation elements can or cannot be planned in advance? What contingency plans should be developed?

4   Successful implementation is an individual development process within certain organizational conditions and strategies (Fullan, 1989, p. 24).

To what extent are individual development factors (for example, commitment, skills, willingness to experiment) important? What are some important organizational conditions?

References

BERMAN, P. and McLAUGHLIN, M.W. (1977) *Federal Programs Supporting Educational Change, Vol. VII: Factors Affecting Implementation and Continuation*, prepared for the US Office of Education, Department of Health, Education and Welfare, Santa Monica, Rand Corporation.

BLAKELY, C. *et al.* (1983) 'The Implementation of Disseminated Educational Innovations: Is the Modified RD and D Model Viable?', paper presented at the Annual Conference of the American Educational Research Association, Montreal.

BRANDT, R. (1989) 'On Curriculum in California: A Conversation with Bill Honig', *Educational Leadership*, **47**, 3.

CLOUGH, E., ASPINWALL, K. and GIBBS, B. (Eds) (1989) *Learning to Change: An LEA School-Focused Initiative*, London, Falmer Press.

CORNBLETH, C. (1990) *Curriculum in Context*, London, Falmer Press.
DALIN, P. and MCLAUGHLIN, M.W. (1975) 'Strategies for Innovations in Higher Education', Educational Research Symposium on Strategies for Research and Development in Higher Education, Stockholm.
ERAUT, M., GOAD, L., SMITH, G. (1975) *The Analysis of Curriculum Materials*, Brighton, University of Sussex.
FARRAR, E., DESANCTIS, J.E. and COHEN, D.K. (1980) 'Views From Below: Implementation Research in Education', *Teachers College Record*, **82**, 1.
FULLAN, M. (1982) *The Meaning of Educational Change*, New York, Teachers College Press.
FULLAN, M. (1989) *Implementing Educational Change: What We Know*, Ottawa, Education and Employment Division, Population and Human Resources Department, World Bank.
FULLAN, M. and POMFRET, A. (1977) 'Research of Curriculum and Instruction Implementation', *Review of Educational Research*, **47**, 2.
GLATTHORN, A.A. (1987) *Curriculum Leadership*, Glenview, Scott Foresman.
HALL, G.E. and LOUCKS, S.F. (1978) *Innovation Configurations: Analyzing the Adaptations of Innovations*, Procedures for Adopting Educational Innovations Programme, Austin, Research and Development Center, University of Texas.
HOUSE, E.R. (1979) 'Technology versus Craft: A Ten-Year Perspective on Innovation', *Journal of Curriculum Studies*, **11**, 1.
KIMPSTON, R.D. (1983) 'Curriculum Fidelity and Implementation Tasks Employed by Teachers', paper presented at the Annual Conference of the American Educational Research Association, Montreal.
LEITHWOOD, K.A. (1981) 'Managing the Implementation of Curriculum Innovations', *Knowledge, Creation, Diffusion, Utilization*, **2**, 3.
LIGHTHALL, F.F. and ALLAN, S.D. (1989) *Local Realities, Local Adaptations*, London, Falmer Press.
LOUCKS, S.F. and CRANDALL, D.P. (1982) *The Practice Profile: An All-Purpose Tool for Program Communication, Staff Development, Evaluation and Implementation*, Andover, MA, The Network.
MACDONALD, B. and WALKER, R. (1976) *Changing the Curriculum*, London, Open Books.
MCLAUGHLIN, M.W. (1987) 'Learning from Experience: Lessons from Policy Implementation', *Educational Evaluation and Policy Analysis*, **9**, 2.
PARSONS, C. (1987) *The Curriculum Change Game*, London, Falmer Press.
PIPER, K. (1976) *Evaluation and the Social Sciences*, Canberra, AGPS.
ROITMAN, D.B. and MAYER, J.P. (1982) 'Fidelity and Reinvention in the Implementation of Innovations', paper presented at the Annual Conference of the American Psychological Association, Washington, DC.
RUDDUCK, J. (1976) 'Dissemination as Acculturation Research', *SSRC Newsletter*, October.

Part 5

Curriculum Ideology

Chapter 26

Curriculum History

Curriculum history provides well-documented accounts of curriculum as it has occurred at specific periods in the past. Studies of curriculum history can include:

(a) accounts of major national curriculum projects in the USA and UK in the 1960s (for example, Nuffield Science, Man: A Course of Study);

(b) accounts of major persons and scholars (for example, biographical accounts of John Dewey);

(c) accounts of schools and schooling at particular time periods (for example, using school records, Franklin's (1986) study of Minneapolis 1917–1950);

(d) studies of examination syllabuses and examination board records, Her Majesty's Inspectors (HMI) reports and Department of Education and Science (DES) reports (for example, Goodson, 1987);

(e) studies of subject teaching associations (for example, Geographical Association, Goodson, 1985);

(f) studies of major conferences and curriculum association meetings (for example, Tanner and Tanner, 1975);

(g) studies of published books and articles on curriculum (for example, Schubert, 1980).

Uses of Curriculum History

It is argued that studies of curriculum history have value because:

(a) They provide a broader perspective on curriculum in that they provide some insights not only about *how* a curriculum was taught in a particular historical period but also *why* and for *whom*.

(b) They provide insights about the complex relationships between the past, present and future (Seddon and Pope, 1989). We don't just recapture the past, but use curriculum history knowledge to make decisions about the present and to inform our future goals.

(c) They provide details of the human processes and motivations behind the formal structures of school subjects and timetables (Goodson, 1985). Seddon and Pope (1989), in a similar vein, refer to the wide range of actors who participate in curriculum (for example, teachers, parents, students, employers, politicians) who are portrayed in curriculum histories.

(d) They provide understandings to appreciate current models of curriculum (Tanner, 1982). Tanner argues that the development of knowledge in the curriculum field is incremental and we need to understand these historical, evolutionary developments to appreciate what we have achieved at the present time.

Examples

Curriculum history specialists have already made valuable contributions. For example, a number of scholars have demonstrated that the curriculum field has been dominated over the decades by *technological* emphases, concentrating upon efficiency, control and predictability.

Kliebard (1986) suggests that schooling in past decades has been dominated by a factory metaphor. This is a very narrow orientation and emphasizes the use of standardized means to achieve predetermined ends.

Olson (1989) argues that technical rationality has persisted over the decades because school administrators and teachers need it. They use technical rationality as a basis for decision-making because it makes their actions less hazardous — they have acted in accordance with scientifically warranted procedures.

Child-centred education is an interesting example. Child-centred education, progressive education, and similar titles have appeared and reappeared in the curriculum history literature. It is a classic example of an issue which seems to be destined to be recycled every decade or so, as revealed by peaks in the 1890s, 1920s, 1930s, 1960s, not counting earlier appearances due to the efforts of Rousseau, Pestalozzi and others.

Child-centred curricula can have very different meanings. The term can refer to:

(a) individualized teaching;
(b) learning through practical operation or doing;
(c) *laissez faire* — no organized curricula at all but based on the momentary interests of children;
(d) creative self-expression by students;
(e) practically oriented activities directed toward the needs of society;
(f) a collective term which refers to the rejection of teaching-directed learning — 'freedom from teacher domination, freedom from the millstone of subject matter, freedom from adult-imposed curriculum goals' (Tanner and Tanner, 1975).

Educators in the US created new directions for child-centred approaches in the early decades of the twentieth century. Dewey advocated a form of child-centred education whereby children's practical activities could be directed toward social needs. His writings were influential both in the US and overseas.

Advocates of individualized learning approaches in the US produced successful schemes such as the Gary Plan (1918, activity-oriented, social needs); the Dalton Plan (1925, use of student worksheets and subject laboratories); and the Winnetka Plan (1927, curriculum divided into 'tool subjects' and 'activities subjects', independent self-instruction in tool subjects).

Other attempts to introduce child-centred curricula gave rise to the establishment of experimental schools. Dewey had commenced a laboratory school at the University of Chicago in 1896 and many other educators followed suit at other universities.

The Progressive Education movement in the US split in different directions during the 1930s and 1940s. One such subgroup were social reconstructionists who proposed that their curriculum would provide an end to the Great Depression and also that it would prevent any future social and economic crises. Few of the Progressive Education adherents were prepared to face up to Count's challenge in a widely publicized speech 'Dare Progressive Education be progressive?' Most of the supporters were only prepared to promote cooperative spirit and group-mindedness in schools and were not willing to take a stand on crucial social issues.

One major success in the 1930s for the Progressive Education Association was the initiation of the Eight-Year Study in which thirty schools adopted child-centred curricula over a period of eight years. A comparison of their graduates who entered university with graduates from normal high schools revealed that the students in the experimental group were not handicapped but in fact scored higher grades in university and achieved higher results on tests of creativity, thinking, and social awareness. But this was only one of the singular successes for the Progressive Education Association. Competing goals within the organization caused it to lose momentum and the advent of World War II hastened its demise.

However, another peak for child-centred curricula was to reappear again in the Plowden Report in 1967, this time in the UK (Nias, 1990). This major report into primary education recommended informal learning for children as revealed in such statements as:

> the school is a community in which children learn to live first and
> foremost as children and then as future adults,

and

> we should encourage the development of the whole personality of
> children, to satisfy their curiosity and develop their confidence,
> perseverance and alertness.

Many educators in Australia and the US were stimulated by the Plowden Report and by the accounts of 'lighthouse' schools in various English counties (especially Leicestershire); they rallied to the slogans of 'open education' and 'open plan' classrooms. Various books promoted this approach. Prominent among these writers were romantic critics such as Holt (*How Children Fail*, 1964) and Silberman (*Crisis in the Classroom*, 1970; *The Open Classroom Reader*, 1973).

The swing of the pendulum began to turn in the late 1970s as empirical studies revealed that basic mastery in literacy and numeracy was not achieved as well in open classrooms as in conventional classrooms (Bennett, 1976; Angus, 1979). A new era of public opinion favouring mastery of basic skills became apparent in the 1970s and it has been maintained in the 1980s and 90s.

The octogenarian Tyler, reminiscing in 1978 on many cycles of curriculum 'fads' he had personally witnessed, remarked that

> surely we can learn from historical studies of these occasions about the climate of opinion in which these pressures develop, about the attempts made, or not made, by educational leaders to get the relevant facts before the public, and to get better public understanding of the curriculum and the rationale for its offerings.

Reflections and Issues

1   Read two books on curriculum, one written in the 1920s or 1930s and one written in the 1960s. Make a note of the different points of emphasis and breadth of coverage.

2   Studies of curriculum history are useful in examining wide-ranging educational topics, such as the use of ability groupings over the decades, but they have limited value in studying small scale phenomena such as an upper secondary class.

Discuss.

3   Curriculum history is a valuable field of inquiry. It uses methods (for example, searching for evidence, inferencing from facts, imaginative reconstruction of events, hypothesizing and selecting defensible explanations) that are specialized and valuable to furthering the curriculum field.

4   Do you consider that there has been an historical period in which major advances were made in curriculum? Give details of the advances that occurred and the reasons why you think that this was an outstanding period (see, for example, Smith *et al.*, 1988).

5   Critics of curriculum assert that studies of curriculum history simply eulogize great thinkers of the past and that they do not provide us with evidence and examples to help understand contemporary problems.

Discuss.

6   If history is to fulfil its potential as a comprehensive synthesis of social understanding, it must take more seriously its base in action theory, for much of it is an ill-formed combination of psychological and social determinism (Gilbert, 1984, p. 228).

Argue a case for whether this statement does or does not apply to curriculum history.

References

ANGUS, M.J. *et al.* (1979) *Open Area Schools: an Evaluative Study of Teaching and Learning in Primary Schools of Conventional and Open Area Design in Australia*, Canberra, ERDC.

BENNETT, N. (1976) *Teaching Styles and Pupil Progress*, London, Open Books.

FRANKLIN, B.M. (1986) *Building the American Community*, London, Falmer Press.

GILBERT, R. (1984) *The Impotent Image: Reflections of Ideology in the Secondary Curriculum*, London, Falmer Press.

GOODSON, I.F. (Ed.) (1985) *Social Histories of the Secondary Curriculum*, London, Falmer Press.

GOODSON, I.F. (1987) *School Subjects and Curriculum Change*, London, Falmer Press.

HOLT, J. (1964) *How Children Fail*, New York, Pitman.

KLIEBARD, H.M. (1986) *The Struggle for the American Curriculum 1893–1958*, Boston, Routledge and Kegan Paul.

NIAS, D.J. (1990) 'Informal Primary Education in Action: Teachers' Accounts', in CONNER, C. and LOFTHOUSE, B., *The Study of Primary Education, A Source Book, Vol. 1, Perspectives*, London, Falmer Press.

OLSON, J. (1989) 'The Persistance of Technical Rationality', in MILBURN, G. *et al.* (Eds) *Re-Interpreting Curriculum Research: Images and Arguments*, London, Falmer Press.

PLOWDEN, LADY B. (1967) *Children and Their Primary Schools, Report of the Central Advisory Council for Education, 1 and 2*, London, HMSO.

SCHUBERT, W.H. (1980) *Curriculum Books: The First Eighty Years*, New York, University Press of America.

SEDDON, T. and POPE, B. (1989) 'Curriculum History: Contribution to Current Curriculum Debate', *Curriculum Perspectives*, **9**, 1.

SILBERMAN, C.E. (1970) *Crisis in the Classroom*, New York, Random House.

SILBERMAN, C.E. (Ed.) (1973) *The Open Classroom Reader*, New York, Vintage Books.

SMITH, L.M., DWYER, D.C., PRUNTY, J.J. and KLEINE, P.F. (1988) *Innovation and Change in Schooling: History, Politics and Agency*, London, Falmer Press.

TANNER, D. and TANNER, L.N. (1975) *Curriculum Development*, New York, Macmillan.

TANNER, L.N. (1982) 'Curriculum History as Useable Knowledge', *Curriculum Inquiry*, **12**, 4.

TYLER, R.W. (1978) 'Trends in Curriculum Development', paper presented at the Annual Conference of the American Research Association, Toronto.

Chapter 27

School Subjects

Recent research studies, especially in the United Kingdom, reveal that curriculum change is both gradual and continuous and that by giving attention to specific *school subjects* it is possible to delineate and explain these changes. A leading researcher in this area is Ivor Goodson (1983a, 1983b, 1985, 1987a, 1987b, 1988) who argues that:

(a) Attention needs to be given to historical studies which examine complex changes over time rather than 'snapshots' of unique events which may be entirely aberrant.

(b) By focusing upon the recurrence of events over time it is possible to discern explanatory frameworks.

(c) Studies of school subjects enable important research to be undertaken using methodologies of the sociologists, historians and curriculum theorists but the dominant approach needs to be provided by the *curriculum historian*.

Hargreaves (1989) takes a similar stance when he notes that

school subjects are more than just groupings of intellectual thought. They are social systems too. They compete for power, prestige, recognition and reward within the secondary or high school system (p. 56).

Other writers who have contributed to this area include Smith (1984, 1986), Ball (1984) and Reid (1984).

School Subjects as Social Systems

In the United Kingdom, Goodson (1983a) argues that *examination boards*, controlled by the universities, have always dominated the school curriculum. The growth of *subject associations* have also wielded considerable power over recent decades. These forces at work need to be considered against the backdrop of major changes to the UK educational system such as the tripartite system developed in the 1940s, the rise and fall of secondary modern schools, growth of comprehensive schools, and the political decisions which greatly reduced the number of grammar schools.

Within this context three traditions about subjects have evolved, the academic, the utilitarian and the pedagogic:

— *Academic* subjects are those whose content is tested by acceptable written examinations which guarantee them high status.
— *Utilitarian* subjects deal with practical knowledge which is not always subjected to high-level written examinations and hence is of low status.
— The *Pedagogic* tradition places major importance upon the way children learn and consequently subject content and methodologies are devised which pursue a preferred pedagogic orientation, such as child-centred, discovery learning.

Examples

In a major study of curriculum history, Goodson (1983a) undertook a series of historical case studies of three school subjects, namely biology, geography and rural studies. He unravels within this volume:

(a) the process by which each of these fields of study over time became a school subject;
(b) the issues, conflicts and compromises which occurred in the promotion of these subjects;
(c) the importance of a socio-historical approach to curriculum studies.

He puts forward three hypotheses which he tests out by using historical data, namely:

(a) that school subjects are not monolithic entities but shifting amalgamations of sub-groups and traditions;
(b) that in the process of establishing a school subject, a subject group moves from promoting pedagogic and utilitarian traditions to an academic tradition;
(c) that much of the curriculum debate that occurs about a school subject over time can be interpreted in terms of conflict between subjects over status, resources and territory.

As a case study example, Goodson (1983a) traces the development of *geography* from the nineteenth century emphasis upon reciting names and statistics, to regional approaches in the 1920s, to quantitative approaches in the 1960s. He highlights some of the tensions and conflicts:

(a)   a drive by geography associations to get geography accepted as a university subject;

(b)   a change in emphasis from a subject which stressed utilitarian values such as citizenship to an emphasis upon academic rigour;

(c)   various arguments and changing positions occurred over the decades about such matters as the role of fieldwork, hostility within university departments about the placement of physical geography, difficulties in setting appropriate theoretical and practical examinations, the expansiveness of school geography and its tendency to swallow up other subjects (see also Bailey, 1989);

(d)   the drive for higher status for geography has brought about more finances and resources for it in schools (for example, better staffing ratios, higher salaries, better career paths).

In a revised and extended edition, Goodson (1987b) concludes that:

(a)   in the case of geography which represents a *field* rather than a *form* of knowledge, there have been shifting sets of sub-groups, all pursuing different objectives and certainly far from a monolithic entity. Examples of three major sub-groups were regional geographers, field geographers and 'new' (quantitative) geographers.

(b)   there was often a time lag between the accepted emphasis in universities and that in schools. For example, a long time after the 'new' geography was established in universities, regional geography was still retained in schools.

(c)   once geography had evolved toward an academic emphasis (rather than practical or pedagogical), university scholars ensured that they defined and legitimated its disciplinary content.

(d)   the Geographical Association played a key role in mediating the views and activities of university scholars and geography teachers.

(e)   the evidence reveals that it was teachers' material self-interest in their working lives (higher status, promotional interests) that caused them to acquiesce to university demands rather than teacher socialization to these dominant groups.

(f)   a school subject still needs to be accepted as a 'vocational' qualification in order to survive and to appeal at a pedagogical level to learners.

Gilbert (1984) also undertook a study of the social subjects (geography, history, economics) in schools in the United Kingdom over the nineteenth and twentieth centuries and with a focus upon social images. He concluded that:

(a)   authors of textbooks concentrated upon social problems that were largely material and consensual ones and dealt with efficiency and harmony; controversial problems were excluded.

(b)   values analysis is rarely included in geography textbooks.

(c) textbook writers explain social events in objective terms, free of any explicit value stance.

Cooper (1983, 1985) undertook an historico-sociological study of secondary school mathematics in the 1950s and 1960s in the United Kingdom. He concluded that:

(a) new curriculum projects in the 1960s were only successful if they did not challenge the differentiation of mathematics curriculum on the grounds of ability and gender (i.e. geometry and algebra for the more able, usually boys; arithmetic for the less able).
(b) mathematics associations and teachers wanted a differentiated curriculum with a foundation list of topics which are practical and relevant for lower ability students.
(c) any attempts to include more abstract mathematics in the curriculum for the average student was strongly resisted by schools, industry and the media.

Reflections and Issues

1 In bringing about change in school subjects, the role played by subject associations and networks should not be underestimated. Comment on this statement in the light of your experiences.

2 The historical study of school subjects enables a researcher to pursue an understanding of the complexity of curriculum action and negotiation over time [and] is a meaningful sequence through which to test and formulate theory (Goodson, 1985, p. 345).

Discuss.

3 Academic subjects for able students are accorded the highest status and resources (Goodson, 1988, p. 140).

Do you accept this point of view? Give examples.

4 Studies of school subjects provide *par excellence* a context where antecedent structures collide with contemporary action; the school subject provides one obvious manifestation of historical legacies with which contemporary actors have to work (Goodson, 1983b, p. 13).

Discuss.

5 In the long run, the sub-group and the version of the subject which is likely to be successfully promoted is that most in harmony with the material interests of the subject's scholars and teachers (Goodson, 1987a, pp. 195–6).

Discuss this statement with reference to one or more subjects.

6   Images in the present subjects are remnants of the past, related to social structures of the time (Gilbert, 1984, p. 229).

Analyze some images of subjects with which you are familiar. In what period of time do you consider that they were promoted? What is the relevance of these images today?

References

BAILEY, P. (1989) 'Geography: New Subject, New Curricular Contributions', in WIEGAND, P. and RAYNER, M. (Eds) *Curriculum Progress 5–16: School Subjects and the National Curriculum Debate*, London, Falmer Press.

BALL, S.J. (1984) 'Imperialism, Social Control and the Colonial Curriculum in Africa', in GOODSON, I.F. and BALL, S.J. (Eds) *Defining the Curriculum: Histories and Ethnographies*, London, Falmer Press.

COOPER, B. (1983) 'On Explaining Change in School Subjects', *British Journal of Sociology of Education*, 4, 3.

COOPER, B. (1985) 'Secondary School Mathematics Since 1905: Reconstructing Differentiation', in GOODSON, I.F. (Ed.) *Social Histories of the Secondary Curriculum: Subjects for Study*, London, Falmer Press.

GILBERT, R. (1984) *The Impotent Image: Reflections of Ideology in the Secondary School Curriculum*, London, Falmer Press.

GOODSON, I.F. (1983a) *School Subjects and Curriculum Change*, London, Croom Helm.

GOODSON, I.F. (1983b) 'History, Context and Qualitative Methods in the Study of Curriculum', paper presented at the SSRC Conference, London.

GOODSON, I.F. (Ed.) (1985) *Social Histories of the Secondary Curriculum*, London, Falmer Press.

GOODSON, I.F. (Ed.) (1987a) *International Perspectives and Curriculum History*, London, Croom Helm.

GOODSON, I.F. (1987b) *School Subjects and Curriculum Change*, London, Falmer Press.

GOODSON, I.F. (1988) *The Making of Curriculum: Collected Essays*, London, Falmer Press.

GOODSON, I.F. and BALL, S.J. (Eds) (1984) *Defining the Curriculum: Histories and Ethnographies*, London, Falmer Press.

HARGREAVES, A. (1989) *Curriculum and Assessment Reform*, Milton Keynes, Open University Press.

REID, W.A. (1984) 'Curricular Topics as Institutional Categories: Implications for Theory and Research in the History and Sociology of School Subjects', in GOODSON, I.F. and BALL, S.J. (Eds) *Defining the Curriculum: Histories and Ethnographies*, London, Falmer Press.

SMITH, L.M. (1984) 'Ethnographic and Historical Method in the Study of Schooling', in GOODSON, I.F. and BALL, S.J. (Eds) *Defining the Curriculum: Histories and Ethnographies*, London, Falmer Press.

SMITH, L.M. *et al.* (Eds) (1986) *Innovation and Change in Schooling: History, Politics and Agency*, London, Falmer Press.

Chapter 28

Curriculum Theorizing and the Reconceptualists

Curriculum theorizing refers to the process of reflecting — thoughtfulness about curriculum matters and seeking meaning and direction to curriculum experiences. The emphasis is more upon reflection and processes of thinking than the production of documents, curriculum plans or theories.

Theorizing Principles of the Reconceptualists

The term *theorizing* is used frequently in the literature now but in the 1970s it was first used by William Pinar (1975) in his book *Curriculum Theorizing: The Reconceptualists*. In this book, Pinar tried to demonstrate that certain scholars were using different values and methods to portray curriculum — they all had a commitment to *transform* or *reconceptualize* the existing curriculum field. The writers in this book shared two common purposes:

(a) a denunciation of rational, means-end approaches to curriculum;
(b) the use of European theoretical traditions (for example, existential-ism, phenomenology, psychoanalysis and neo-Marxism).

According to Klohr (1980) some of the main principles used by reconceptual-ists in their theorizing endeavours include the following:

(a) Curriculum must be perceived as a holistic and organic view of people and their relation to nature.
(b) The individual is the chief agent in the construction of knowledge; he/she is a culture creator as well as a culture bearer.
(c) We get meaning by drawing on our own experiential base — it is necessary to reconstruct and reorganize experiences by individuals and groups.
(d) The preconscious realms of experience are important in developing meaning about curriculum.
(e) Personal liberty and the attainment of higher levels of conscious-ness are central values.

(f) Diversity and pluralism are characteristics both of the social ends and the means proposed to attain these ends.

(g) New language forms are needed to bring out new meanings and insights about curriculum. Examples include 'autobiographical method' (using past experiences to inform one of current principles) and 'currere' (making meaning of personal experiences by remembering and reflecting upon one's past histories in schools and projecting one's hopes for the future).

Yet, it is also important to note that the term *reconceptualist* is misleading. It does not indicate something finished or final — ideas and methods are still evolving. Also, there are major divergences within the group. Rather, there are at least four sub-groups.

Some writers (for example, Kliebard, Apple and Franklin) have used *historical critique* to examine critically assumptions accepted in the past about schools and schooling. They have developed forms of inquiry which widen the connections between forces at work in the educational scene. Then again, writers such as Huebner, Greene, Macdonald, Apple, Giroux and Popkewitz, to name just a few, have used *social/political critique* to analyze vigorously and reveal social justice problems such as domination, alienation and repression. Still others have used an *aesthetic/philosophic critique* (for example, Eisner, McCutcheon, Greene, Huebner) to focus on the total educational environment and to illuminate and portray expressive forms of classroom action which are typically ignored by traditional educators. A fourth sub-group, *psychoanalytic critique*, as developed by Pinar and Grumet, uses autobiography to stress the need to focus upon the individual. Each individual needs to return to his/her past as well as to consider the present and possible futures, in comprehending the dynamics of his/her psychological life.

The school curriculum is formed and shaped ideologically. The dominant forms of school curriculum reflect the dominant ideological forms in society (Kemmis, 1986). In contemporary schooling, the vocational/neoclassical orientation remains dominant.

Socially-critical orientations work against the grain of these dominant forms. They encourage action as empowerment — developing interactions with others which will emancipate teachers, students and parents from irrationality, injustice and coercion (see module 6).

Achievements and Problems

In general, reconceptualists (despite their differences as noted above) have achieved a number of major advances in curriculum theorizing.

(a) They have raised serious challenges about traditional approaches to curriculum.

(b) They have generated new concepts and a new language to theorize about curriculum. A new language was needed to explain adequately different perspectives and relationships. Pinar and colleagues use such new technical terms as *hermeneutics* (process of interpretation), *praxis* (accepted activities of problem posing and problem solving), *reflexivity* (self-analysis), *phenomenological* (phenomena as consciously experienced), *problematic* (defining a conceptual field of study not only in terms of what is included but also what is excluded).

(c) They have assisted greatly in the demotion of quantitative methods of evaluating education practices from their position of pre-eminence. They have highlighted the qualitative aspects of educational experiences and have broadened the interpretation of evaluation processes and evaluative judgments (see Sherman and Webb, 1988).

Their achievements can be criticized on the following grounds, however:

(a) that their work is predominantly prose rather than analysis and hence it provides minimal practical insights (Van Manen, 1978). Although readers might be stimulated by the writings they are equally likely to be frustrated by what it means in terms of classroom practice. 'Consciousness and transcendence is an enchanting prospect' (Feinberg, 1985, p. 92) but what does this mean for classroom teaching or teacher training practices?

(b) that autobiographical accounts do not provide generalized principles which can explain their validity to a wider audience of scholars and teachers.

(c) that self-report methods minimize the effects of ideology. It could be that individuals are unaware of and do not recognize latent structures that affect their lived experiences. According to Mazza (1982) and Sharp and Green (1975) too much trust is placed on the power of reflexivity to penetrate the powerful ideological influences upon teachers' and students' actions.

Reflections and Issues

1 Is it appropriate for teachers to be curriculum theorizers? Should a teacher support an education system and the wider society or critique it?

2 Teachers must promote a critical consciousness committed equally to (moral, political, and social) reflection and committed action, aimed at a more just, human, satisfying environment (Beyer, 1988, p. 241).

To what extent is this a desirable goal for curriculum theorizing endeavours? How might this be translated into specific school aims?

3 What freedoms or restrictions do you have as a teacher? What opportunities do you have to critique policies and procedures? Which

values or principles would you consider are of major importance to you?

4   Critical empirical studies of curriculum and efforts to reform curriculum consistent with values of human possibility and social justice have tended to focus on curriculum documents such as syllabi and textbooks rather than curriculum practice ... There must be greater attention to context and contextualized social processes (Cornbleth, 1990, p. 198).

Do you agree that critical empirical studies have given too much attention to curriculum documents? What are important contextual factors and processes that also need attention?

5   Teachers ... must be given the theoretical and conceptual tools to combat all forms of mystification and alienation (Giroux, 1981, p. 156).

What theoretical tools are needed to penetrate the surface realities of teaching? To what extent can teachers generate their own meanings and develop these within frameworks of social justice and social action?

6   Most of what has been, and still is, taught in schools is *information*. ... Much of what is taught in schools is *labels* for ideas, rather than the ideas themselves (Smith and Lovat, 1990, p. 198).

Do you agree? How can curriculum theorizing help us to overcome this perceived deficiency?

7   Teachers and school communities are participants in curriculum theorizing, not the recipients of state-endorsed curriculum theories or the curriculum theories of the academy (Kemmis, 1986, p. 106).

In your experience, is this the case?
If not, what processes might be established to bring this about?

8   Gilbert (1984) argues that major curriculum theory issues revolve around a greater understanding of the relationships between social knowledge, social practice and the individual. What social knowledge is conveyed in school textbooks and what are its theoretical bases? How do these texts relate to current social practices and to the roles and responsibilities of individuals in society?

9   We need to develop curriculum theories which investigate systematically how existing curriculum originates, is reproduced, metamorphoses and responds to new prescriptions (Goodson, 1991, p. 167).

Explain how curricula undergo metamorphosis by various professional groups.

Is it possible to theorize about the patterns of action, reaction and interaction which occur between these individuals and groups?

References

BEYER, L.E. (1988) *Knowing and Acting: Inquiry, Ideology and Educational Studies*, London, Falmer Press.

CORNBLETH, C. (1990) *Curriculum in Context*, London, Falmer Press.

FEINBERG, P.R. (1985) 'Four Curriculum Theorists: A Critique in the Light of Martin Buber's Philosophy of Education', *Journal of Curriculum Theorizing*, 6, 1.

GILBERT, R. (1984) *The Impotent Image*, London, Falmer Press.

GIROUX, H.A. (1981) *Ideology, Culture and the Process of Schooling*, London, Falmer Press.

GOODSON, I.F. (1991) 'On Understanding Curriculum: The Alienation of Curriculum Theory', in GOODSON, I.F. and WALKER, R., *Biography, Identity and Schooling: Episodes in Educational Research*, London, Falmer Press.

KEMMIS, S. (1986) *Curriculum Theorizing: Beyond Reproduction Theory*, Geelong, Deakin University Press.

KLOHR, P.R. (1980) 'The Curriculum Field — Gritty and Ragged?', *Curriculum Perspectives*, 1, 1.

MAZZA, K.A. (1982) 'Reconceptual Inquiry as an Alternative Mode of Curriculum Theory and Practice: A Critical Study', *Journal of Curriculum Theorizing*, 4, 2.

PINAR, W.F. (Ed.) (1975) *Curriculum Theorizing: The Reconceptualists*, Berkeley, CA, McCutchan.

SHARP, R. and GREEN, A. (1975) *Education and Social Control: A Study in Progressive Primary Education*, London, Routledge and Kegan Paul.

SHERMAN, R.R. and WEBB, R.B. (Eds) (1988) *Qualitative Research in Education: Focus and Methods*, London, Falmer Press.

SMITH, D.L. and LOVAT, T.J. (1990) *Curriculum: Action on Reflection*, Sydney, Social Science Press.

VAN MANEN, M. (1978) 'Reconceptualist Curriculum Thought: A Review of Recent Literature', *Curriculum Inquiry*, 8, 4.

Chapter 29

Sociology of Knowledge Approach to Curriculum

Philosophers such as Hirst (1965) and Phenix (1964) state that there are particular forms of knowledge (for example, physical sciences, history, literature and the fine arts) which exist independent of societies' actions. This knowledge is relatively objective, non-problematic and it is verifiable.

Sociologists over the last two decades (Young, 1971; Bowles and Gintis, 1976; Apple, 1982; Giroux, 1982) advocate that what counts as 'knowledge' is defined and organized by the dominant groups in society. Knowledge is socially constructed. It is basically subjective, relative and political. This is the Sociology of Knowledge approach.

Proponents and Their Principles

The basis for this approach can be traced back to eighteenth century writers. For example, Marx (in Althusser, 1969) argued that since knowledge is a function of social groups then different groups in society have different forms of knowledge. Marx related this argument, however, to class struggle and did not give particular attention to how forms of knowledge affected people in their everyday lives.

It is argued that schools reproduce the values and attitudes needed to maintain dominant social groups. They do this through their formal and informal curricula. There is little opportunity given to students to generate their own meanings about knowledge. Knowledge is imposed overtly upon students or covertly via the subtle interactions of the 'hidden curriculum'. Under these circumstances, learning is a mode of control and domination.

The term *hegemony* is useful to portray how particular areas of knowledge become legitimated in society. According to Giroux (1981), hegemonic processes include:

(a) attempts by a dominant class to obtain control over the resources of society mainly via the mass media and the educational system.

(b) the dominant class controls other classes so that the preferred view of the world becomes all inclusive and universal.

(c) force and consent are used to shape and incorporate the views of the subordinate groups.

(d) the dominant group places limits on the oppositional discussions and practices that are permitted to occur.

Giroux argues that schools support and practice a number of hegemonic principles but that many of them are not made explicit. Examples include the rights of students versus the rights of teachers. De Castell *et al.* (1989) suggest that textbooks, literature for children and instructional approaches are dominated by the world views and ideological perspectives of hegemonic groups.

Knowledge in schools is treated as a realm of objective 'facts' (Giroux, 1979). It is not questioned, analyzed or negotiated. Rather it is something to be managed and mastered. In schools there is little opportunity for students to generate their own meanings. The purpose of knowledge in schools becomes a matter of accumulation and categorization. Schools should be seen as part of the dominant society. They reproduce the cultural values and social relationships of the larger social order.

Sociology of Knowledge proponents tend to use very different and technical terms in their offensive against mainstream curriculum practices, including:

hegemony	— organized assemblage of meanings and practices, typically wielded by ruling groups;
cultural capital	— the ability of certain groups in society to transform culture into a commodity, and to accumulate it;
reflexivity	— self-analysis;
problematic	— the defining of a conceptual field not only in terms of what is included but what is excluded.

They maintain, with some justification, that a new technical language is needed to provide different insights and interpretations about existing phenomena and structures.

Researchers in the 1970s and 1980s undertook empirical research studies to explore overt and covert knowledge found in school settings. As an example, Anyon (1981) observed and interviewed teachers and students in two working-class primary schools, two middle-class primary schools and two affluent primary schools in the USA. In the two working-class schools, most work activity involved following set procedures and rote learning. In the middle-class schools there was more opportunity for student choice. In the affluent school, work activity commonly involved creative activity carried out independently by the students. She concluded that children from different social classes do not have equal opportunity to knowledge.

Another example can be found in Willis (1977), who used participant observation techniques with a group of working class boys attending a secondary school in an industrial city in the United Kingdom. He paints vivid descriptions of the rituals and cultural forms which permeated the lives of this group of boys. The boys developed their own counter-culture as a reaction to the official culture of the school curriculum. They took every opportunity to subvert the routines and practices of their teachers — they rejected the established culture of the school.

Taking a more recent example, Hargreaves (1989) suggests that the national curriculum introduced into the United Kingdom in 1989 is unambiguously subject-based. There is no attempt to include broader areas of educational experience such as aesthetic, practical, social or personal subjects. That is, the new national curriculum will continue to differentiate students on academic subject lines. It will reinforce the existing culture of teaching and favour and reproduce the middle classes' dominance. It will limit still further the educational opportunities for students from poorly resourced backgrounds.

Achievements and Problems

Merits of Sociology of Knowledge Approach

(a) It recognizes the connections between curriculum and different factors of production in society.

(b) It raises questions about 'rational' value-free approaches to curriculum planning.

(c) It develops new terms and conceptual structures to understand curriculum processes.

Unresolved Problems with the Sociology of Knowledge Approach

(a) *Relativism* — If the content of knowledge is directly related to social conditions, then as social conditions vary so must truth and knowledge. Can truth, as a vital part of knowledge vary? Doesn't this destroy the very being of teachers and schooling if there are no objective truths?

(b) *Cultural differences* — Knowledge cannot be the exclusive property of any one culture. Knowledge and truth must be extra-cultural.

(c) *Ideology* — Marxist ideas tend to be offered as the solution to dominance by major social groups. Is this the only solution? Is it a desirable alternative?

(d) *Evidence* — Much of what is presented is assertion rather than evidence of what actually happens in schools. Is the rhetoric more powerful than the facts? Have the links with classroom practices really been established?

Reflections and Issues

1   We must develop a mode of curriculum that cultivates critical theoretical discourse about the quality and purpose of schooling and human life (Giroux 1979, p. 253).

Discuss.

2   The Sociology of Knowledge approach is strong on its denunciation of the traditional curriculum paradigm but contributes little to specific, alternative programmes or structures.

Discuss.

3   Those in positions of power are able to determine largely what counts as the 'real' world, including what counts as 'education' and 'educational problems' (Young, 1971).

Discuss.

4   Why and how are particular aspects of our culture represented in schools as objective, factual knowledge? Consider some specific examples to clarify your stand.

5   Public examinations have a major role in controlling school knowledge (Whitty, 1985).

Explain.

References

ALTHUSSER, L. (1969) *For Marx*, London, Penguin Books.

ANYON, J. (1981) 'Educational Equity and School Instruction', *Social Education*, **45**, 4.

APPLE, M.W. (1982) *Education and Power*, Boston, Routledge and Kegan Paul.

BOWLES, S. and GINTIS, H. (1976) *Schooling in Capitalist America*, London, Routledge and Kegan Paul.

DE CASTELL, S., LUKE, A. and LUKE, C. (Eds) (1989) *Language, Authority and Criticism: Readings on the School Textbook*, London, Falmer Press.

EISNER, E.W. (1979) *The Educational Imagination*, New York, Macmillan.

GIROUX, H.A. (1979) 'Toward a New Sociology of Curriculum', *Educational Leadership*, **37**, 3, pp. 248–53.

GIROUX, H.A. (1981) *Ideology, Culture and the Process of Schooling*, London, Falmer Press.

GIROUX, H. (1982) 'Power and Resistance in the New Sociology of Education: Beyond Theories of Social and Cultural Reproduction', *Curriculum Perspectives*, **2**, 3, pp. 1–15.

GOODSON, I.F. (1983) *School Subjects and Curriculum Change*, London, Croom Helm.

HARGREAVES, A. (1989) 'Curriculum Policy and the Culture of Teaching', in MILBURN, G., GOODSON, I.F. and CLARK, R.J. (Eds) *Re-interpreting Curriculum Research: Images and Arguments*, London, Falmer Press.

HIRST, P.H. (1965) 'Liberal Education and the Nature of Knowledge', in ARCHAMBAULT, R.D. (Ed.) *Philosophical Analysis in Education*, London, Routledge and Kegan Paul.

PHENIX, P.H. (1964) *Realms of Meaning: A Philosophy of the Curriculum for General Education*, New York, McGraw Hill.
WHITTY, G. (1985) *Sociology and School Knowledge*, London, Methuen.
WILLIS, P. (1977) *Learning to Labour*, London, Saxon House.
YOUNG, M.F.D. (Ed.) (1971) *Knowledge and Control*, London, Collier-Macmillan.

Chapter 30

Curriculum Reform

Proposals for reforms in education appear frequently in the literature and especially proposals for curriculum reform. Presumably this means that there are problems to be solved. Because of the frequency of reform proposals this would seem to indicate that previous reforms did not remove the problems they were intended to solve.

Proposals for curriculum reform can come from various sources including:

teachers,
teacher unions,
policy-makers,
academics,
politicians,
media and
pressure groups.

Some examples of curriculum reform proposals include:

(a)   the need for a stronger academic programme;
(b)   the need for special programmes for the disadvantaged;
(c)   the need for higher standards of student achievement in core subjects.

Ideology Stances

It is very evident that reform proposals represent very different frames of reference about curriculum in schools. For example, the current reform movement in the US, with its emphasis upon excellence, has the nation's productivity as a major goal. Although supported by many groups there are others who object strongly to reforms that will reindustrialize — in the name of making the US more competitive.

Apple (1988) argues that these reforms are not the appropriate ones. He maintains that reforms should concentrate on the relationship between schooling and the larger society and on the structure of inequalities in society — the deskilling of jobs, and the lowering of wages and benefits.

Reform Reports

Reform reports are often a popular means of bringing a purported problem to the consciousness of the public. The reports tend to focus on one or two key elements, often dramatizing the problems so as to elicit the solutions. Examples of reform reports include:

> *The American High School Today* (Conant, 1959)
> *The Process of Education* (Bruner, 1960)
> *A Nation at Risk: The Imperative for Educational Reform* (National Com mission on Excellence in Education, 1983)
> *High School: A Report on Secondary Education in America* (Boyer, 1983)
> *Horace's Compromise: The Dilemma of the American High School* (Sizer, 1984)

According to Presseisen (1989), these reform reports may be high on rhetoric but they tend to be deficient in such matters as:

(a) including research data to support their assertions,
(b) providing reasoned consideration of options,
(c) presenting supporting evidence and argumentation for well-specified proposals.

Further, it should be noted that making reform proposals is only part of the process and that there are many problems in getting reforms implemented. The factors affecting innovations and change, and implementation, as noted in modules 20 and 25, are most pertinent.

Types of Reforms

Reforms can vary enormously in terms of their scope and impact. Plank (1988) suggests that there are four main types which he categorizes as *additive reforms*, *external reforms*, *regulatory reforms*, and *structural reforms* (see table 30.1). By far the most difficult to achieve are the structural reforms.

Additive reforms are relatively easy to implement because they involve additional resources and do not affect the organizational character of schools. An example would be a fully-funded computer literacy programme.

External reforms also have little effect on the structure of schools, as they concentrate upon teachers entering the system or students leaving the system. Examples include higher tests for preservice teachers or more stringent requirements for high school graduation. These types of reforms are typically welcomed by school boards and teachers' unions.

Table 30.1: Types of curriculum reforms and examples

Additive	External	Regulatory	Structural
• increased salaries	• preserve teacher tests	• longer school day	• smaller classes
• pre-school initiatives	• new high school graduation requirements	• longer school year	• vouchers/tax credits
• computer literacy programme	• certification changes	• more basic skills	• merit pay plans
		• state-wide assessment	• competency tests for teachers

(After Plank, 1988)

Regulatory reforms seek changes in schools but not necessarily affecting the basic structure. The emphasis is upon more time and effort to achieve higher student achievements. Examples include longer school days and school years, core curriculum, statewide testing.

Structural reforms require alterations to the structure and operation of schools. They question current school structures and have the potential to be extremely disruptive to teachers and students. Examples include merit pay plans and voucher systems for parents to use at schools of their choice.

Taxonomy of Reform Proposals

In the USA over recent years, various reforms have been advocated via official reports but also through state legislation. It is not all integrated into one major reform policy, and in fact, some authors such as Cibulka (1990) argue that some of the reform proposals are not consistent and are even contradictory. Cibulka suggests that there are some major or core proposals which have occurred in most states (for example, state mandates) and ancillary proposals (for example, greater choice of schools) which have been advocated by some pressure groups in some states (see table 30.2).

These proposals represent a *pluralist* approach to reform and because of the inconsistencies between different policies there is little shared consensus over ends or means. These pluralist bargaining games may create a lot of media publicity but the lack of unity could mean limited chances of success.

By contrast, reforms in the United Kingdom have coherence and have been implemented as a total package of reform, despite widespread criticism. The ruling Tory party under the leadership of Prime Minister Margaret Thatcher produced reforms that were aimed at raising standards of all students. The creation of core and foundation subjects, key stages, attainment targets and standard assessment tasks have been carefully orchestrated to achieve this end (see table 30.3). Notwithstanding, it is far from clear

Table 30.2: Taxonomy of reform proposals in the USA during the 1980s

Core proposals
(a) higher standards through mandates passed by state legislatures and state boards of education;
(b) improved salaries for teachers to enable teaching to become more of a profession;
(c) higher-order thinking skills;
(d) reducing drop-out rates in high schools.

Ancillary proposals
(e) performance incentives to 'quality' teachers;
(f) removing state and federal regulations from schools;
(g) increased use of standardized tests to make comparisons among schools and school districts;
(h) school empowerment to empower other stakeholders such as parents and students;
(i) to give parents greater choice over the type and location of schools they want for their children.

(After Cibulka, 1990)

Table 30.3: Reform proposals and their implementation in the UK during the 1980s

The following proposals were included in a series of Education Reform Acts passed by Parliament during the period 1987–88.

A National Curriculum will be introduced to achieve consistently high standards for students by providing:
(a) a balanced and broadly based curriculum.
(b) spiritual, moral, cultural, mental and physical development.
(c) development in all the main areas of learning and experience (3 core subjects — English, mathematics, science; 7 foundation subjects — history, geography, technology, music, art, physical education, modern foreign language).
(d) students with the opportunities, responsibilities and experiences of adult life.

The National Curriculum was implemented in 1989 using:
(a) the core and foundation subjects.
(b) four key stages have been used as phases of learning:
key stage 1 — the two infant years,
key stage 2 — the four junior years,
key stage 3 — the first three years of secondary schooling,
key stage 4 — the final two years of compulsory schooling.
(c) attainment targets including up to ten levels of attainment cover the four key stages for each subject.
(d) standard assessment tasks have been designed for each key stage and overall school results will be published.

whether these reforms will be accepted and implemented appropriately by teachers.

Reflections and Issues

1   Educational reform cannot progress without financial resources. People, time and materials are necessary costs that are not considered to any great degree in most reform reports (Presseisen, 1989, p. 135).

Why is it that reform reports rarely include detailed budgets? Who should determine priorities for finance for reform proposals?

2   Compare and contrast the following statements:

> The school reform movement in the US has been the most sustained and far-reaching reform effort in modern times (Boyd, 1987, p. 28).

> Most of the reforms that have been adopted in the US in the past five years have not significantly altered the traditional structure and functioning of American public school systems. (Plank, 1988, p. 143).

3   Some of the most difficult dilemmas we face currently have been around for a long time.

Give examples of reforms that have been proposed over the decades to solve a particular curriculum problem. Have any proposals been more successful than others? Give reasons.

4   Do schools exist to increase the nation's productivity or for other equally important personal and social goals (Passow, 1988, p. 254)? What is your stance on this matter?

5   The reform proposals in the US reflect and help perpetuate practices that are at odds with equity and excellence goals (Cornbleth and Gottlieb, 1988, p. 11).

Why do you consider that equity goals which were being advanced in the 1960s and 70s are not being given a high priority in the 1980s and 90s? Are equity and excellence diametrically opposed goals?

6   Problems of logical consistency among the elements of American educational reform abound ... If we ask how these all fit together, the answer is that they do not ... What this analysis suggests is that a shotgun approach to reform, so characteristic of Americans in the past and once again being played out, is very risky, indeed. If Americans wish to succeed in their current reforms, their pragmatism must include more careful consideration of how to maximise the interdependent elements in these educational reform strategies rather than approaching them piecemeal (Cibulka, 1990, p. 108).

Critically discuss.

References

APPLE, M.W. (1988) 'What Reform Talk Does: Creating Inequalities in Education', *Educational Administration Quarterly*, **24**, 3.

BOYD, W.L. (1987) 'Rhetoric and Symbolic Politics: President Reagan's School Reform Agenda', *Education Week*, March.

Boyer, E.L. (1983) *High School: A Report on Secondary Education in America*, New York, Harper and Row.

Bruner, J.S. (1960) *The Process of Education*, New York, Vintage Books.

Cibulka, J. (1990) 'American Educational Reform and Government Power', *Educational Review*, **42**, 2.

Conant, J.B. (1959) *The American High School Today*, New York, McGraw Hill.

Cornbleth, C. and Gottlieb, E.E. (1988) 'Reform, Discourse and Curriculum Reform', paper presented at the Annual Conference of the American Educational Research Association, New Orleans.

National Commission on Excellence in Education (1983) *A Nation At Risk: The Imperative for Educational Reform*, Washington DC, Government Printing Office.

Passow, A.H. (1988) 'Whither (or Wither)? School Reform?', *Educational Administration Quarterly*, **24**, 3.

Plank, D.N. (1988) 'Why School Reform Doesn't Change Schools: Political and Organizational Perspectives' in Boyd, W.L. and Kerchner, C.T. (Eds) *The Politics of Excellence and Choice in Education*, London, Falmer Press.

Presseisen, B.Z. (1989) *Unlearned Lessons: Current and Past Reforms for School Improvement*, London, Falmer Press.

Sizer, T.R. (1984) *Horace's Compromise: The Dilemma of the American High School*, Boston, Houghton Mifflin.

Concluding Issues

It is important to reflect upon what has been achieved by reading about these thirty concepts. Some relevant questions which might be asked include:

To what extent did the information provided about each concept add to your understanding of curriculum matters?

Were there matters left unstated that troubled you? Were you unable to follow up these unresolved aspects in the references supplied?

Has a reading of these concepts added to your understanding of what should be taught, to whom, when and how?

Schools are very complex organizations. Over recent years we have gained a number of insights about the processes and factors involved in curriculum planning and development and this has been due in no small measure to our use of conceptual structures and particular concepts. Concepts are powerful tools for exploring and reflecting upon relationships between major actors and events in the school environment.

There are no 'right' answers in curriculum. Analyses of events and problems using appropriate concepts is certainly preferable to a slavish rendering of factual accounts and the reproduction of particular recipes of action.

Curriculum workers need to develop balanced, informed and justifiable answers to major curriculum issues which they are prepared to uphold and value. If readers are even beginning to reflect and develop along these lines then the key concepts approach to curriculum is vindicated.

Index

academic subjects, 197
Action Research, 116–122
  examples, 117–118
  impact on schools, 120
  processes, 116–117, 118–119
Adams, M., 175–177
Adelman, C., 116, 121
adoption, 138
aims, 85, 86–87
Alexander, K., 165
Althuser, L., 206
Angus, M., 194
Anyon, J., 207
Apple, M., 21, 45, 141, 202, 206, 211
assessment, 102–105
  criterion referenced, 103
  diagnostic, 102–103
  formative, 102–103
  norm referenced, 103
  summative, 102–103
  techniques, 103–105

Ball, S., 196
Barrow, R., 142
Becher, T., 171
Bennett, N., 194
Bennis, W., 143
Berman, P., 161, 185
Boomer, G., 45
Brady, L., 2–4
Broadfoot, P., 38
Brown, D., 156

Caldwell, B., 149–156
Canadian provinces, 76, 125
CATS, 76

change, planned, 137
  agents, 142
  phases, 137–140
  strategies and tactics, 143–146
Cibulka, J., 213–214
Clark, D., 47, 162
Clough, E., 141
Collaborative School Management
  Model, 149–157
  advantages and disadvantages, 155
  phases, 150–155
concept building, 1
Conner, C., 98
Cooper, B., 199
Cornbleth, C., 183
Crandall, D., 143, 161, 162, 184
Cumming, J., 174, 175, 178
curriculum
  alignment, 186
  centrally based, 123–127
  development, 4, 6
  frameworks, 73–78
  gender, 25–31
  generic, 124
  hidden, 20–24
  history, 191–195
  ideology, 4, 8–9, 211–212
  implementation, 180–188
  management, 4, 7
  materials, 52
  planning, 4, 6
  reform, 211–215
  reform reports, 212
  school-based, 128–133
  theorizing, 201–205
Curriculum Development Centre, 27

Dalin, P., 185
Davidson, A., 93, 96
Davies, L., 34
Day, C., 67, 156, 172, 175
De Castell, L., 207
Deem, R., 166
deliberation, 112–115
diffusion, 142
dissemination, 142

Ebbutt, D., 117
Edmonds, R., 158
Education Reform Act, 28, 75, 98, 124,
    156, 166, 208, 214
effective schools, 158–160
    examples, 159–160
    factors, 158–159
Eisner, E., 86, 88, 110, 202
Elliott, J., 116
English, F., 81
environment
    physical, 16–18
Eraut, M., 184
examinations, 38–41

Farrar, E., 184, 185
Feinberg, P., 203
Flude, M., 124
Franklin, B., 191, 202
Fraser, B., 16
Fullan, M., 139, 180, 181–182

Gall, M., 56
GCSE, 39–40, 171
Gilbert, R., 198
Giroux, H., 45, 202, 206–207
Glatthorn, A., 186
goals, 85–89
Goodlad, J., 88–89
Goodson, I., 191, 192, 196–200
grading, 102
Gray, T., 138
Green, B., 45, 46
Greene, M., 202
GRIDS, 175
Griffiths, B., 34
Grumet, M., 202
Grundy, S., 107, 110, 118

Hall, G., 60, 143, 184
Hammer, M., 124

Hardy, T., 74
Hargreaves, A., 46, 124, 196, 208
Harrison, M., 128–129
Havelock, R., 140
hegemony, 206–207
Henderson, J., 140
hermeneutics, 203
Hillman, W., 27
Hirst, P., 206
history, curriculum, 191–195
    examples, 192–194
    uses, 191–192
Holly, P., 171, 175
House, E., 182
Huberman, M., 124, 143

implementation, 139, 180–188
    factors affecting, 181–182
    fidelity perspective, 184–185
    problems of measuring, 182–184
    process perspective, 185–186
innovations, 137
    characteristics, 140
    contexts, 141
inquiry, 95
institutionalization, 139
interest inventories, 103–104

Johnston, V., 125

Kelly, A., 2–3
Kelly, P., 142
Kemmis, S., 116–117, 119, 202
Kennedy, K., 112
Kerr, D., 73
Kimpston, R., 184
Kliebard, H., 192, 202
Klohr, P., 201

Lawton, D., 98
leadership, 58–59
learning environment, 15–19
Leithwood, K., 60, 62, 143, 180
Levacic, R., 156
Lighthall, F., 141, 172, 185
Lippit, R., 137
Little, J., 47
Loucks, S., 138, 184
Lustig-Selzer, A., 27
Lutz, F., 165
Lynch, K., 21

MacDonald, B., 185
MacKenzie, D., 159
Manning, J., 166
Marland, M., 64
Marsh, C., 2, 105, 109, 124, 130
Mazza, K., 203
McCutcheon, G., 46, 202
McLaughlin, M., 161, 185
McMahon, A., 175, 176
McNeil, J., 2–3, 45
McTaggart, R., 116–117
methods, 93–100
  imparting content, 93–96
  organising content, 96–99
Miles, M., 140
Mort, P., 140
Mortimore, P., 158–160
My Class Inventory, 16

National Curriculum Council 124
Naturalistic Model, 112–115
needs assessment, 79, 81–83
Nias, J., 46

objectives, 85, 88–90
Oliva, P., 83
Olson, J., 192
Orpwood, G., 112

parents, 165–168
  as decision makers, 167–168
Parker, L., 27
Parsons, C., 182–187
Pereira, P., 114
Pettit, D., 165
Phenix, P., 206
phenomenological, 203
Pinar, W., 201, 202
Piper, K., 184
Plank, D., 212–213
Plowden Report, 166, 193
Pomfret, A., 139, 180
Pope, B., 191–192
Popkewitz, T., 202
Porter, P., 25
Presseisen, B., 212, 213
principal, 58–63
  inservice programmes, 60
  styles, 59–60
problem solving, 95

rating scales, 106
reconceptualists, 201
reflexivity, 203, 207
Reid, W., 196
Reynolds, J., 79–80
Roberts-Gray, C., 138
Robinson, F., 2–3
Robinson, V., 175
Roby, T., 112
Rogers, E., 140, 142
Roitman, D., 184
role plays, 95
Rosenau, R., 143, 144–145
Rudduck, J., 142, 185

Sallis, J., 166
SATS, 75, 76
SBCD, 128–133
  problems and issues, 131–132
  types and characteristics, 128–130
Schofield, H., 165
school councils, 165–170
school evaluations, 171–179
  examples, 173–178
  reasons, 171–172
  techniques, 172–173
school governors, 165–170
school improvement, 160–162
  factors, 161–162
  tárgets, 160–161
school management, 149
school reviews, 171–179
school subjects, 196–200
Schools Educational Assessment
  Council, 124
Schubert, W., 1–3, 191
scope, 96
Seddon, T., 20, 191, 192
semantic differential, 104
sequence, 96
Sharp, R., 203
Sherman, R., 203
Simons, H., 131, 172, 175, 178
situational analysis, 79–81
Skilbeck, M., 79–80, 128
Smith, L., 196
sociology of knowledge, 206
Soliman, I., 79–81
Spinks, J., 149–156
Stafford, K., 109
Stedman, K., 160

Stenhouse, L., 116
Straton, R., 175
students, 4
  needs, 15
  participation levels, 32–36
  role in decision making, 32–37
subjects, school, 196–200
  academic, 197
  pedagogic, 197
  utilitarian, 197
Sunderland, R., 160
synoptic textbooks, 1–4

textbooks, 1, 51–57
  and disempowerment, 45–46
  and empowerment, 45–50
testing, 102
teachers, 4
  appraisal, 64–69
  appraisal criteria, 66–67
  as researchers, 116–122
  talks, 95
Tripp, D., 118
Tanner, D., 191

Tanner, L., 191, 192
Turner, G., 64, 178
Turner, G., 22
Thomson, M., 116
Thomas, N., 64
Tyler, R., 107–111

Valdez, G., 46
Vanterpool, M., 141

Walker, D., 112–115
Walker, R., 185
Walton, J., 129
Whitty, G., 22, 209
Willis, P., 21, 208
Wilson, J., 171
Wragg, E., 66
Wringe, C., 86
Wyn, J., 26

Young, M., 206

Zaltman, G., 142